Gateways to Worship

A YEAR OF WORSHIP EXPERIENCES FOR YOUNG CHILDREN

Carolyn C. Brown

ABINGDON PRESS
NASHVILLE

CONTENTS

*Starred sessions should be scheduled to fit seasons, holidays, or congregational events.

WHAT IS THIS BOOK, AND HOW CAN I USE IT?

Worship is the heart of the Christian life. As we sing, pray, and hear the Word read and proclaimed, we get in touch with the meaning of life. We celebrate who we are and what we are called to be. We find the inspiration and power to live out our calling. If people participate in only one part of the life of the church, it will most likely be worship.

Worshiping is one distinctive sign of being human. Yet, what goes on in most congregations on Sunday morning does not come naturally. Where else do we sit in one place with so little movement for one hour? Where else do we listen to one person speak without interruption for twenty or more minutes? What other music carries the rhythms and forms that hymns carry? Where else do we use the prayers and musical responses that are part of worship? Though we may be worshipers by our God-created nature, we need to learn our congregation's worship ways and claim them as our own.

Gateways to Worship describes a fifty-two-Sundays-a-year program of worship activities designed to help kindergarten children grow as worshipers and to equip them to participate in the congregation's Sunday worship services. It's goals are (1) to offer children an opportunity to worship God in their own kindergarten way and (2) to introduce children to worship in the sanctuary by doing the following.

*exploring the five movements of worship (praise, confession, proclamation, petition, and dedication)
*exploring and observing the sacraments
*learning the Lord's Prayer and the doxology
*hearing church music and learning a few hymns
*exploring the seasons of the church year

To these ends, kindergarten children gather during the worship hour every week for group activities in their own room and for occasional visits to the congregation as it worships in the sanctuary. Beginning at Easter time, the children join their families each week for the first ten to fifteen minutes of the worship service. At the end of the year, children should be ready to remain with their families for the entire worship service.

Disclaimer: This ministry is not a replacement for but an addition to church school. In church school children are introduced to the biblical stories and the full scope of the life of the church. This program is unapologetically and narrowly focused on worship.

How Children Learn to Worship

Worship is a mystery. It is not a collection of skills to be mastered or a body of knowledge to be understood. It is an experience to be lived. We learn to worship by worshiping. Ask an older member of your congregation what the Lord's Supper means and he or she will tell you the highlights of a lifetime of experience with the Lord's Supper and his or her interpretation of those experiences. So one way children learn to worship is by collecting experiences of worship.

We help children most when we help them enter as fully as possible into the worship life of the congregation. We help when we worship with them, being present to answer questions about what is going on and why we do it that way.

Young children approach worship on the feeling or attitude level. Their sense of wonder about the natural order enables them to respond to God's world with praise. The opportunity to confess and be forgiven is welcomed because they know already that they need it. They can share the quiet hope of Christmas and the trumpet-loud joy of Easter. Our task is to help them identify and interpret the deep movements within every worship service and within the seasons of the church year.

The second way we help children is by equipping them to participate in the worship of the community so that they truly feel themselves part of God's people. This means helping them learn the prayers and responses so that they can pray and sing with God's people. Just to be able to say or sing the words allows children to participate in worship as more than an observer. If they can say and sing them with an understanding of the mood and general thrust of what is meant, children can participate still more fully. Then, if as their ability for critical thinking develops in later childhood and youth, and they are able to define the detailed meaning of songs and prayers they have understood on a feeling level for years, they will worship in a still richer way.

How the Church Introduces Children to Worship

Few people in the church today would disagree with these goals. However, there are two schools of thought about how to accomplish them. According to one school, young children need to be provided with worship opportunities that are geared to their particular needs, interests, and abilities. Since that cannot be done in the sanctuary, this school advocates separate worship experiences for children through the early or even middle elementary years. The other school claims that because worship is a mystery, children will best grow into it by being in the sanctuary from the earliest possible age. Advocates of this school urge acceptance of childhood wiggles and planning worship experiences that take the children's presence into account. They focus their attention on training the parents and worship leaders how to make the children welcome in the sanctuary.

In theory, I side with the "keep them in the sanctuary" school. I agree that elementary-aged children need to be in congregational worship regularly. I also believe that we are just beginning to explore possibilities for making our worship both more child-accessible and more meaningful for adults. But in practice I have found that in a large congregation with an open but formal worship service, an hour in the sanctuary was seldom a worship experience for five- and six-year-olds or their parents. *Gateways to Worship* is an attempt to devote a year to easing into worship. At the end of the year, children will be equipped to participate on their level in the congregation's worship and will be at an age when structured activities, such as those in the sanctuary, are more comfortable.

At What Age Are Children Ready for the Gateway?

These materials were developed for kindergarten children, most of whom attend fairly high structured weekday preschool programs. Therefore, the children were accustomed to group activities even as they began their kindergarten year. Not all kindergarten children have this background. If yours do not, you might consider making this a first-grade experience. Only you can decide what is best for your children. The one caution I offer is that almost all four-year-olds are too young for this experience, and almost all second-graders would find many of the activities insultingly babyish.

What Kinds of Leaders Do We Need?

This program requires the weekly leadership of two adults to work with ten to fifteen children. Some churches may want to enlist a team of three adults with the expectation that two of the three would be with the children on any given Sunday. Avoid the temptation of enlisting parents to take one month or an occasional Sunday. Fragmented leadership produces a fragmented experience for the children.
    Look for people with three qualifications.

1. Leaders should be people who know the worship practices of your congregation well and who have a deep love for worship. Their knowledge will enable them to be effective planners. Their attitudes toward worship will teach as much as the activities they lead.
2. Leaders should be people who like children and whom children like. The leaders should respect children for the people they are now and enjoy being with them rather than delight in their "cuteness." (If your congregation has only one Sunday worship service, leaders will be giving up regular Sunday worship in order to lead worship with the children. This will be acceptable to worship lovers only if they can truly feel that they worship in an especially meaningful way when they worship with the children.)
3. At least one of the leaders needs to be comfortable leading the children in singing. This does not mean they need to have a solo voice and musical training. It simply means that they must be comfortable singing with the children and teaching them some of the songs of the church. The leaders' attitudes toward worship music will shape the attitudes of the children. This team of leaders will need the support of others in the congregation. For special occasions, they will need a visiting musician to play an instrument as the children learn a song. Someone able to get letters to parents at three or four times during the year would be great support. At Christmas and Easter extra hands will be needed if crowds are expected. Parents are great sources of such support, but do not overlook other members of the congregation who would be happy to take care of the children in this more limited way.

Setting Up the Calendar for the Year

This course is laid out in three sections: (1) an introductory unit of ten sessions, (2) a unit on the seasons of the church year, and (3) a collection of sessions that stand alone. *You will not lead the sessions in the order in which they are presented in this book.* Therefore, your first task will be to plan out the order in which you will present them. Use the chart on page 11 with its fifty-two divisions to make and keep up with your calendar.
    To set the calendar, first fill in the dates for this year, putting the date of your first Sunday with the children at the top of the first column, the second Sunday's date just below it, and so on to the last date in the space at the bottom of the second column.
    Second, in the "notes" column, identify special events that occur at that time. Be sure to include Advent (the four Sundays before Christmas), Christmas (the day of or first Sunday after Christmas Day), Epiphany (the Sunday after Christmas Sunday), Lent (six Sundays before Easter), Easter, Pentecost (the sixth Sunday after Easter), and Thanksgiving. Do not panic if you've never heard of some of these days. For now just write them in the appropriate space. You will learn a lot this year that will enrich your worship. Ask your minister for help with this, if needed.
    Also identify special Sundays in your congregation. If officers are installed on Sunday morning, note the date for that. If you have a Homecoming or Reunion Sunday, note it. If your congregation sets aside a Sunday to dedicate financial promises to the church, find out when it will be this year. Note the

Sundays on which your congregation will celebrate the Lord's Supper and, if you know in advance, when there will be baptisms.

Finally, write in the title of one session by each date. Begin by writing in the six sessions related to Christmas, the Lent sessions before Easter, the two sessions for the Easter season, and the one for Pentecost. (The table of contents will help.)

There are two sessions each on baptism and the Lord's Supper. Each of these should be done on a Sunday when the children can observe the sacrament in the sanctuary. You may have to wait until baptisms are announced to schedule the baptism sessions.

Fill in sessions for other special dates from the collection of one-Sunday sessions.

Next decide where to place the ten session introductory unit. Obviously, you should do it as close to the beginning of the year as possible. Feel free to interrupt it if necessary for a special event.

Finally fill in the remaining Sundays with the single Sunday events.

A calendar for a year that begins in September might look like this.

Sept.–early Nov.	Introductory Unit with break for Halloween session
Mid-November	Thanksgiving sessions
Last of Nov.–Dec.	Advent and Christmas sessions
Jan.–Feb.	Epiphany, Officer Installation, and several single sessions
Feb.–March	Lent sessions
April–May	Easter and Pentecost sessions
June–August	Single sessions

Time in the Sanctuary

Because we want our children to learn *to* worship rather than to learn *about* worship, it is important for them to begin participating in the congregation's worship. At the beginning of this course you will find suggestions for nonintrusive visits to the sanctuary to participate in or observe a specific part of worship. The Advent decorations and music make December an ideal time for children to attend the first ten to fifteen minutes of worship with their families. By spring, the children will be prepared to spend part of every week in the sanctuary with their families. Palm Sunday and Easter can be the beginning of this change. After Easter children will attend worship with their families, departing at a designated point to pursue children's worship activities. If your church has a children's sermon, the kindergarten children may leave for children's church after the children's sermon. Another smooth exit point is during a second hymn. The familiar adult leader will stand quietly at the front of the sanctuary during the hymn, the children will join the leader, and they will all leave together. Be sure to include directions for this departure in each week's order of worship.

If in your church kindergarten children generally attend the first part of worship, there is no need to interrupt this practice for the first half of the year. Simply adjust the plans to fit the amount of time available. In the introductory unit especially, this may require omitting one or two of the activities each week.

A Place to Worship and Learn

The children need a regular meeting room. The room should be large enough to hold two work areas for your children—a large rug or circle of chairs in which to meet as a group, and tables and chairs for individual work. Select a room that is neither too small nor too large for the number of children you expect. If space is at a premium, remember that children can do artwork on the floor. In cold weather they can sit or lie around the edges of the rug to work on the hard surface of the floor or the seats of chairs.

If possible use a room that may be used only by your group—on Sunday, at least. If this is not possible, try to find a space other than that of the children's Sunday school classes. The children need a

CALENDAR FOR THE YEAR

Date	Notes	# and Session Title	Date	Notes	# and Session Title

change of place to emphasize that this is not an extension of Sunday school. Avoid using a room that is filled with distractions, such as the learning centers or play centers that children use in other groups. It is often easier for children's worship groups to share space with adults or older children than with another preschool group.

Some Basic Supplies and Equipment

These sessions use simple, familiar supplies and equipment that are available at most churches or homes. It will be helpful to store the following basics in or near your room.

> crayons
> manila drawing paper
> construction paper (variety of colors)
> children's scissors
> glue sticks or paste (your preference)
> powdered tempera paints and brushes

Most of these items are available in discount or grocery stores. However, it may be worth a trip to a school or art supply store at the beginning of the year to get good prices on the items above and to pick up one roll of white chart paper (36″ wide) and a collection of poster boards in two or three colors.

Buy or borrow an instant camera (one that produces photographs instantly) for frequent use. Also stay alert for sales on film for it. You will use lots of the film during the year to help children see themselves as worshipers.

If your church has rhythm instruments, find out where they are and how to borrow them. If you do not and money is available, consider buying a set. (Check school supply catalogs or stores.) If money is scarce, make your own set of rhythm instruments. Make rattles by putting small pebbles in plastic or metal cans. Oatmeal boxes or lidded plastic bowls or boxes make drums. Pan lids make cymbals, which may be banged together or tapped with a metal spoon. Tack rough sandpaper onto sanded scraps of wood to make wood blocks. Stitch jingle bells onto elastic bracelets to ring.

Remember that children appreciate things that both sound and look beautiful. So experiment to find "instruments" that make appealing sounds and decorate your instruments to make them look as fine as they sound. Cover some with Contact paper or paint. (An older child or youth may be happy to create these instruments to earn a scout badge or as a class service project.)

Locate any old church school curriculum or teaching pictures that are gathering dust in closets. After checking to be sure that no one else claims them, add them to your stores for making charts and illustrating stories.

Last, you need two medium-sized boxes. Cover one with Contact paper or a collage of magazine pictures and a sign "leave picture magazines here." Place that box just outside your door or wherever people are likely to see it and contribute to it. At the beginning of the year, ask parents and members of the congregation to contribute magazines with pretty pictures for the children to cut out and use in learning about worship. The other box is to store charts, pictures, and other resources that you can use during the year. Be sure to put your name and a request that its contents not be thrown away on the box.

The People Behind the Ministry

This curriculum grew out of four years' work by many folks at First Presbyterian Church in Nashville, Tennessee. Throughout the session plans you will see the names of Nan Russell, Lindy Judd, Lynette Johnson, and Shelley DeVault. Each one in turn brought her special gifts to the program and contributed unique songs, stories, and activities. Over the years their work has become so intertwined that it is hard to tell what each one gave. So I give them the credit they richly deserve here and with the songs and stories we know to be their unique contributions.

During my years as Director of Christian Education at First Presbyterian, I planned and worked with each of these people. Since then, I have dug through the huge black notebook of our session plans, revising, omitting, adding to, and totally redoing our work to create the organized, complete curriculum we all dreamed about but never had time to develop. That is this book.

EXPLORING FIVE MOVEMENTS WITHIN WORSHIP

UNIT INTRODUCTION

We begin the year with a ten-Sunday unit in which we devote two Sundays to each of the five major movements in worship. We begin with praise, which is probably the most natural response to God. The second movement is confession. The third is proclamation—celebrating and affirming God's story. The fourth is petition—asking help for ourselves and others. The fifth is dedication—giving ourselves in response to God.

If possible, begin with praise and move through the movements in the order presented. Check your calendar to know when your stewardship emphasis will be. Rearrange sessions as necessary so that you will do the dedication Sundays during the stewardship emphasis.

PRAISE

Session 1

Worship Focus: We praise God!

Worship services begin with praise—that is, they begin by recalling and restating with joy who God is and what God does. This appreciation for God ripples out into appreciation for all God creates, even us. It is no accident that such praise often takes the form of a song. Praise involves so much wonder and deep happiness that it takes more than words to express. Music, dancing (or at least marching in), and other arts are called into service.

This mood of celebration is our focus with the children. Praise often comes naturally. Our task is to help children express it in their own terms and to help children claim as their own the ways we praise God in the sanctuary. Today that means learning the word *praise*, beginning to learn the doxology, and expressing their own praises in their own ways.

Time	Worship Activity	Materials/Resources
5 min.	1. Define *praise*	Praise card
10 min.	2. Singing praises	
20 min.	3. Doxology Song Book	poster board magazine pictures glue or paste
5 min.	4. "Praising God" game	
15 min.	5. Praise rubbings	rubbing cards paper and crayons masking tape
5 min.	6. Line out Psalm 100 and sing to close	

Getting Ready

For your first class song book—the doxology—you will need four sheets of poster board in a pastel color and three metal rings or some yarn or cloth ribbon. Prepare each page as on page 19, printing with a marking pen or crayon:

PAGE 1   PAGE 2   PAGE 3   PAGE 4

The word *praise* should be made with the outline letters in the Craft Patterns section. It should look the same on each page. Prepare pages one and two as shown.

The children will complete pages one and two by adding magazine pictures, which you have cut out in advance. You need two piles of pictures with about one and a half times as many pictures as expected children. One pile should be pictures of all kinds of blessings God bestows. Include pictures of different kinds of food, of people in special relationships with one another, pets, nature scenes, fun activities, and so on. The second pile is pictures of people of all ages, races, sexes, and dress. Before class, spread these piles on two different tables or counters to be ready for the children's use.

On page three, mount pictures of an angel or several angels from old teaching picture files.

Though you will not use it until the next session, prepare page four while you work on the first three. To illustrate "Father," find a picture of the natural world God created. For "Son" find a picture of Jesus from old teaching files or Sunday school books. To illustrate "Holy Ghost," find a picture of people praying or reading the Bible, a choir with happy faces singing together, or anything else that indicates a sense of God's presence. Arrange your pictures on the page and write the words of the phrase around them. Do not mount the pictures now.

Punch three holes down the side of each poster page, being sure you punch the correct side for the book to read in the proper order. Thread the metal rings or ribbon or several strands of yarn through each hole after the children finish making the whole book. Save this book for use in later sessions.

The other resource to make is a set of cards with raised letters and patterns using the pattern on page 207. The children will lay thin drawing paper over these cards and scribble over the raised places to make the word *praise* and the patterns appear on their paper. Any shirt board or cardboard or old poster board will make a good base. Cut letters and patterns out of very thick poster board. (Picture frame matting scraps are great for this and can usually be picked out of the scrap heap in framing shops for free.) Glue these patterns *firmly* onto a base that is several inches larger than the pattern. You will need one "Praise" card for every five children and approximately one pattern card for every two children to share. Use the pattern page as a starter. Add other patterns you think of. *Save all these cards to use in later sessions.*

Getting Started

As children arrive, one worship leader greets each child, prints the child's name in large letters on a name necklace (index card with holes punched in the upper corners and threaded with about 18″ of yarn), puts it around the child's neck, and invites the child to join the group on the floor. If children are coming with folders and craft projects from Sunday school, help them find a place to leave these until time to go home.

The second leader gathers children in a circle on a rug or in chairs. As the first children come in, the leader gets to know them by asking questions about their families and what they have been doing this morning. When the group has gathered, bring out a "Praise" card. Ask children to identify some of the letters on the card, then ask if anyone can sound out the word. Say the word together a few times. Whisper it. Shout it. Go around the circle, each saying "praise" to the next person. Then ask if anyone knows what *praise* means. If some ideas are offered, discuss them before presenting "What Is Praise Like?" (see pages 201-2). If no one has any ideas, go straight into the reading.

Singing Praises

The mood of the reading will make everyone feel like singing praise songs. Begin with familiar songs of praise. You may want to check with Sunday school teachers to learn the familiar songs for your particular group. Possibilities include "Jesus Loves Me," "Praise Him, All Ye Little Children," "Praise Ye the Lord, Alleluia!" and others. As you sing, ask children to raise their hands every time they sing the word *praise*. Briefly discuss the meaning of each sentence in which it is used.

After singing several familiar songs, introduce the doxology. Present it as a song that Christians all around the world sing in church every Sunday today and have sung for hundreds of years. Note that it has some big, difficult words but that it also has a word they already know.

Sing it for them, asking them to listen for the familiar word *praise*. Sing it again, asking them to raise their hands each time they hear "praise." Sing it again, asking them to count the number of "praises." Sing it again, asking them to clap their hands each time they hear "praise."

Invite them to learn the song by making a big song book together.

Doxology Song Book

Page one. Point to the word *praise* and ask someone to identify it. Read the whole phrase and tell the children that we praise God for all the wonderful things given us. Mention some specific things you praise God for, including such items as your favorite foods, people you love, pets, and activities you enjoy. Ask them to name some blessings they praise God for. Once they understand the idea, invite each child to select one picture of something they praise God for from the first table of pictures cut from magazines. Help them mount the pictures around the words on your poster with paste or glue sticks. When everyone has mounted a picture, say the phrase slowly and ask the children to repeat it. Then begin an informal praise litany by asking each child to point out his or her picture and to tell what she or he likes about it. After each child has spoken, the whole group repeats, "Praise God from whom all blessings flow."

Page two. Point to the word *praise* on the page and ask someone to identify it. Read the rest of the phrase. Explain it by saying, "Guess who a creature is. You are (pointing to a child), and you are (pointing to others until you have pointed at everyone), and I am. We are all creatures. All people are creatures, so our song says we can all praise God." Send everyone to the second table to select a picture of a person to mount on this page. Talk about the people as children glue the pictures in place. (What do they like to eat and do? Where do they live?) If you have an instant camera, take a picture of the group and mount it on the page. Admire your page together. Say the phrase and ask the children to repeat it. Do it several times. Then wonder aloud what it would be like if everyone in the world really did praise God together. To help imagine this (and learn the phrase), one leader says the phrase then motions for the person next to her or him to join in saying it a second time. That person then motions for the next person to join them as they say it a third time, and so on until everyone in the circle is saying it together.

Page three is already made. Show it to the children and explain that not only can "all creatures here below" praise God, but the angels above can as well. Say the phrase and repeat it together several times. (This phrase has several hard words in it. It is best to let children learn the phrase without dealing with the meaning of particular words.)

"Praising God" Game

The children are probably ready to move around, so play "Follow the Praise Leader." Instruct the children to repeat what the leader says and then do it. You may begin with: "Praise God for bodies that stand tall" and stand up. Continue with "Praise God for feet that hop . . . children who skip . . . arms with strong muscles . . . " and so on. Move around the room and even down a hall and back if that is possible. End with some actions that are done sitting back in their circle. Now go straight into the praise rubbing directions.

Praise Rubbings

Using the cards appliqued with the cardboard word *praise* and flowers, stars, and other things for which we give praise, children create rubbings. Broken crayons are used on their sides to shade in an area that centers on a raised appliqué. The result is a sheet of paper with areas of color highlighting outlines of the word *praise* and several of the designs.

Some children will need an adult to hold their paper securely in place while they color. Other children manage well on their own if the design cards are securely taped to the table.

Closing

As children finish their rubbings, one leader helps the last worker, while the other invites other children to the rug. Point to each of the pages of your Doxology Song Book and see who can say the phrase. (Do not expect great results. Be ready to give lots of help.)

When all are on the rug, open a Bible and explain that the Bible is filled with stories about people who praise God and with songs they wrote to praise God. Invite them to read one song with you by repeating what you say after you each line. Read Psalm 100 in short phrases for children to repeat. Then sing again some of the songs you sang at the beginning of the session.

As children leave, help them get their belongings and put their name necklaces near the door for next week.

Looking Ahead

Next week you will need one microwave frozen dinner dish and its cover for each child.

Session 2

Worship Focus: We praise God!
Refer to the background for the first session.

Time	Worship Activity	Materials/Resources
5 min.	1. Define *praise*	"Praise" card
5 min.	2. Sing praise songs	
10 min.	3. Learn the doxology	Doxology Song Book
10 min.	4. Make "Praise God" banner	mop handle big sheet of paper magazine pictures ribbon and glue
10 min.	5. Hear the story of Miriam	
10 min.	6. Make tambourines	frozen dinner trays with covers dried beans/stones "Praise hearts"
10 min.	7. Praise parade	tape-recorded music

Getting Ready

1. To prepare a banner, find an old mop handle or long straight tree branch. Tape on it a big (2′ square) banner pieced together from small strips of shelf paper or cut from a chart paper roll. Write "Praise God" on it in bright colors using the letter patterns in the Craft Patterns. At either end, add ribbon bows with streamers for decoration.

2. Gather a pile of magazine pictures of things for which children could praise God. Gather enough for each child to select two or three pictures.

3. For tambourines you will need a frozen dinner tray *and* its snap-on plastic cover for each child. You may know someone who can supply all you need. If not, parents may be able to gather them for you. Each child will also need two heart-shaped cutouts with "Praise God" printed on them.

Getting Started

As children arrive, one leader meets them at the door to help them find places, to put aside what they bring with them, and to get their name necklaces. The second leader gathers them on the rug to talk about their week. When most have arrived, bring out a "Praise" card from last week. Ask who knows the word *praise*. If necessary, repeat the steps of identifying letters and sounding out the word. When the word is recognized, begin some statements for the children to complete with the word *praise*. (Example: When I run through the grass and feel a cool breeze on my face, I. . . .) Include some sentences about praising God. Then repeat the reading "What Praise Is Like" from last week.

Singing Praises

Sing with the children some of the familiar praise songs from last week. Then sing the doxology. Sing it again, asking children to clap their hands each time they hear the word *praise*. Next ask the children to raise both arms way over their heads and touch the palms of their hands to the hands of the person on each side of them (still over their heads.) Note that together you make sort of a flower facing up at God. This time as you sing the doxology, children clap their neighbors' hands every time you sing "praise." You may want to do this several times for sheer pleasure before God.

Review each phrase of the doxology, using your song book. When you come to the last phrase, mount each picture as you talk about God the Father, the Son, and the Holy Ghost. Don't get bogged down. A sentence about each one and a few comments from the children are all that is needed until children get old enough to understand the intricacies of the Trinity. Invite the children to sing along with you. Ask children to take turns turning the pages of your big book as you sing.

"Praise God" Banner

Ask two children to hold up your "Praise God" banner. Discuss what it says. Then ask children what they praise God for. As soon as ideas get going, invite everyone to go to the table to select two pictures of something that makes them praise God to glue on the banner.

Miriam's Praise Story

Set the banner aside to dry while you share a praise story from the Bible. Invite children to help you tell this story by doing the motions you do.

Once God's people lived in Egypt. They were slaves *(big frown)*. They had to work all day in the hot sun *(fan yourself)*. At night they trudged home tired *(pantomime trudging)* and hungry *(rub stomach)*.

But there was no clean soft bed *(hands on hips)*, and there was hardly any food *(rub stomach harder)*.

And it never changed. Sometimes people put their heads in their hands and cried, "It is not fair" *(do as you say)*.

Sometimes they raised their hands to heaven and said, "God, do something. Help us! Save us!" *(Do as you say.)*

Then Moses came. Moses said *(hand to ear)*, "God has heard you. He sent me to take you to a new land."

When the king heard Moses, he said, "No, they can't go. I need slaves" *(thumbs down)*.

Moses said, "If you don't let us go, God will send flies ZZZZZZZZZ!"

The king said "No! I am not afraid of flies!" *(thumbs down)*

ZZZZZZZZZZZZZZZZZZZ! *(buzz)*

"Okay! Go!" said the king. "But stop these flies" *(point finger)*.

Once the flies were gone, the king said, "No, you can't go. I need slaves" *(thumbs down)*.

Moses replied, "Let us go or God will send frogs—lots of frogs!" *(Jump your hand up and down on your leg like a frog.)*

"I'm not afraid of frogs!" And soon there were frogs everywhere—on your feet, in your pockets, in your hair *(jump those frogs)*.

The king said, "Go, but take the frogs!" *(Point finger.)*

Again, when the frogs were gone, the king said, "No!" *(Thumbs down.)*

Seven more times God sent trouble *(hold up seven fingers)*.

Seven more times the king changed his mind *(shake head sadly)*.

But the last trouble was so terrible that while the king was still crying, God's people got away *(hide face in hands)*.

God's people were happy. They pitched their tents by the water *(form tent with hands and arms)*.

But one of them looked back toward Egypt. *(Shade eyes)* Way off, but coming fast, was . . . the king's army! *(Hands up in panic.)* He had changed his mind again! *(Thumbs down, shaking head sadly.)*

What could they do? They were trapped! The king would kill them! *(Hands up in panic.)*

Moses said, "God has a plan. It is all right" *(hands in calming position)*. As he stretched his hand over the water, the wind blew *(stretch out hands, palms down)*. The water cleared away, and they walked across on dry land *(point finger)*.

But when the king came, God stopped the wind *(hold out hand to stop)*. The water came back—and the king was gone forever *(rippling motions with hands)*.

Miriam and all the women grabbed their tambourines and sang, "God has saved us!" *(Wave hands over head.)* "God saved us from the king!" *(Repeat.)* "God loves us!" *(Repeat.)* "God takes care of us!" *(Repeat.)* "Praise God! Praise God forever!" *(Repeat.)*

Then look at your hands, noting that they are not tambourines. Talk about what a tambourine is and give instructions for making one.

Making Tambourines

Each child glues one "praise heart" to the bottom of his or her frozen dinner tray and one to the top of its cover. Drop a handful of beans or stones into each plate and snap the cover into place. If a cover is loose, secure it by applying a little glue around the rim of the plate.

Closing

Hold a Praise Parade. Form a line with two children carrying the "Praise God" banner at the front and the others with their tambourines following. Line out Psalm 100 like a cheer. Then turn on a praise record and march around to the music. As you turn off the record say, "Praise God!"

If you have time and the children enjoyed Miriam's praise story, retell the end of Miriam's story, shaking your tambourines to accompany the last lines.

As the children leave, help them get all their belongings and return their name necklaces to their place near the door.

CONFESSION

Session 3

Worship Focus: We can make choices. When we choose to do wrong things, we are forgiven when we say, "I'm sorry."

For kindergarten children, sin is doing something wrong, something you were not supposed to do. They need to know that everyone of all ages does wrong and that when we do there are unhappy consequences. More important, they need to know that the guilt and unhappiness need not last forever. We can say, "I'm sorry." When we say "I'm sorry," God promises to forgive, to say it's okay. Most people who love us will do the same.

Focus on love, forgiveness, and reconciliation rather than on sin, confession, and guilt because it is our trust in God's love and the love of our family and friends that allows us to say "I'm sorry" and try again.

In this session we will explore the fact that we all make choices. Most of the time is devoted to celebrating our ability to make choices. But the heart of the session is the stories, prayer, and song in which the children look at what happens when we make wrong choices.

Time	Worship Activity	Materials/Resources
10 min.	1. Conversation about breakfast sharing grapes singing praise	name necklaces bowl of grapes
15 min.	2. Making things with clay	clay prepared plate to take clay home clean-up supplies
5 min.	3. Praising God for choices	
10 min.	4. Bad choices: stories song: "Jesus Loves Me" "As High as the Sky"	magic slate
15 min.	5. Making a gift to share	selected art supplies prepared sign
5 min.	6. "Promise hearts"	prepared hearts

Getting Ready

1. Prepare seedless grapes to share with the group in the opening. One grape per child is enough.

2. Buy or make clay that will dry. At a school supply store buy real potting clay. This is often sold only in large boxes. If your church is large enough that the clay will be used by other groups in the next six months, it's worth the investment. If you question whether it will be used again, make your own clay by mixing one part flour with one part salt, then adding enough water to make a smooth, pliable dough.

The children will want to work the clay on the table top, but they will need a firm surface on which to take their masterpieces home. Sturdy paper or Styrofoam plates do the job. To explain to the parents how this clay object is part of the child's worship experience, copy the following note or a similar one of your own writing and mount it to one side of the top of the plate.

> Dear Parent,
> We have been thinking about making choices today. Your child chose to make this object out of a lump of clay. We praised God for choices. We also talked about the unhappy consequences of wrong choices and God's promise to forgive when we say ''I'm sorry.''
>   (sign your name)

3. Buy a magic slate to use today and in the future. Magic slates are toy "clipboards" on which a carbon-like backing is topped by two thin sheets of plastic. Using a wooden or plastic stylus, draw pictures on the plastic sheets. The pictures are erased when the sheets are lifted and lose contact with the backing. Magic slates can be found in toy stores or in the toy section of discount stores.

4. Prepare several (one for each child) large stencils cut from poster board or cardboard patterns of stars, flowers, hearts, and butterflies. Make the patterns approximately 12″ square so that you can fill the sidewalk or a large piece of chart paper within the available time. Use patterns in the back of the book as a guide. Enlist the help of an artistic member of the church to make these for you, if necessary. You will use the stencils several times during the year.

Decide whether to work on the sidewalk or on a mural to post in a hallway indoors. If the weather cooperates, the sidewalk drawing is more interesting to the children. There will be plenty of opportunities to paint indoors during the year.

If you are going to work on the sidewalk, you need colored chalk. If you are going to work indoors on a mural, cut sponges into 1″ × 12″ pieces so that each child can have a piece, and pour tempera paints mixed with a squirt of liquid detergent in shallow dishes. Be sure the children wear paint aprons (see directions for making aprons in the Craft Patterns.

Make a large sign that says, "We love you" and have every person in your group sign it. Post it near your work for the rest of the congregation to see.

5. Use the heart pattern in the Craft Patterns to cut out a red construction paper "Promise Heart" for each child. On one side write "God loves you." On the other write "God will forgive you." You will need another set of "Promise Hearts" next Sunday. Make all of them today, if you want to get ahead.

Getting Started

One leader greets the children at the door to help them find safe places for their belongings and to put on their name necklaces. The other leader gathers the children on the rug for conversation about what they ate for breakfast that morning and what they like to eat for breakfast.

When all of the children have arrived, open your bowl of grapes, noting that all the talk about food has made you hungry. Pretend to consider whether you will eat the grapes by yourself or share them. Decide to share and offer each child a grape. As you eat your grapes, point out that we all make lots of choices. You had to decide whether to eat all the grapes or share them. Note that God allows each of us to make choices. Part of what makes us special is the choices we make. Use breakfast preferences as examples of this.

Sing the doxology as a way of praising God for creating us able to make choices. Sing one or two other praise songs the children know and enjoy.

GATEWAYS TO WORSHIP

Making Things with Clay

Send the children to their work tables where a lump of clay has been set out for each child. Allow plenty of time for the children to enjoy the clay and try out whatever they want in shaping it. As they begin to work on something to take home, give each one a prepared plate on which to put their masterpieces. As they finish, be sure to write each child's name on the edge of the parent's note on the plate.

Praising God for Choices

As the children finish working with the clay, one leader gathers them on the rug to sing favorite songs. When all are on the rug, invite the children to go with you on a tour of all the things they have made with clay. Clasp your hands behind your back and instruct the children to do the same. This is a look-not-touch tour. As you walk around, let each child say one thing about what he or she has made.

Back on the rug invite the children to join you in a litany prayer.

God, we all started with lumps of clay that looked alike, but we made them into . . . *(list some of the items made by your children).*

Thank you, God, for choices.

God, we all like to eat breakfast. But when we can choose, some of us choose . . *(list some of the breakfast preferences).*

Thank you, God, for choices.

God, some days we want to run and shout and play outside. On other days we want to read and be quiet inside. There are so many different good things to enjoy!

Thank you, God, for choices.

God, it is fun to play with friends, laughing and working together, *and* it is good to play alone, working quietly on things we like to do.

Thank you, God, for choices.

Amen.

Bad Choices

Point out that some choices are easy, while others are harder to make. Then tell this story using the slate.

(Draw two "cookies"—two circles on your slate—as you begin telling this story.) Preston was hungry. All the way home from school, he sat in the back of the car and thought about the cookies that were always waiting for him and his brother Bailey. As soon as the door opened, Preston ran straight to the kitchen. There on a plate were two big chocolate iced cookies—his favorite! He did not take long to choose. He took them both. He stuffed one in his mouth and went to his room with the other one.

"Hi, Mom!" he heard Bailey call. "Where's the cookies?" Just as Preston was swallowing the last bite of the second cookie, Bailey and Mother came into his room. Bailey had two graham crackers in his hand.

"Thanks a lot, Preston Pig," Bailey said unhappily, showing Preston the crackers. "I like chocolate cookies, too." And with that he stomped off down the hall.

Mother looked at Preston sadly, closed his bedroom door, and walked back to the kitchen. There was still some chocolate icing on his lips, but it did not taste so good anymore. The house was quiet. Preston sat on his bed thinking. Usually he and Bailey played in the tree house together, but he guessed Bailey wouldn't want to play with him today. He heard the television come on. But he bet Bailey would not even watch television with him. So he just sat in his room and thought. He thought about those two cookies.

Finally, he opened his door. Bailey was watching TV. Quietly he sat down just inside the room. When the commercial came on Bailey looked at Preston.

"I'm sorry, Bailey. I shouldn't have eaten your cookie." Preston paused. "Tomorrow you can have mine."

Bailey was quiet a minute. Then he smiled a little smile. "Oh, that's okay. I don't want to eat yours. Let's just eat our own, all right?"

"Okay," said Preston. Then they watched TV together.

Point out that when Preston saw the cookies he made a choice. Ask the children to tell you about the choice and how Preston felt after he had made it. Ask questions to find out what Preston had to say before he could be friends with Bailey again.

Pick up your slate, erase the cookies, and say that when we say we are sorry God promises to erase all of our wrong choices. Teach the "As High as the Sky" assurance of forgiveness (see page 202).

Do the motions expansively to get the feeling of all our wrongs being taken far, far away. There are big words in these verses. For today it is sufficient to define *transgressions* as wrong choices and concentrate on the feeling of God's taking far away all the bad feelings that follow wrong choices. Once the children begin to know the verses, say them together one last time to remind Preston that when he says "I'm sorry" Bailey and God will forgive him.

To conclude your thinking about forgiveness, introduce the song "Forgive Me, God, for Things I Do," which you will use frequently during the year (see page 204). Sing it for the children once. Then line it out with them once or twice.

Making a Gift

Show the children the stencils and chalk or sponge painting supplies. Let the children choose between making pictures to take home or to share with other people in your church family by using the chalk to draw on the church sidewalk or painting a mural to put up in the hall.

To decorate the sidewalk, tape the stencils in place on the sidewalk. Several children can work together on coloring in each stencil. As they finish one stencil, it can be moved, and the children can begin work on a different stencil with a different color. Hang on a nearby tree branch or place in a chair your sign identifying the work.

To make a mural, lay the stencils on a long strip of chart paper or shelf paper. Position the stencils around the edges so that they can be securely taped to the floor on one side. (Tape tends to tear the chart paper as you remove the stencil.) Children dip the sponge pieces into shallow dishes of paint and then press the sponges several times on the paper in the center of the stencils. Again several children can work together on one stencil and then move on to another stencil. (Remember to wear paint aprons.)

Whichever activity your group does, keep an eye on the clock to be sure that you have time for the closing.

"Promise Heart" Closing

Close with a prayer in which you thank God for the choices we can make, apologize for the times we make wrong choices, and ask for help in making good choices. As a reminder that God always forgives us, give each child a "promise heart," saying: "_____ (name), God loves you and will forgive you always." Hug each child as you distribute the hearts. Help them fold the hearts into their pockets or slip them into one of their shoes. Repeat the "As High as the Sky" assurance of forgiveness with its motions.

Session 4

Worship Focus: Rules help us live and work together happily. When we break rules and say "I'm sorry," God promises to forgive us.

Another way children can understand sin is that it is breaking rules. As they enter school, children become increasingly aware of rules. In early childhood all rules are accepted as indisputable when presented by trusted adults. Evaluation of rules will come later.

The majority of the session will be spent exploring and celebrating the rules in the children's lives and introducing Jesus' two great rules. But the section about broken rules will be the heart of the session.

Time	Worship Activity	Materials/Resources
5 min.	1. Conversation about rules	
15 min.	2. Painting pictures of what we do at home or school or . . .	tempera paints brushes and paper aprons clean-up supplies
5 min.	4. Game with rules	
5 min.	3. Litany: Thanks for Rules	
10 min.	5. Breaking rules: Story "Forgive Me, God . . . " song "As High as the Sky"	
15 min.	6. Two Good Rules belt	pre-cut belt sections ribbons stapler and staples
5 min.	7. "Promise Heart" closing	prepared hearts

Getting Ready

1. Mix powdered tempera paints with water and a squirt of liquid detergent. Pour the paint into the bowls of egg cartons that have been cut into four-bowl sections. One section filled with four different colors will serve four children. Fill a jar with water for rinsing brushes. If you have a small number of children you may prefer to purchase individual water paint trays from a discount store. Don't forget the painting aprons!

2. Select a game the children know and like to play. Consider "Duck-Duck-Goose," "Simon Says," "Follow the Leader," or any other game. Be sure you know the details and rules of how your children play the game; rules differ.

3. To make the belt, cut a 36″ piece of paper gift ribbon for each child. From the Pattern Section, copy one page of belt pieces for each child. If possible copy the pattern pages on two colors of paper that are as stiff as possible. Cut out the belt pieces and cut the slashes through which the children will weave their ribbons. Be sure that the slashes are wide enough for the ribbons to pass through easily.

4. See the directions for making "Promise Hearts" (page 25) in Session 3 and repeat them for this session.

Getting Started

One leader greets the children and their parents at the door, puts aside belongings, and finds a name necklace for each child. The other leader gathers the children on the rug for conversation about "rules" or "how we do things" at the children's schools. Compare rules for what you do when you arrive in the morning, how the group goes to the playground, who may speak when the class is together, and the like. Give as many children as possible a chance to tell how they do things at their schools. When all of the children have arrived, point out that it is good to have rules about how to do things. Rules help us work and play together happily.

Painting My School

Invite the children to paint a picture of something they do at their schools. Older children will be able to paint pictures showing how they keep a particular rule at their schools. Younger children will paint pictures of their classes in action. The leaders' job is to identify the rules that lie behind the pictures through conversation with the artists.

As pictures are finished, write the artists' names in a corner of the page in pencil. Leave the paintings on the tables to dry flat.

Playing a Game with Rules

As the children finish their work and clean up, gather them on the rug to sing. When all have arrived on the rug introduce and play the game you have selected. As you play, refer frequently to the rules and note how they make the game fun: "Aren't we lucky to have the rule that tells us which way to run when the goose tags our heads? Without that rule we would bump right into one another."

Praise God for Rules That Help Us Be Happy Together

As you finish the game, begin the following litany with one leader speaking the prayer and the other responding with the children.

Thank you, God, for_____ *(insert name of the game you played and add a brief description of a part of it that the group enjoyed)*.

Thank you, God.

Thank you, God, for_____ *(list all the different schools your children attend)*.

Thank you, God.

Thank you for teachers who tell us what to do as we work and play together.

Thank you, God.

Thank you for the rules that help us work and play happily together.

Thank you, God.

Amen.

Sing several praise songs, such as the doxology, "Jesus Loves Me," and "Praise Him, All Ye Little Children."

Thinking About Breaking Rules

Tell the following story.

Kim Breaks a Rule

"Amanda and Becky are mean, mean, mean," Kim said to herself as they walked away from her on the playround. "Bert is mean, mean, mean," she said as she remembered the name he had called her. "Mrs.

29

Baird is mean, mean, mean. She didn't let me be first in the line. This whole school is mean, mean, mean. I don't like it here anymore." The longer she thought about it the madder she got.

The bell rang to go back inside, but Kim did not go. She quietly walked around the big bush beside the building and started running for home. She'd show them. She wouldn't stay at their mean old school. She was a big girl. She knew the way home.

Or she thought she knew the way home. When she came to the corner, Kim followed the sidewalk down the street. She chased a squirrel up the sidewalk until it climbed a tree. The further she got from that school the better Kim felt. She looked around. The houses looked different. She had never seen these houses before. But she kept walking. She was sure she knew the way home. She walked a long time. She was getting hungry. At school it would be snack time. And her legs were getting tired. Kim sat down on some steps in front of a house.

An angry looking man opened the front door and scowled at her. "Get out of here!" he yelled. "I don't want any children in *my* yard. Get going *now!*"

Kim started to run again, but she did not know where to go. She just ran. Finally she stopped and sat on the curb. She was lost. Big tears started sliding down her cheeks and splashing on her knees.

Someone sat down beside her. Kim looked up and saw the Library Lady from school.

"Are you okay, Kim?" the Library Lady asked quietly. Kim nodded her head. "What are you doing here?"

Kim explained about the mean morning in her class. When she got to the part about leaving the school, she stopped. "I'm sorry," she said. "I broke a rule."

The Library Lady smiled a little. "Yes, you did. Kim, do you know why we have the rule not to leave school alone?"

Kim thought a minute. "Because you can get lost?" she asked.

The Library Lady nodded. "We don't want you to get lost or hurt. That is why the rule says not to leave school alone. I think it's a good rule. What about you?"

Kim nodded.

"Let's go back to school. Everyone is worried about you."

The Library Lady and Kim walked back to the school and down the hall to her room. She even stayed while Kim explained to Mrs. Baird what had happened. "I'm sorry," Kim said again. "I broke the rule, but I won't do it again."

"I hope not," said Mrs. Baird, giving Kim a little hug. "We don't want you to get lost or hurt."

To explore the story, ask such questions as:

* Why did Kim have to say "I'm sorry"?
* What rule did she break?
* How did she feel when she broke the rule?
* How did she feel after she talked to the Library Lady and Mrs. Baird?

Point out that we all occasionally break rules. The children may want to tell stories of other broken rules. Hear them out. As you respond, be careful to accept broken rules as understandable, but also let the children know that breaking rules is wrong.

Teach the children this verse of "Jesus Loves Me."

> Jesus loves me when I'm good,
> When I do the things I should.
> Jesus loves me when I'm bad,
> Even though it makes him sad.

After singing this verse several times to build familiarity with it, invite the children to join you in the "As High as the Sky" promise of forgiveness learned last week. Say it once for Kim and once for all the times we break rules.

Two Good Rules Belt

Show the children a completed "Two Good Rules" belt. Open the Bible in your worship center to Matthew 22:37-38 and tell the children that Jesus said that there are two good rules to keep wherever we are. Read them from the Bible and restate the rules as "love God" and "love one another." Point out the connection between the shapes on the belt and the two rules. Then give each child the materials with which to weave a belt. If the tables are still covered with drying paintings, do this weaving on the floor.

You may have a few minutes left to play the game you played earlier or another game the children enjoy before the closing.

"Promise Heart" Closing

Close with a prayer in which you thank God for the rules that help us work and play happily together. Apologize for the times we have broken rules and ask for help in keeping them. As a reminder that God always forgives us, give each child a "promise heart," saying: "_____(name), God loves you and will forgive you always." Hug each child as you distribute the hearts. Help them fold the hearts into their pockets or slip them into one of their shoes. Repeat the "As High as the Sky" assurance of forgiveness with its motions.

Evaluation and Looking Ahead

This concludes our section on confession. We have looked at sin as making wrong choices and breaking rules. Which seemed most meaningful to your children? How could you incorporate it into your classroom discipline?

Do your children seem to understand the sequence of feelings involved in sin, confession, and forgiveness? In the weeks to come many sessions will include confession and forgiveness activities that focus on feelings. This is perhaps the best way for kindergarten children to begin their experience with confession and forgiveness in worship.

PROCLAMATION

Session 5

Worship Focus: In worship each week we listen to God's Word read from the Bible. The preacher helps us understand God's Word and apply it to our lives.

We are focusing this year on what *we* say and do in worship so that the children can begin saying and doing those things with us. One of the things we do is listen to God. One way we listen is to read and ponder the Bible. In public worship each week, one or more passages are read and the preacher leads the congregation in reflecting on them. Sometimes our attention is focused on what God has done. At other times we focus on what God calls us to do.

Though the sermon will be one of the last parts of worship the children will share in fully, they can link it to listening to God's Word in the Scripture and in their own hearts.

Time	Worship Activity	Materials/Resources
8 min.	1. Singing and praise litany	
7 min.	2. "Hiding" confession	
5 min.	3. Listening to God: Bible	poster pictures of pulpit
15 min.	4. Making finger puppets	basic puppet forms marking pens
10 min.	5. Puppet skits	child-made puppets
10 min.	6. Closing: "Tell Me the Old, Old Story" "Jesus Loves Zacchaeus"	
	OPTIONAL	
10 min.	Go see pulpit and Bible	

Getting Ready

1. In the upper left-hand corner of a colored poster board, mount pictures of all sorts of people. In the center mount a big picture of an open Bible. (You may find one among old teaching pictures or take a picture of the Bible in your sanctuary, lying open in its usual place.) In the lower right-hand corner mount a picture of people taking care of others or in some way living out the Bible's message. With a marking pen, draw an arrow from the people in the upper left to the Bible and from the Bible to the people in the lower right.

2. Using the finger puppet pattern (see the Craft Patterns section), cut puppet outlines from a tan poster board. You will need two for each child. Fingernail scissors with curved points are great for cutting the finger holes.

Gather fine-tip marking pens for the children to "color in" the puppets. Crayons are fine, but pens are brighter and more satisfying.

Getting Started

As one leader welcomes the children and helps them put away their belongings, the other gathers the children on the rug to sing some of the praise songs the group has been learning. When most of the group has gathered, begin a conversation with the question, "How do you know about God?" Together identify people, books, videos, and places where they learn about God. If none of the children mentions the Bible, mention it yourself. Add a Bible to your worship center as a permanent fixture. Conclude your conversation by turning the things mentioned into a praise litany. The leader mentions one of the ways we know God, to which the children reply, "Thank you, God, for letting us know you." Conclude by singing the doxology.

Confession and Assurance of Pardon

Invite the children to do with their bodies what you do with yours.

Praising God puts a smile on our faces. *(smile)*
Praising God makes us hold our heads high. *(smile and hold head high)*
Praising God makes us sit up straight. *(sit up straight)*
Sometimes, praising God makes us clap our hands *(clap)*
or snap our fingers *(snap)*
or even whistle. *(whistle a line from doxology)*
BUT sometimes I can't praise God.
I feel all wrong inside.
I want to hide my eyes, so God can't see me. *(hide eyes)*
I want to hang my head *(hang head)*
and turn my back *(turn back)*
so God won't notice me.
I wish I was so small that even God could not find me. *(make self small)*
I want to hide because
I said mean things. . . . *(pause)*
I did what I should not have done. . . . *(pause)*
I have not done what I should have done. . . . *(pause)*
I have broken God's holy laws. *(pause)*
But God tells us that we never have to hide.
We can tell God about *anything* we have done.
When we say we are sorry, God promises to forgive.
In your heart, tell God about what you have done wrong. *(pause)* Now remember that God loves us so much that we do not have to hide.

Go from child to child, lifting each one's face, and say, "_____(name), God forgives you and wants to be able always to look at your face." Or straighten them and say, "_____(name), God wants you to stand tall always and never hide."

You know what? This makes me feel like praising God again! I want to smile *(smile)* and hold my head up high *(hold head high)* and sit up straight *(sit tall)* and clap my hands *(clap)* and snap my fingers *(snap fingers)* and even whistle *(whistle doxology)*.

Listening for God's Word in the Bible

If you have a chapel that is not used during this hour, visit it to see the pulpit and to find all the Bibles in the room. Talk about who uses which Bibles and why they are where they are. You may want to do the poster-based story in the chapel before returning to your room.

Recall that the Bible is one of the ways we learn about God. Present the poster and explain that we read the Bible every Sunday in church because all of us need to listen to God. Then we go home and to school and do what we have heard in the Bible. Use the Golden Rule as an example. Point it out to the children (Matt. 22:39) and read it from the Bible. Then ask the children how they might follow that rule this week. Together list specific ways of showing love. (The lower picture on the poster may be a good starter.) Then invite the children to practice this, using finger puppets that they will make.

Making Puppets

Give each child one boy and one girl puppet to color.

Puppet Shows: Putting the Bible into Action

Gather the children with their puppets on the rug again. Show them how to put one puppet on two fingers of one hand and make it walk around on their knees. When all are comfortable manipulating their puppets, invite them to be part of a puppet show with you. Explain that they will all be in the first part of the show. Then different one will perform different parts. When it is not their turn, they are to watch and listen quietly.

The show begins as they all go to church.

Everyone was going to church. They walked around saying "hello" to one another *(lead the way by making your puppets walk around on your knees and speak to puppets on either side of you)*. Then they found their seats *(one puppet-child on each knee)*. They stood up to sing praises to God. They sat down and bowed their heads to confess their sins to God and be forgiven. Then they sat up straight to hear God's Word from the Bible. The minister read, "Do unto others as you would have them do unto you." He talked a long time about what that meant. Many of the boys and girls could not remember everything the preacher had said. But they could remember what the Bible said *(pause to invite children to say the verse with you)*: "Do unto others as you would have them do unto you."

After the worship was over, they all got up, said good-bye to their friends, and started home. In some cars *(point to several children to act out this scene with both of their puppets)* there were two children in the back seat—like Bobby *(point to the brother puppets)* and Shannon *(point to the sister puppets)*. As the car went around the corner just a little fast, Shannon fell over into Bobby. Bobby shoved back *hard*. "Stay on your own side, Shrimp!" he yelled.

"I didn't mean to," said Shannon, starting to cry.

Then Bobby remembered what the Bible said *(pause for children to repeat the verse with you)*. "I'm sorry," he said. "I know you didn't mean to. It was an accident."

"That's okay," Shannon replied with just a little bit of a smile.

At another house *(point to several other children)*, Pearl *(point to the sister puppets)* and Paul *(point to the brother puppets)* jumped out of the car and raced for the new basketball Grandpa had brought them yesterday.

"I got it," shouted Paul.

But Pearl had a good grip on it, too, and was just about to shout, "It's mine, too!" when she remembered what she had heard in church *(children all repeat verse)*. She let go of the ball and went inside.

But Pearl was not the only one who had been listening in church. Paul remembered it, too *(repeat again)*. So after lunch he said, "Pearl, I had the ball before lunch. Now it's your turn."

Marilyn *(point to several sister puppets)* and Joe *(point to their brothers)* are twins. They were both thinking about what they had heard at church. They remembered *(all repeat the verse)*, so they winked at each other, then set the table for lunch without being asked to do it. After lunch Marilyn was drying the last dish and Joe was wiping off the table when their mother said, "We have worked so well together, I think we ought to go swimming this afternoon"—and they did.

Rosey *(point to several new sister puppets)* was hiding when Brad *(point to their brother puppets)* came back into his room and found the big splat of green paint on his best model.

"Rosey!" he yelled. "Rosey, don't you ever come in my room again. I told you to stay away from my model. But you didn't, and now it's ruined—ruined! Get out of here and don't you ever come back!"

Rosey cried in her room for a while. Then she remembered what she had heard in church that morning *(all repeat the verse)*. Brad was right. He had told her not to mess with his model, and she had ruined it. It was an accident, but she shouldn't have been looking in his paint bottle. So she went to the door of his room. "Brad, I'm sorry. I didn't mean to ruin your model, and I promise I'll never come in your room ever again."

"That's all right, Rosey." Brad had remembered the verse, too. "I shouldn't have yelled at you like that. I'm sorry, too. And you can come in my room—just don't mess with my models, okay?"

"Okay," Rosey replied.

And that night when all the boys and girls snuggled down into their beds, they all had smiles on their faces. It had been a good day and would be a good week if they could just remember what the Bible said. *(All repeat the verse one more time.)*

Closing

Laying aside your puppets, tell the children that this show makes you think of a song about the stories in the Bible. Sing the chorus of "Tell Me the Old, Old Story" once. Ask the children to sing it with you, adding a different rhythmic accompaniment each time. First, clap as you sing. Then pat your legs as you sing. Then snap your fingers. Combine them by assigning different groups of children to do different rhythms as you all sing. Or clap as you sing the first phrase, pat your legs as you sing the second phrase, snap your fingers as you sing the third phrase, point up as you sing "of Jesus," and throw your arms out to embrace the whole world as you sing "and his love."

If you have time, tell the children one of your favorite stories about Jesus. You might want to tell the story of Zacchaeus (Luke 19:1-10). Whatever story you tell, open the Bible to the place it is found as you tell the story.

Close by reminding the children of the difference it made to the children in the puppet shows to have heard God's Word in the Bible. Give each child two small Bible stickers to glue on their puppets' hands. Then give them another Bible sticker to put on themselves to remind them of the verse they heard. Repeat the Golden Rule one more time.

Visit the Bible in the Sanctuary (optional)

If it is possible, sometime during this session visit the sanctuary of a small chapel (if your church has one) to get a close look at whatever Bible is displayed in the worship center there. Be sure each child gets to see the book. Talk about why the Bible is placed where it is and how it is used.

If the only way to make this trip is to have the children at a side door of the sanctuary, ready to go in as soon as the worship is over, leave a big sign on your classroom door, telling parents where you have gone and where they should pick up their children.

Looking Ahead

Next Sunday you will need a collection of items to spark discussion about creation and either stickers with Jesus' picture on them or small pictures of Jesus cut from old curricula. Other materials should be in the supply closet.

Session 6

Worship Focus: Last Sunday we explored "proclamation" as listening for what God wants us to do. This Sunday we will focus on listening to and affirming all God is and has done.

As we read the Bible in worship, we are reminded of all that God has done and continues to do for us. As we retell the stories of the people of God, we reclaim for ourselves citizenship among those people. In many congregations the scripture reading and sermon are followed by a creed or affirmation of faith said by the congregation. Kindergarten children cannot understand creeds and affirmations, but they can learn to listen to scripture with a sense of "this is my/our story."

To experience this with the children, we will trace the overview of the biblical story. Creation will be tied to praise. Receiving and failing to keep the commandments will be tied to confession and pardon. Then we will enjoy several stories about Jesus and summarize their importance by making a Bible bookmark. In response, children will participate in a simplified version of the Apostles' Creed (more to get the feeling of standing up to say "I believe" than to hear the Apostles' Creed).

Time	Worship Activity	Materials/Resources
10 min.	1. Creation conversation and praise songs	creation items Doxology Song Book
10 min.	2. Ten Commandments and confessing our sins . . . Sing "Forgive Me, God . . . "	
20 min.	3. Stories about Jesus	selected equipment
15 min.	4. "Jesus" bookmarks	bookmark forms stickers or pictures glue or paste fine-tip marking pens yarn
5 min.	5. "I believe . . ."	

Getting Ready

1. Select an item or group of items that will start a conversation with the children about God's creation. An acorn, a small branch of colored leaves, and a picture of a big tree start talk about God's plan for the growth of trees. If you're feeling brave and have access to one, a baby animal will start lots of talk about that animal and its place in God's world. You might even invite a parent or friend with a nature-centered hobby to bring items in and be a part of the discussion about creation.

2. Select at least two stories about Jesus to share with the children. If you have filmstrips, use one. If you have access to Bible videos, plan to show one of them. Look for other stories in children's books about Jesus in your church library or at home. Or prepare to tell in your own words one of your favorite stories about Jesus (save the Christmas and Easter stories for those days). Prepare each story in a different way. Gather and set up whatever equipment or props you need for these stories so that you don't have to interrupt the session.

3. Prepare materials for children to make bookmarks. Cut from attractive poster board one 2″ × 6″ bookmark for each child. At one end punch a hole for the tassel. Each child needs two pictures of Jesus and two hearts. Find stickers or cut from old curriculum resources small pictures of Jesus. Find heart stickers or cut small hearts from red construction paper. The children will also need two pictures of themselves. One or both of these could be cut from instantly developed photos taken in groups of two or three as the children arrive. Or the children could draw self-portraits using fine-tip marking pens (crayons are too big for this space). Decide how you will do the self-portraits and gather the necessary materials. Finally cut each child a 4″ strand of colored yarn to tie on the bookmark as a tassel.

Getting Started and Singing Praises

As one leader greets children at the door and helps them settle their belongings, the other leader gathers children on the rug for conversation about the creation items you have brought. Talk about growth and God's plan. Hear children's ideas about each item and generally enjoy them. When most of the children have arrived, place the items on your worship center. Open the Bible to Genesis and read, "In the beginning God created the heavens and the earth. . . . And God saw everything that he had made, and behold, it was very good." (Gen. 1:1 and 31*a*). Tell them that this makes you feel like singing songs for God and invite them to sing several of your praise songs with you. Point out how creation is one of the "blessings" which flow from God.

Ten Commandments and Confession

Tell a story.

After creating the world, God did not just say, "Whew! That's done" and go look for something else to do. No way. God loved the world. God especially loved the people. God watched over and knew each one. God watched children being born and growing up and going to school and getting married and having children of their own. Most of the time, this made God very happy, but not all of the time. When God's people were mean to one another or called one another names or hurt one another or fought, God was unhappy, and the people were unhappy.

One day God had an idea. God told the people, "If you want to be my happy people, you will need to follow some rules. If you follow these rules, we will all be happy together." All the people gathered around to hear God's rules. This is what God said.

I am your God.
Don't make pictures or statues of me. I'm bigger and more different than you can imagine)
Say my name with love and respect.
Remember that Sunday is a special day.
Honor your parents.
Don't kill.
Love your family always.
Don't steal.
Don't tell lies.
Don't be jealous of things other people have.

If you had been there, would those rules have sounded good to you? *(Discuss the rules if the children want to ask questions about any of them.)* The people thought the rules sounded pretty good. So God said, "Let's make some promises." *(Ask the children to pretend that they are with the people. After you say each of the rules, the children are to stand up to reply, "I'll do that." Before each rule say, "Do you promise to . . . ."*

The people did like the rules, and they tried to follow them. But it wasn't easy. Sometimes they broke the rules. And we do, too. We do fine with some of them—I guess none of us has ever killed anyone. But we do tell lies—I know I do. And we do get jealous of good things other people have. Sometimes, we get so jealous that we grab them for ourselves—that is stealing. And when we do these things, there is only one thing to do. What is it? *(Children's answers should lead to the idea that we must confess. They may even mention the prayer about breaking laws. If they do not, conclude the discussion by mentioning the prayer and inviting the children to line it out with you.)*

Dear God, we have broken your holy rules. We have left undone those things we ought to have done. We have done things we ought not to have done. We are very sorry. Amen.

Teach the children the song "Forgive Me, God, for Things I Do" by singing it through, then having them say the words after you and finally singing it several times.

Remind the children that God forgives us when we confess. Then do the "As High as the Sky" assurance of pardon.

Telling the Stories of Jesus

Sing the chorus "Tell Me the Old, Old Story" with the rhythmic sounds. You may want to go through the whole process of adding claps and finger snaps one at a time as described in the last lesson. Then share the stories about Jesus you have selected. Between each story sing the hymn chorus together. The whole point is to enjoy hearing and retelling stories of Jesus. Children may also volunteer to tell a story they know about Jesus.

Making "Jesus" Bookmarks

Show the children a completed bookmark and show how it can be used to mark stories about Jesus in the Bible. Point out how tricky it is to get the stickers and pictures in the right order on each side and urge the children to follow your directions carefully as you work to make your bookmarks.

Give each child a bookmark to take to a table. Instruct them to place their bookmarks with the hole at the bottom on the table in front of them.

Give each child a sticker or small picture of Jesus to place at the top of the page.

When those are in place, give them hearts to mount in the middle of the bookmark.

When those are in place, give them the picture of themselves or the pens with which to draw a picture of themselves for the bottom of the bookmark.

"Read" the message together. Then tell the children to turn their bookmarks over, keeping the holes at the bottom. Repeat the process above, putting the self-portrait first, then the heart, then the picture of Jesus. "Read" that message.

When both sides are done, children may wish to decorate them with colored marking pens. Finally, give each child 4″ of colored yarn to tie through the hole as a tassel.

Closing: I Believe

If any children say the Pledge of Allegiance at their schools, ask them to describe how it is said and what it means. Use their answers as a starting point for standing up straight and tall to say what we know and love about God. Then invite them to join you in lining out the sentences below.

I love God, who created the world.
I love Jesus.
He was born in a barn to Mary.
He. . . . *(say a sentence about each of the stories told today)*
I love the church of God's people.
Amen.

Spend any remaining time singing songs about Jesus.

PETITION

Session 7

Worship Focus: We can share with God anything that is important to us.

Just as God's love is big enough to handle our sin, so also it is big enough to handle all our joys, sorrows, worries, needs, and fears. There is nothing that is important to us that we cannot share with God. So we are free to tell God about everything and to ask God's help for ourselves and for others.

Today we will focus on sharing our feelings with God. We will try sharing some happy feelings and some unhappy ones as one way of dealing with feelings. Next week we will be ready to explore prayers of concern for others.

Time	Worship Activity	Materials/Resources
10 min.	1. Conversation and singing	
15 min.	2. Mounting happy faces Saying happy prayers	pre-cut Happy Face magazine pictures colored paper glue or paste or tacks
5 min.	3. Birthday feelings and prayers	birthday banner
10 min.	4. Enjoy a game and tell God about it	
15 min.	5. Scared feelings pictures	black construction paper scraps of colored paper paste or glue sticks
5 min.	6. Closing: Psalm 139:1-6 and singing	

Getting Ready

1. From the Craft Patterns section, cut out and mount on stiff paper the "feelings faces." Save them all for later use.

2. From magazines, cut out a collection of pictures of different kinds of places and seasons, family pictures, friendship pictures, and the like that could make children feel happy. Cut out at least one and one half times as many pictures as the number of children you expect.

3. Gather a sheet of dark construction paper for each child, scraps of colored construction paper, and paste or glue sticks. Make a torn paper picture of something that frightens you; make your figure large and simple.

4. Buy or make a "happy birthday" streamer or banner to post on your happy board.

Getting Started

As one leader greets children and settles their belongings, the other leader gathers children on the rug to look at "feelings faces." Ask each child which face he or she feels more like at the moment. You may ask what has happened to make them feel that way. Accept all answers without judgment.

Sing several homegrown verses of the old song "If You're Happy and You Know It." Each verse describes one feeling using the following format.

If you're _____ and you know it, _____.
(do something with hands or feet, such as clap your hands or clench your fists as you sing what you do)

(Repeat first line.)

If you're _____ and you know it,
Then your face will surely show it. *(make appropriate face)*

(Repeat first line.)

Sing verses, picking up on the feelings most children identified with in the picture faces.

After pointing out that God loves us no matter what we are feeling, sing some songs about God's love ("Jesus Loves Me," "Jesus Loves the Little Children of the World," "He's Got the Whole World in His Hands," and the doxology).

Joyful Feelings and Praise

1. When the group has arrived, present the happy face and ask the children to identify the feeling. Try it on yourselves. Show how your mouth looks, how you walk, and how your feel all over when you are joyful. Then invite each child to select one picture that makes them feel joyful from the collection of pictures on the table. After they have selected their pictures, encourage them to select a "happy colored" piece of construction paper on which to mount their pictures. (Remember we each see different colors as "happy"—no right answers here!).

As the children finish their work, invite them to bring their pictures to the circle. Challenge each child to think of a prayer about that happy picture. (These will be brief statements of what they like about their pictures more than formal prayers. That is a great beginning!) As each child offers his or her prayer, mount his or her picture around the happy face on a bulletin board or door and lead the group in responding, "Praise God from whom all blessings flow!" You need not wait until all the children have completed their picture to begin hearing happy prayers and mounting the pictures.

2. Unroll a length of a crêpe paper birthday banner (store-bought or homemade) and ask: Who has had a birthday? Who likes having a birthday? Who likes going to someone else's birthday party? Go around your circle, asking each child to say one happy thing about birthdays. Add the banner to

your door or bulletin board of happy things. Then ask everyone to join you in a prayer about birthdays. Line out (leader says a phrase and the children repeat) a prayer that grows out of what the children have talked about, thanking God for birthday fun and happy feelings about birthdays.

3. Talk about games that the children like to play. Play one of the games they mention. ("Duck-Duck-Goose" or "Drop the Handkerchief" are good to remember if the children need help naming a game to enjoy in the classroom.) After enjoying the game for a while, sit down, get quiet, then lead a prayer to thank God for the fun of playing games together. Comment that it is fun to share happy feelings with God, and it almost makes us happier when we do. Go on to note that God likes sharing happy feelings as much as we like feeling happy, but that God also wants us to share the unhappy times and feelings.

Feeling Scared

1. Tell the children to sit on their hands because you are going to ask some questions for them to think about but not answer.

> Have you ever thought you saw a monster in your room at night? *(pause)*
> Have you ever been alone and afraid that someone was going to hurt you? *(pause)*
> Have you ever been afraid that you had been left behind and no one would come back for you? *(pause)*
> Have you ever seen a really scary movie or TV show that scared you every time you thought of it? *(pause)*

Tell them that everyone is scared some of the time. Then invite them to make pictures of something really scary. Give each child a piece of black construction paper. On each table, place a pile of construction paper scraps and some paste or glue sticks. Make the pictures by gluing torn paper shapes onto the black paper. Show your sample to the children so that they may get the idea. As pictures are completed, post them around the frightened face on a door or wall. Encourage discussion about the pictures as they are posted. (Yes, you will probably get a number of monster pictures that look like the products of active, confident imaginations on the loose. That is fine.)

2. Gather the children on the rug to remind them that everyone gets scared. Open your Bible to Matthew 26 and tell the story of Jesus' prayer in Gethsemane.

> Jesus was frightened. He knew he had strong, angry enemies. His enemies did not like what Jesus said and did. They had been following him around. And Jesus knew there was trouble ahead. They were going to hurt him. They wanted to kill him. That is why Jesus was frightened.
> After dinner, Jesus and his friends went to a park. Jesus went off by himself to talk to God. He told God all about his fear. He prayed, "Father, if it is possible, don't let this happen."
> But he also said something else. After telling God that he did not want to be hurt and killed, Jesus remembered how much he loved and trusted God. He said, "Still, not what I want but what you want. Even if they hurt me, even if they kill me, I know you love me and care for me. So if that is what you want, I will do it."
> And he did. A few minutes later his enemies came with soldiers and arrested him. Jesus met them quietly. He was very calm and brave because he knew that God was with him no matter what.

Point to the children's pictures and tell them that just as God was with Jesus when Jesus was afraid, so also God is with us even when . . . *(list some of the frightening events in the pictures).*

Closing

Point to each of the feeling faces and to your displays about happy feelings and fear. Remind the children that there is nothing we cannot share with God. Open the Bible to Psalm 139 and line out verses 1-6 a phrase at a time with the children. Close by rephrasing "If You're Happy and You Know It" one more time. This time sing the verses below.

> If you're _____ and you know it, *(everyone make appropriate faces)*
> Tell it to God. *(fold hands in prayer)*

(Repeat line one)

If you're _____ and you know it,
God who made you wants to share it.
If you're _____ and you know it,
Tell it to God.

Looking Ahead

Next week's session begins with praise using instruments. If there is a trumpet, guitar, or flute player in your congregation, invite that person to visit with his or her instrument (see "Getting Ready" before issuing the invitation). You will also have to gather vegetables, paints, and paper towels to make stamp pad note cards.

Session 8

Worship Focus: When we pray for other people we become partners with God in loving them.

We can tell God not only about ourselves and our needs, but also we can tell God about other people who need love and care. So we pray for others, both people we know personally and those we know at a distance. When we pray for people, we become partners with God in caring for them. Asking God to help them leads us to do what we can for them.

Time	Worship Activity	Materials/Resources
10 min.	1. Praising with instruments	rhythm instruments guitar and guest (?)
5 min.	2. Confessing	
10 min.	3. "Musical Prayers"	prayer pictures record player and record
5 min.	4. Praying for one another	
5 min.	5. Chicken pox story	
20 min.	6. Making cards for the sick	stamps and pads pre-folded cards paper for design
5 min.	7. Closing: Jesus' prayer and ours for friends	

Getting Ready

1. Read Psalm 150. Gather your rhythm instruments. Be sure to find drums and cymbals or bells. Borrow a guitar, if possible. Invite a guest trumpeter or flute player to join you for the beginning of your session. With some warning and a copy of the music, your guest may be willing to learn one of your songs to play while the children sing as well as to play at the appropriate place when you line out Psalm 150.

2. Around your room at a child's eye level post pictures of people in a variety of situations—some happy, others unhappy. Be sure to have one picture for each child. These are the "chairs" for the game "Musical Prayers," which is modeled on "Musical Chairs." You will also need recorded Christian music.

3. To make stamps for children to use in making cards, cut carrots into 4″ sticks (makes round balls); cut stalks of celery into 4″ sticks (makes half moon shapes); section an orange or two (makes leaf and petal shapes); and, if you feel adventurous, carve chunks of potato into stars, hearts, and the like. Using these stamps, children may make free-form designs or recognizable pictures for their cards by combining different stamps. For example, a flower can be made with a carrot stamp center surrounded by orange section petals. To make stamp pads, pour thick tempera paint over pads of folded paper towels until they are just soaked through. Set the pads in jar lids or saucers. **Warning:** the pads will dry out if prepared too far in advance. Two or three (at the most) colors of paint are ample. You will also need pre-folded cards for the children to decorate and some half sheets of paper on which the children can make designs to take home.

Getting Started with Praise

As one leader greets children and gets their belongings settled, the other gathers children on the rug to introduce whatever instruments you have and pass them out to the children. Use the instruments to accompany yourselves as you sing familiar praise songs. If you have a guest trumpeter or flute player, introduce your guest and his or her instrument. Sing a song as the guest plays.

When everyone has had a chance to play at least one of the instruments, read Psalm 150. Put away all the rhythm instruments except the ones for the psalm. Introduce the guitar and its place as the "lute" in the psalm. Assign each instrument to a player. Then line out the psalm, pointing to the appropriate instruments when they are to be played. Pass the instruments to new players and repeat the psalm a time or two. Thank your guest for helping. (The guest may want to leave for worship or stay for the rest of the session.)

While putting away the remaining instruments, point out that even without instruments we can praise God because God made us with built-in instruments—clapping hands, snapping fingers, slapping our knees, and sliding our hands back and forth like sandpaper blocks are our instruments. Make an orchestra by assigning one "instrument" to each group of children. Together sing one of the praise songs with an adult serving as conductor, pointing to groups when they are to play. (There is no right way to conduct. Just give each group a chance on different phrases of the song.) Finally, rephrase Psalm 150 to use your body instruments—for example, "Praise God with clapping hands."

Confession and Forgiveness

Raise your arms over your head and clap your hands several times. Look up and keep your hands up as you say the following.

> When we praise you, oh God, we are happy. We want to be near you. We know that you are good, good, good and that you love best of all. We want to give you a big hug. *(Drop your hands into your lap and bow your head.)*
>
> But sometimes we have to look away because we have not been good and loving. We have not done what we should have done. We have done what we should not have done. We have refused to listen or share. We have called people names and said mean things in anger. Over and over we have had to say "I'm sorry" to our friends and people in our families. And now we each need to say "I'm sorry" to you, God.
>
> *(Pause briefly for children to say a silent "I'm sorry prayer." Then invite them to sing "Forgive Me, God, for Things I Do." Then look up and put your hand up over your head.)*
>
> "What does God promise will happen when we say we are sorry?" *(Go into the "As High as the Sky" assurance of pardon with motions.)*

Musical Prayers

Remind the children that last week we learned that we can tell God anything about ourselves. Explain that we can also tell God about other people and what they need. Then instruct each child to stand in front of one of the pictures around the room. Tell them to look at the picture and make up a prayer for one of the people in it. Suggest that the prayer might begin, "God, help. . . . " Get a few children to say what their prayers would be and why until you feel the children have caught on to the idea. Then invite them to play "Musical Prayers." When the music starts, the players move around the room, touching each picture as they pass it. When the music stops, each player puts a hand on a picture. Only one child can claim a picture. Ask one or two children to say a prayer for a person in that picture, then start the music again. Call on a variety of children and give attention to a variety of pictures. (In this game, unlike "Musical Chairs," no pictures are removed between rounds so that every player gets a picture every time the music stops.)

Praying for One Another

As interest in the game begins to wane, call everyone to sit in a circle on the rug. Note that in the game they were making up prayers for people they did not know. Invite them to help make up prayers for people they do know—one another. Ask one child to stand and step back from the circle. Say a short sentence to thank God for something special about that child and have the rest of the group repeat it. The next child stands up, and the prayer process is repeated until every child in the circle has been prayed for.

Pose the question, "If I had thanked God for ———'s *(name something about one child for which the group had thanked God)*, but the next time I saw her I said something really mean or shoved her or grabbed something she was working with, would I really be very thankful for ———?" Once conversation has made the point that our actions must match our prayers, proceed to the story.

Chicken Pox and Prayers*

Mary was five years old when she got the chicken pox. Who here has had the chicken pox? *(pause for show of hands)* You will agree that having chicken pox isn't fun. Mary did not feel well at all! The night she got sick, Mary's mother and father prayed, "God, Mary has the chicken pox. She doesn't feel well at all. Please, help her."

Mary's father took her to the doctor the next day. The doctor gave her some medicine and said for Mary to stay quiet and try not to scratch all the little itchy sores. Mary's father brought her home and helped her into bed. Mary really was tired. Her mother gave her the medicine. That night Mary's father and mother prayed again, "God, Mary has the chicken pox. She doesn't feel well at all. Please, help her."

The next day Mary's mother gave her more of the medicine. Then when Mary had slept as much as she could, Mother brought her chocolate pudding (her favorite!) and some quiet games. They worked a puzzle together for a while. That night Mary's father and mother prayed for her again, "God, Mary has the chicken pox. Please, help her."

Finally Mary was beginning to feel better. She got dressed and even went outside for a little while. The red spots were beginning to go away. That night her father brought home a big, hot pizza for supper because he was so glad Mary was feeling better. Later that night Mary's mother and father prayed, "Mary is feeling better now, God. Thank you."

Questions for discussion. (1) When Mary got the chicken pox, her parents began to pray for her. What else did they do? (2) What if they had just prayed for God to help Mary but had not taken her to the doctor or given her the medicine or kept the house quiet so she could sleep or played quiet games with her?

Note that when we pray for someone we become partners with God in taking care of that person.

———
*Written by Lindy Judd. Used by permission.

Mary's parents were partners with God in taking care of her. And we can be God's partners in taking care of people around us.

Making Cards for the Sick

Tell the children that every week in worship our whole church prays for people who are sick. Then during the week we do whatever we can to help take care of them. Invite the children to join the work by making cards that can be sent to people who are sick.

Show children how the stamping process works and how they can make designs using the different stamps. Give them each one small piece of paper on which to make a design to keep and a card on which to make a design for someone who is sick. If you know of people in your church who are sick, tell the children about them while they work.

Closing

Gather back on the rug. Tell the children that Jesus often prayed for other people. Open your Bible to John 17 and tell them that one night just before Jesus was going to be killed, he had a wonderful dinner with his friends. After dinner he prayed for his friends. He said, "Father, keep them safe. I love them and have protected them. I have given them your message of love to give to the whole world. Help them."

Put the Bible back on your worship center and say something like, "We can pray in that same way for people we know and love. Let's bow our heads and close our eyes. I'll pray out loud and say some things for you to pray about silently." Pray for the people who will receive your cards. Then thank God for the special people you know and suggest one at a time types of people (parents, friends, pets, someone at school, etc.) they can pray for. Pause briefly after each suggestion. If you have extra time, sing some favorite songs.

DEDICATION

Session 9

Worship Focus: In response to God's love we set aside buildings, equipment, books, and our own lives to be used in God's work.

In worship, we praise God; we confess our sins, accepting God's promised forgiveness; and we listen to the stories of God's love, claiming them as our own. Our natural response is to give something back to God in love and appreciation. So we dedicate our talents and our resources to God. Today we will explore what it means to set things (everything from buildings to our lives) aside for God's use. Next week we will look at the offering taken in our worship service and what happens to money dedicated to God. When (if) your church officers are installed in Sunday worship, you may want to use session 33, "Officer Installation Sunday," to explore how church officers dedicate their time to doing God's work.

Time	Worship Activity	Materials/Resources
10 min.	1. Tape interviews about talents Prayer litany	tape recorder with microphone
10 min.	2. Confession about talents	
20 min.	3. Dedication Walk	
10 min.	4. Dedication Mobile	hangers pre-cut, punched cards string or thread
5 min.	5. Learn "Take My Life and Let It Be Consecrated"	song board
5 min.	6. Closing: prayer based on opening interviews	recorded interviews

46

Getting Ready

1. Be sure you have a tape recorder and blank tape on hand to record statements from the children. Practice operating the recorder so that you can record, play, and stop easily.

2. The "big event" of this session is a "Dedication Walk," a tour of items around your church that are dedicated to the glory of God and some special use. Plan for this tour by listing what dedicated items you have. Do you have a cornerstone dedicating your sanctuary, any room with a sign saying what it is dedicated to, a communion set inscribed with a dedication, inscribed flower vases, Bibles or hymnbooks with bookplates indicating that they are dedicated, and books in the church library with dedication bookplates? Plan your itinerary, being sure that you have keys for locked closets if necessary.

3. To make a Dedication Mobile, you will need one wire coat hanger for every six children in your group. On each one tape a sign that says "Dedicated" in bright bold letters. Cut out a variety of shapes of colored poster board, all about 4″ × 6″. In each one punch a hole through which you will tie a 20″ piece of thread or string. Tie or hook the first hanger to the ceiling near your worship center. Tie the second hanger onto the middle of the crossbar of the first hanger with three cards on each side, and so on.

4. Begin a poster board song book for "Take My Life and Let It Be Consecrated." You will need one page for each of the two verses. Reproduce the pages below on your poster board, using broad-tipped marking pens. The words beside the page are added for your interpretation.

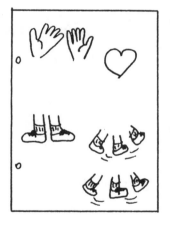

Take my hands and let them move
At the impulse of thy love.

Take my feet and let them be
Swift and beautiful for Thee,
Swift and beautiful for Thee.

Take my voice and let me sing
Always only for my King.

Take my lips and let them be
filled with messages from Thee,
filled with messages from Thee.

Getting Started

While one leader greets children at the door and helps settle their belongings, the other gathers the children on the rug to conduct interviews about what they do well. Begin by defining *talents*. Move quickly into recording a brief statement by each child about his or her own talents. Avoid taping anything but the children's actual comments. (The leader at the door can help by greeting children in a whisper, telling them that the group is recording, and asking them to join the group silently to await their turn.)

When everyone has made a statement, turn the tape into a prayer by playing it back and stopping after each statement to say as a class, "Thank you, God."

Sing the doxology, pointing out that the things we can do well are some of the blessings that come from God. Enjoy singing other praise songs together.

Confession About Using Our Talents

Tell this story of a little boy who did not use his talent.

Helio's Talent

Grandma was coming to live with them. Everyone was excited, *and* everyone was working hard to welcome her.

Papa was building a long ramp by the back steps. Grandma had trouble walking, and the ramp would make it easy for her to get in and out of the house. Helio watched Papa measure and cut and nail.

"Why don't you go draw Grandma a welcome picture," Papa suggested. Helio drew very well. Several of his pictures were chosen to be in a school art show. Helio shrugged his shoulders. "Think I'll go ride my bike," he said. And he did.

Mother was fixing a room for Grandma. She washed the curtains and cleaned out the drawers. She dusted the shelves and even washed the rug. Out in the hall was the big new chair that would go into Grandma's room for reading. When Helio looked in to see what she was doing, Mother said, "Helio, you know what this room needs is a nice picture to put on the wall." Helio knew who she thought should draw it. But he said, "Think I'll go watch television."

Maria was sitting by the big bookshelf. A small pile of books lay on the floor beside her.

"What are you doing?" Helio asked.

"Picking out books about other countries for Grandma's room," Maria said, adding a book about Mexico to the pile. Grandma loved to read about other countries. Maria was studying about other countries in the fifth grade. So she could find the right books. "You know, Helio, you could draw a picture to put on her bookshelf."

"Yeah, I could," and Helio turned on the TV.

The next day when Grandma came to live with them, she said, "Oh, my goodness! Oh, my goodness!" over and over again when she saw the ramp Papa had built. She smiled and hugged Papa tight as they walked up it for the first time.

When she came into her room, she sat in her new chair, looked all around, and smiled. She squeezed Mother's hand, "Someone has done a lot of work getting ready for me."

When she saw the bookshelf, she got out her glasses to read the titles. "Someone knows what I like to read," she said looking happily at Maria.

Helio watched from the door. He felt kind of sad and lonely inside. Everyone but he had done something to welcome Grandma.

Help the children identify what each member of the family did to welcome Grandma. Talk about their talents and how they used them. Then talk about Helio's failure to use his talent. Discuss how he felt when Grandma came.

Use this as a springboard to pointing out that all of us have talents that we can use—or *not* use. Recall some of the talents that were mentioned in the recorded interviews. Pray a brief prayer, confessing that sometimes we do not use and enjoy the gifts God gives us. Sing "Forgive Me, God, for Things I Do." Then tell the children that the story about Helio does not end there.

Helio walked back into his room. He thought about Papa's ramp and Mother's clean room and Maria's pile of books. And he thought about the picture he *could* draw. Then he got out his crayons and a big piece of paper. He drew their house. Inside he drew Papa and Mother and Maria and Helio and Grandma. It was a good picture. He gave it to Grandma that night at supper. She liked it so much that the very next day she bought a picture frame and hung Helio's picture on her wall. She gave him a big hug and said, "Now I will always remember that this is my home." Helio hugged Grandma. He was glad that she was going to live with them, too.

Dedication Walk

Introduce the word *dedicated*. Ask the children to repeat it after you, then say it one after the other all the way around your circle. Once they can say the word, ask whether anyone knows what it means. Lead conversation to the idea that a thing that is dedicated is set apart for God's use.

Go on a walking tour of some of the "dedicated" items around your church. At each one discuss how it is used for God.

Dedication Mobile

When you return to your classroom, show the children the frame for your mobile. Then ask each child to think of one dedicated thing he or she saw and to draw a picture of it for the mobile. Ask each child to say what she or he is going to draw as you give them one of the pre-cut cards on their way to the tables. As children finish their drawings, tie the drawings to the mobile.

Learning "Take My Life and Let It Be Consecrated"

Teach the children the first verse of "Take My Life and Let It Be Consecrated" on the song poster you have prepared. Begin by pointing out that we can dedicate not only buildings and books to God, but we can also dedicate ourselves to God. We can dedicate our bodies and our gifts to God. We can dance and play music and do sports and sing for God. Line out the words one phrase at a time. Be sure children understand the meanings of the phrases.

Sing the verse once and point to the appropriate pictures as you sing. Invite the children to sing with you. Again, point to the pictures as you sing. Sing the verse several times.

Closing Prayer of Dedication

If you have time, replay the taped statements from the opening of this session. After each child's statement, stop the tape to offer a one-sentence prayer, such as "God, help Tony sing for you" or "Help Lee remember that you make her strong."

If time is short, ask the children to bow their heads and close their eyes and remember what they said on the tape. Pause for a moment, then pray, "God, we thank you for all our different gifts and talents. Help us to dedicate them to you. We love you, God. Amen."

Looking Ahead

Next week your group goes to the sanctuary to watch the offering being collected. Read the directions for the trip now and contact your minister to plan for this visit.

You will also need to make a big "map" that shows where the offering money goes.

Session 10

Worship Focus: We dedicate our gifts of money and talents to God.

In response to God's love, we offer all our financial resources and talents for God's work. Bringing those gifts is part of our community worship. The collection of the offering is not a break in the order of worship but an important part of it. In many congregations, the offering follows the scripture readings and sermon, thus emphasizing the fact that we give in response to God's love.

You will devote much time to the details of how we take up the offering today. Your children will have many questions as they observe the offering in the sanctuary and follow the journey of the "dedicated dollars." That is good, but remember that the most important concept for them to grasp is that our motivation for giving is not an "ought" but our free response to God's love.

Time	Worship Activity	Materials/Resources
8 min.	1. Praise for loving things others do for us	
7 min.	2. Confession story and prayer	
10 min.	3. Act out the offering	offering plate play money
10 min.	4. Watch the offering in the sanctuary	coins for children camera
10 min.	5. Journey of "dedicated dollars"	"map"
15 min.	6. My offering	prepared sheet song chart offering plate

Getting Ready

1. Be sure you know how the offering is collected during your worship service. When is the prayer of dedication prayed? Who passes the plates? If the doxology is used, at what point is it sung in the service?

Borrow an offering plate. Check old teaching picture files for a picture of the offering being collected. Buy or make some play money. (To make it, cut "dollars" from green construction paper.)

2. Plan your visit to the sanctuary to watch the offering. Find out from your minister at what time the offering is usually taken. Clear with the minister where the children will stand. Since it is important for them to see well, two good places for the children to stand are a side door near the front of the sanctuary (at the appropriate time, open the door and, with the children, step quietly inside) or on the back pews (ask ushers to save these for you). Remember, the presence of quiet children, even standing in a corner up front, is an addition, not a distraction, to worship for most people.

If the children will be watching from a place to which the offering plate will be passed, be sure each child has a coin (not play money) to put into the plate.

Once you know when you will visit the sanctuary, rearrange the plan for the other activities as needed.

Your minister might want to put a note about your visit in the bulletin, especially if this is your group's first visit to the sanctuary during worship. This lets people know what is going on in children's worship and introduces them to this ministry of the church.

3. Make a "map" that traces the journey of the money that is put in the offering plates. Following the outline below, (1) draw a picture of an offering plate filled with money or glue some play money onto a circle; (2) mount a drawing or photograph of the money bags or safe at the church; (3) mount a picture of the bank to which it is deposited; (4) mount a picture of the people in your church who decide how to spend the money; and (5) mount a column of pictures or items that represent some of the things for

which your church spends money—pictures of staff, a drawing of the church building, covers from Sunday school books, pictures of mission projects, and so on.

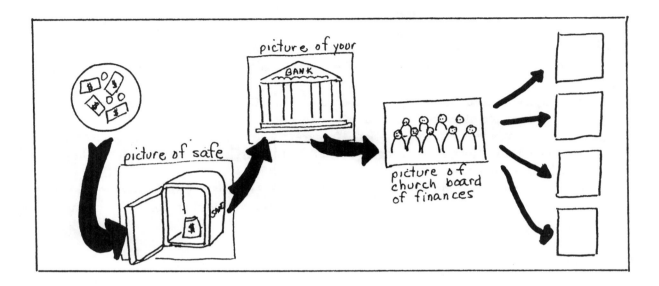

4. At the top of a sheet of drawing paper, write, "For God." At the bottom write, "Love, _____" (children will sign their own names). Make one sheet for each child to use.

Getting Started

As one leader greets children and their parents at the door and helps the children settle their belongings, the other leader gathers children on the rug for conversation about nice things other people have done for us. Give each child a chance to tell about something nice someone has done. The leader may have to start with an example. Once most of the children have gathered and had a chance to add to the conversation, inform them that you know an important secret about God. Then explain that one way God does nice things for us is to send a person to do it for God. So when someone does something nice for us it means not only that that person loves us, but it also means that God loves us! Use some of the stories the children have told as examples of God's loving us through other people. Conclude with a litany of praise for the God who loves us. The children's response is "Thank you, God, for loving us." The leader offers lines like these, which grow from your group conversation:

When a friend lets us go first though we didn't ask, we say . . .
When my sister cleans up our whole room, not just her side, I say . . .
When Daddy tucks me in and reads an extra story and tells me I am very special, I say . . .
When someone says, "My, how fine you look today," we say . . .

Acting Out the Offering

Point out to the children that one way we help God do good things for others is to take an offering. Ask if anyone has seen what happens in church when the money plates are passed to collect the offering. Combine what they already know with what you know to walk through the process. Include a prayer of dedication and sing the doxology and an offertory hymn, if they are part of your worship. Talk about the offering, using a teaching picture if one is available.

Then act it out. Sit in rows as if in pews. Take turns being the people who pass the plates, the people in the pews filling the plates, and the person who prays about the money's use. Sing the doxology at the appropriate time. You may want to do this several times so that the children may try out several roles.

Observing the Offering in the Sanctuary

Take the children to a place just outside the sanctuary a few minutes before time for the offering. One leader listens for the time to go in while the other sings or talks quietly with the children while you wait.

If this is your first visit to the sanctuary as a group, be sure the children understand what they will see and what is expected of them. Tell them where to stand or sit. Explain that they may not talk, whisper, or wave to people in the congregation. They are to watch and listen to what happens. Prepare children to sing the doxology with the congregation. Be sure each child has a coin to put in the offering plate if it will come your way.

After your visit, be sure to congratulate the children on their behavior and correct misbehavior if needed. Remember a first trip to the sanctuary may easily involve some mistakes. Enlist parental help in teaching children proper worship behavior.

The Journey of the Dedicated Dollars

If the filled offering plates are carried out of the sanctuary immediately, follow them to the place they are taken and talk to the person in charge about what is done with the money next. Take a picture of that person and the money with your instant camera to add to your "map." If the money is left in the sanctuary, return immediately to your room.

Using your map, follow the journey of the money from the offering plate to its use for God's work.

My Offering

Using the song chart from last week, work on relearning one verse of "Take My Life and Let It Be Consecrated."

After singing it several times, point out to the children that though none of them has much money to give God, they do have many gifts they can give. Discuss gifts they can give with their mouths and feet as in the song. Make the point that one gift we give God is loving and taking care of others. Summarize your conversation by saying in your own words Matthew 25:40, "Whatever you do for the least important of my brothers or sisters, you do for me."

Then give each child a prepared offering paper on which to draw a picture of something they plan to do today as an offering to God. When all pictures are drawn and signed, gather near the worship center. Say Matthew 25:40 again, sing your verse of "Take My Life and Let It Be Consecrated," collect the pictures in the offering plate, pray a prayer of dedication, and sing the doxology together. Return the drawings to the children as reminders that the offering is not really finished until they have done what they promised to God.

Evaluation

This concludes the introductory unit. The aim of the unit was to expose the children to the five acts or moods that are part of all worship. Which one do the children understand most fully? Which ones do you want to focus more energy on during the remainder of the year?

Consult your year-long calendar to identify the next sessions.

ENTERING INTO WORSHIP SEASONS

UNIT INTRODUCTION

This curriculum includes two sessions on thanksgiving. The first session focuses on developing gratitude, the inclination toward giving thanks. The second session focuses on sharing as a natural response to giving thanks. You may want to use both of these sessions during the Thanksgiving season, or you may want to use only one of them. To make your decision find out what your congregation's Thanksgiving plans are. Will the Sunday before Thanksgiving be an especially festive service with extra choirs singing? Is there a Thanksgiving sharing project, such as a food collection? If so, when and where will the collection place be? Based on this information decide: (1) whether the children should attend at least part of a service with their families or as a class and (2) which of the thanksgiving sessions to do on which Sunday. Remember that Advent starts the Sunday immediately after Thanksgiving and that giving thanks is not limited to one time of the year. So saving one or both of these sessions for another Sunday is fine.

THANKSGIVING

Session 11: Saying Thank You to God

Worship Focus: Thanking God for the gifts God gives us makes God happy and makes us happy, too.

At Thanksgiving we make special efforts to cultivate in ourselves a natural sense of gratitude. With the children this means identifying what they truly are thankful for, practicing saying thank you to God, and learning some of the church's songs and prayers of thanksgiving. When all of this is undertaken in a spirit of joy and when children are given freedom to identify the people and things for which they are truly thankful, they learn that being grateful is not a duty but a happy way of living.

Today we will begin by looking at thankfulness. Then we will plan and carry out ways of saying thank you to God.

Time	*Worship Activity*	*Materials/Resources*
10 min.	1. Treat gift and singing	treat for each child
5 min.	2. Story of the ten lepers Prepare "Thank You" for God	Arch Book or Bible
10 min.	3. Learn "For the Beauty of the Earth"	prepared song book pre-cut pictures glue or paste
15 min.	4. Draw ten things I like	prepared drawing sheets crayons
5 min.	5. Set up your Order of Worship	Bible 2 song books blank drawing sheet
15 min.	6. Giving thanks to God	selected musical instrument

Getting Ready

1. You will need a small treat to give each child upon arrival. Choose a piece of candy or a bite-sized piece of fruit. Check your bookshelves or local book store for a copy of the Arch book *He Remembered to Say Thank You,* or be sure your Bible is handy to read the story about the ten lepers. Select one of your rhythm instruments to use in the prayer. A triangle or a bell that is struck are the best choices because one strike can be the rule. (If you cannot imagine your children doing this step of the prayer with reverence, omit it, but try it if possible. It can be very effective.)

2. To make the song book "For the Beauty of the Earth," you will need two pastel colored poster boards with holes punched in the sides, threaded with metal rings or yarn. On page one write the title with a broad-tipped marker. On page two write, "For the beauty of the earth." On page three write, "For the beauty of the sky." On page four write, "For the love which from our birth over and around us lies." Cut out in advance three piles of magazine pictures of the earth, of all kinds of skies, and of scenes depicting love in a variety of families.

3. With a dark marking pen, divide large sheets of drawing paper into ten equal windows and title the page "Ten Things I Like." Prepare one for each child you expect.

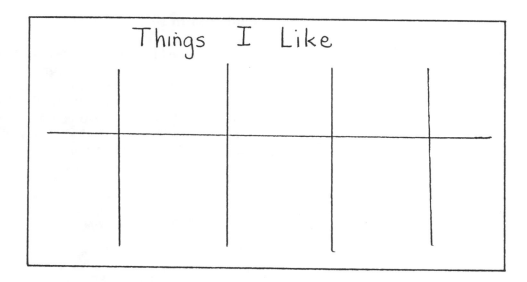

Getting Started

Today one leader greets the children, helps them settle their belongings, and then gives each one a piece of candy or a bite-sized piece of fruit. The leader should give the gift without comment as a no-strings-attached gift. The second leader gathers the children on the rug to sing songs of praise and thanksgiving ("Praise Him, All Ye Little Children," "Praise Ye the Lord, Alleluia!" the doxology).

When all the children have arrived, the leader at the door joins the group on the rug to discuss the children's response to the candy gift they have received. Use some of the questions below.

Did I owe any of you a treat?
Were any of you expecting me to give you a treat?
Was anyone disappointed to get the treat?
Was anyone happy to get the treat?
How did you show that you were happy?
  Did you show your candy to anyone else?
  Did you smile?
  Did you tell me that the candy made you happy?
  Did the surprise make you feel more like singing?

As you talk, avoid discussing how the children *ought* to have acted and what they *ought* to have said. Instead help them to examine what they felt and said. This is not the time for behavior judgments.

The Story of the Ten Lepers

The discussion of the treat sets the stage for the story of the ten lepers. Read the story directly from the *Good News Bible* in Luke 17:11-17. Or read it from Arch Book number 13, *He Remembered to Say Thank You.* Ask the following questions: How did the leper feel when Jesus healed him? Why do you think the leper went back to thank Jesus? How do you think Jesus felt when the man returned? (Focus on the tenth leper, who did return.)

Preparing a Thanksgiving Service "For the Beauty of the Earth"

Explain that today you are going to plan a worship service as a way of saying thank you to God.

Begin learning "For the Beauty of the Earth" by singing the refrain for the children. Ask them to sing it with you several times. Be sure they know what it means.

When the children can sing the refrain with some confidence, work on the phrases by adding illustrations to the pages of your song book. Say the first phrase together a time or two. Then send a group to select a pre-cut magazine picture of one of the beauties of the earth they especially like. Have the children take turns mounting the pictures around the phrase on the song page and have them tell about their pictures as they are added. Repeat the process with the second phrase about the skies. (Send a second group to get pictures for this phrase.) Pointing to your song book pages, sing the first two phrases and the refrain once or twice before illustrating the third line (send a third group this time). Finally, sing the entire first verse and refrain.

Drawing Ten Things I Like

Give each child a prepared "Ten Things I Like" drawing sheet. Tell them that it is fun to think of all the things and people and games we really like. Their job is to draw one of them in each window on their paper. Get them to think by asking them to list things they like. When that person runs out of ideas, call on another until everyone is "primed." While the children draw with crayons, move among them and talk about their pictures, comparing the different things they each enjoy.

Setting Up the Order of Worship

When all have finished their drawings, or have filled at least several windows, gather on the rug. Instruct children to lay their paper on the rug in front of them because you will be using it in your "thank you service." Explain that you will say thank you to God in four different ways and that you are setting up some reminders of what we are going to do next. Lean the following items against the wall near your worship center in this order: a Bible opened to Psalm 100, your "For the Beauty of the Earth" song book, a blank copy of the "Ten Things I Like" sheet, and your Doxology Song Book.

Saying Thank You to God

Tell the children that now we are talking only to God. This is our way of saying thank you. Encourage them to sit up straight, close their eyes, and be quiet for just a moment before you begin. Tell them to open their eyes and say a poem from the Bible for God. Then line out Psalm 100 (GNB) with dramatic inflection. Next, sing "For the Beauty of the Earth," using your song book.

Explain that you are going to make a prayer using your drawing. Each child selects one item to tell God about. Children may say, "Thank you God for . . . " or "God, I like _____ because . . . " or something else of their choosing. Give them a moment of silence to decide what they will pray. To share the prayer, each child in turn says a prayer and plays one tone on the musical instrument. In a small group, the group then sings the refrain of "For the Beauty of the Earth." In a larger group the refrain of "For the Beauty of the Earth" is sung only after all children have offered their prayers. Conclude your worship by singing the doxology.

Session 12: Thanks-Sharing

Worship Focus: Thankful people share. When we recognize ourselves to be the receivers of God's gifts and love, sharing those gifts with others is a natural response. Sharing is no longer a responsibility but a happy privilege. That is one reason why Thanksgiving has become a time for churches to focus energy on mission projects.

This session helps the children to explore the connections between thanksgiving and sharing and between worship and mission. It is effective if it is tied to a sharing effort of your congregation.

Time	Worship Activity	Materials/Resources
10 min.	1. Singing: "For the Beauty of the Earth" Psalm 136	song book Bible
10 min.	2. Confession: full/part measures	box of sand set of measures
5 min.	3. "Gathering Game"	"sticks"
5 min.	4. Ruth and Boaz story	
10 min.	5. Visit your congregation's project	
10 min.	6. Make refrigerator posters	poster forms labels and pictures glue or paste
10 min.	7. Closing: "Now Thank We All . . ." Prayer	

Getting Ready

1. Practice singing Psalm 136 ("A Psalm of Thanksgiving" on page 203). This is like a chant. It takes a little practice to know which note goes with which word of each line.
2. For the confession you will need a large shallow box filled with something dry (sand, rice, or kitty litter would be great) and a set of measuring scoops (kitchen flour scoops of several sizes are fine).
3. You need *lots* of craft sticks or straws for the "Gathering Game." Plan on twenty per child.
4. Learn about your congregation's Thanksgiving mission project. Be sure you know where the collection point is in the building. (The directions for this session refer to food collections. Change your wording to match what you are collecting.)

Prepare a poster form for each child. The poster form needs to identify the items being collected at the top and the words "Thanking God" at the bottom. Then gather pictures of the items to be collected. Cut them from magazines and catalogs. If you are collecting food, gather labels from food packages.

Getting Started

As one leader greets the children at the door and helps them settle their belongings, the other leader gathers the children on the rug to talk about their morning's activities. When enough children have arrived, begin singing songs of thanksgiving together. Use your student-made song book to sing "For the Beauty of the Earth." Enjoy other songs the children know. Last, introduce Psalm 136 by opening to it in the Bible on your worship center. Point out that we often "read" from the Bible, but that we can "sing" some of the Bible as well. Psalm 136 is a song we can sing for God. Teach them their response. Then sing it with a leader singing the verses and the children responding.

Using Measures (confession and pardon)

Remind the children that sometimes we buy things in packages. Sometimes we choose what we want from big bins and then weigh or measure how much we want. Mention places in your community where children may have experienced measuring things out to buy them. Use your measuring box and tools to illustrate this process. Invite several children to come and ask for one of the measures full of rice or cornmeal, whatever is familiar to them. After measuring out several level measures to several children, half fill a measure and give it to a child as if it were full. As children respond to your short-changed measure, talk about both the justice and their feelings about less-than-full measures. Then fill another child's measure to overflowing and discuss that. When the children seem to grasp the use of measures, turn in the Bible to read to the children Luke 6:38 and talk about what Jesus is saying to us. Pray the prayer below with all doing the motions as the leader says the words.

> Dear God, we want to share *(open hands to offer)*, but we do not always do it.
> We grab for ourselves *(close hands tight)*. We hide what we have *(hold hands to your side as if hiding something)*. We share only a little *("drip out" a little from your hand)*.
> We are sorry *(hands open out and up in admission)*. Forgive us *(fold hands in lap)*. Amen.
> God knows this about us and still loves us and promises to pour out overflowing love for each one of us *(cup hands to receive full measure)*. God gives us so much love that we will always have plenty to share *(open arms.)*

Gathering Game

While one leader explains the game, the other scatters craft sticks randomly around the room. Point to the first gatherer (or group of gatherers). They must ask, "May I gather in your field?" You reply, "Yes." If a player omits the question, he or she loses the turn. Give players enough time to gather a small handful of sticks, then call time. Send out the next group. After all groups have had a turn, compare how many sticks players have gathered. Spread out the sticks again. This time send out one player with instructions to get them all before time is called. Allow enough time to get most, but not all, of the sticks. Let one or two more players try to get them all unsuccessfully.

The Story of Ruth and Boaz

Assign groups of children to each of the four parts and explain the action to be done.

1. *Boaz*—stand straight and tall with arms folded across chest.
2. *Cutters*—swing arms back and forth as if cutting grain with a long curved knife.
3. *Gatherers*—act out picking up grain with one hand to fold across the other arm.
4. *Ruth and Naomi*—hands on stomach, look hungry.

Players are also to use their faces to show what people felt. Point to groups at the italicized words.

The Story of Ruth and Boaz*

Boaz was a rich farmer in the village of Bethlehem. He had fields and fields of ripe grain. There was more than he could ever harvest by himself. So, he hired lots of helpers. *He gave some of the helpers long knives* to cut the barley. *Other helpers followed to pick it up* in bundles to take to the barns.

---

*Written by Lynette Johnson. Used by permission.

But not everyone in Bethlehem was a rich farmer or a paid helper. *Young Ruth and Old Naomi* were poor, and they were hungry.

One morning *Ruth* said to *Naomi*, "They will not gather ALL the grain in Boaz's fields. I will go follow the gatherers and pick up what they leave. Maybe, if I work hard and am lucky, I will come home with enough for us to make some bread to eat tonight."

Naomi thought that was a good idea.

So Ruth went to the field. She asked the *gatherers,* "May I pick up what gets left behind and falls from the bundles?"

They said, "Yes, you may." Then *everyone went to work.* All morning Ruth went up and down the field picking up what had been dropped.

About noon *Boaz* came to see how the work was going. He saw Ruth working hard and asked one of the gatherers about her. Then he spoke to Ruth, "I am glad to have you picking up the dropped grain in my field. You are welcome to come every day. When you get thirsty, help yourself to some of the water I bring in jugs for the workers."

Ruth thanked him for his kindness and went back to work. She worked all day. At the end of the day she had a nice big bag of barley to take home to Naomi.

They ground the barley into flour and baked two loaves of fresh bread for their supper.

Ruth went to *Boaz's* fields every day. When Boaz got to know what a fine person Ruth was, he asked her to be his wife. When they were married, Naomi went to live with them. Boaz and Ruth were very happy together. They had a son named Obed and how Naomi loved him! When Obed grew up he had a son named Jesse. When Jesse grew up, he had a son named David. And when David grew up, he became the greatest king of Israel.

Thank the children for their help in telling the story. Then discuss how Boaz shared with Ruth and Naomi. Use this to lead into discussing how your congregation shares food with people who need it.

Your Sharing Project

Visit the food drive collection. Look at posters or pictures of where the food goes and who receives it.

Return to your room to make posters to put on refrigerators at home this week as reminders to bring food for the drive next week. Children paste or glue pictures of food and labels from food packages onto prepared poster sheets.

Closing: Thanks and Giving

Leave posters on the tables while the glue dries. Gather on the rug. Learn the first verse of "Now Thank We All Our God" using the motions.

Now thank we all our God
With hearts *(hands over heart)*
and hands *(display hands, palms out)*
And voices, *(cup hands around mouth)*
Who wondrous things hath done, *(spread arms over head)*
In whom this world rejoices; *(wiggle hands, arms up)*
Who, from our mothers' arms, *(cradling motion)*
Hath blessed us on our way *(hands up in benediction)*
With countless gifts of love, *(arms outstretched, palms up)*
And still is ours today.

Point out that one way we say thank you to God is sharing with others. Identify ways we can do this with our hearts and hands and voices every day. Point out that one way Boaz thanked God was to let Ruth pick up the grain left in his field. Say a brief prayer to thank God for our gifts and to ask God to help us share thankfully as we gather food. Sing the verse of the song again if there is time.

ADVENT, CHRISTMAS, AND EPIPHANY

Many Protestant churches are rediscovering the meaning of the ancient three part Christmas season of the church year. Advent, which begins the fourth Sunday before Christmas, is a time to face up to our hurting world. We are called to recognize that ours is indeed a dark world in need of God's rescue. Advent is a time to prepare our hearts and homes for the coming of God's love. Christmas follows with the celebration of God's love displayed in the baby born in a barn. Epiphany, with its emphasis on the story of the three wise men following the star from foreign lands, begins twelve days after Christmas (January 6) to remind us that God's love includes the whole world. In many denominations Epiphany is the beginning of an emphasis on world missions.

The calendar of our culture omits Advent, jumping straight to Christmas joy immediately after Thanksgiving (or even before) then forgetting the whole business on December 26. So it takes a little effort to make time for Advent and to keep Christmas going through January 6. But most people find it is worth the effort because the celebration is made richer and more meaningful. Children respond quickly if their adult leaders are enthusiastic.

Begin your preparations for this season by finding out exactly what your congregation will be doing to celebrate, especially during worship. When will there be special music? Will an advent wreath be lighted each week during worship? Will there be special decorations in the sanctuary? Will the color purple be used on the pulpit, table, or ministers' robes?

Because there is often a lot to see and hear in worship during this season, it is good for children to spend brief times with their families in the sanctuary during worship. If the advent wreath is lighted at the beginning of the service, children could start each week in the sanctuary with their families (fifteen minutes is usually the limit), then leave with their leaders during the singing of one of the congregational hymns. When the children's choir sings or similar Christmas events are planned, plan for children to be in the sanctuary with their families.

Skim the plans for all the sessions and mesh them with the plans of your congregation. Once you develop a schedule, write a letter to parents, telling them of your plans (underline details that involve changes in normal Sunday patterns), explaining the use of the Advent calendar chain their children will receive, and enlisting their support. Your church office may be willing to copy this letter and mail it for you. If not, get help from a parent.

Finally, remember that as Christmas gets closer children get both more excitable and more tired.

You may also get larger crowds. Extra parent or youth helpers can make the difference in a session that is simply survived and one that is truly worshipful. Get extra help EARLY!

Advent is the first of seven seasons of the church year. This curriculum will introduce the seasons, their colors, and special traditions and concerns as we move through the year. You may have as much to learn about it as the children do. If so, you are in for a treat as you grow in your worship life. Each season will be explained in some detail in the "Worship Focus" section at the beginning of the season. If you are not sure about your congregation's practices for any season, call your pastor. You may even discover a new tradition to introduce to your congregation on behalf of the children—and the rest of the congregation.

Session 13: The First Sunday of Advent

Worship Focus: "Wait" is the theme of Advent. For adults, waiting focuses on longing for the day when God's kingdom is a reality on earth, when love and justice and peace on earth are not ideals but the God-given state of the world. Children spend all of Advent waiting for the good things that come with Christmas. The growing edge for them is learning to prepare themselves to be more loving as they wait. So we will celebrate waiting. Though we will use the biblical Christmas stories, teaching them is not the focus. Exploring the theme of waiting and learning the worship practices of the congregation are.

Basic Information About Advent

Advent begins with the fourth Sunday before Christmas and ends at midnight on Christmas Eve. The color for Advent is purple—the color of kings—because we wait for a king. An Advent wreath is a circle of four candles. The candles may all be purple, or the fourth may be pink. One candle is lighted on the first Sunday of Advent, two on the second, and so on. In the center of the circle is a tall white candle (the Christ candle), which is lighted on Christmas Day or Christmas Eve. Churches often light wreathes during worship with readings from the prophets and the stories leading up to Jesus' birth. Some families have wreathes at home that are lighted on Sundays and during evening meals during the week. Candles may be set in purchased Advent wreath candle rings or in wreaths of greenery.

Today we will be introducing Advent, its color, and its theme of waiting and preparation.

Time	Worship Activity	Materials/Resources
5 min.	1. Conversation about Thanksgiving and Introduction to Advent	Church year calendar
15 min.	2. Putting up purple	purple paint/paper pictures for display
10 min.	3. "The Purple Game"	soft purple stuff to hide and find
10 min.	4. Getting Ready with John	*Godspell* record
15 min.	5. Starting the Advent Calendar Chain	paper paints or crayons chains in bags one purple marker
5 min.	6. Wreath, and "O Come, O Come, Emmanuel"	candles and base for Advent wreath matches

Getting Ready

1. There are two big items for you to make for the Advent season. This would be a good chance to solicit the help of some parents or the youth group.

The first item is a poster calendar with space for each Sunday of the year on which children can glue a pre-cut patch of appropriately colored construction paper. Turn the poster board sideways to lay out the months in four columns of three months each. Draw a square for each day of the week. (You will need to work with a calendar for the coming year to get the beginning and ending of each month on the correct day.) Write in the name of each month (for the sake of the adults using the calendar). Cut out squares of construction paper the size of the daily space. You will need nine purple patches, eleven white patches, two red patches, and thirty green patches if you follow the general pattern. Cut a few extra squares of each color. Put the patches and a capped glue stick in a ziplock bag. Paper-clip the bag to the poster board so that it will be ready to use each week.

The second project is an Advent chain for each child to use at home. Directions and instructions that go on each chain link are on pages 66-69. This is a big job and is best tackled by a group. (Do not plan on the children assembling the chains. Paste and glue sticks do not hold and there are never enough staplers to do the job fast enough to suit kindergarten attention spans.) Be sure to make enough for possible Christmas visitors.

2. Gather supplies to make an Advent wreath for your group. A Styrofoam ring can be used as the base for the ring of candles; candles are easily pushed down into the Styrofoam. Add plastic greenery. Find or borrow a copy of the record *Godspell*, the source of the song "Prepare Ye the Way of the Lord." Gather purple paint and/or paper for your decorating projects. **Warning:** purple poster or chart paper is one of the harder colors to find. It might be easier to paint, even finger-paint, than to track it down. But purple paint is difficult to get out of clothes. So add some liquid detergent *and* don't forget the paint aprons!

Getting Started

While one leader greets the children at the door and helps them settle their belongings (have extra name necklaces handy for Thanksgiving weekend visitors), the second leader gathers the children on the rug to talk about Thanksgiving. When most have arrived, lead conversation toward Christmas plans. Hear any plans and hopes children want to share, then introduce Advent.

Introducing the Church Year and Advent

Briefly show the children the calendar and explain that the church celebrates special times of the year. Introduce Advent as the time of getting ready for Christmas. Introduce purple, the color of kings, as the color of Advent. If you are going into the sanctuary for part of the service, instruct the children to look for purple there. Help one child glue a purple patch on the square for today and explain to the group that we will be recording the color for each Sunday from now on.

Choose some of the following activities as ways for the children to fill their room with purple to remind them that they are waiting for a king.

1. Cover a door and/or a bulletin board with a purple paper background. A memorable way to do this is to have the children don painting aprons to paint with brushes or to finger-paint white paper until it is all purple. When the background is up, add cut-out pictures of people getting ready for Christmas. (Leave space to add more during the coming weeks.) Title the display "Advent Is for Waiting."

2. Cover your worship center with purple cloth.

Purple Game

Show the children a piece of soft purple cloth, a purple stuffed animal, or a wad of purple paper (last resort). Then tell everyone to close their eyes while you hide it somewhere in the room with at least part of it in plain view. When it is hidden, children will move around the room without touching or opening anything to look for it. As soon as a player finds it, she or he sits down. The first person to find it gets to hide it next.

Getting Ready with John

Gather the children again on the rug and invite them to imagine that they are waiting for a king to come. Play the song "Prepare Ye the Way of the Lord" from *Godspell*. Then open a Bible on your lap to tell the following story about John the Baptist.

> The Bible tells us that there was a man named John who wanted to prepare the way of the Lord. John went everywhere and told whoever would listen to him, "Prepare the way for the Lord! You say you are good people. But you do bad things in secret. You think God will not see. But God does see. You must change. You must make the world a loving place to live. You must prepare a place that is good enough for God to stay, because our Savior is coming. So prepare the way of the Lord!"
>
> He said it over and over again. Some people did not listen. But some people did listen. They believed John. They did make changes. They began to prepare a way for the Lord. They began to get ready for the Savior John knew was coming soon.

Reinforce the story by learning the following choral reading together. Divide the class into two groups. Teach Group One to *whisper* the following words in the indicated rhythm.

Then teach Group Two to *say* the following in rhythm.

After each group has practiced, assume the role of John for the litany below. Each part should be spoken quickly after the other to keep the rhythm and intensity.

Leader:	*(strong loud voice)* Prepare the Way of the Lord!
Group 1:	*(whispered)* Get ready! Get ready!
Group 2:	*(spoken)* Jesus is coming soon!
Leader:	Stop being mean to one another!
Group 1:	Get ready! Get ready!
Group 2:	Jesus is coming soon!
Leader:	Share God's love!
Group 1:	Get ready! Get ready!
Group 2:	Jesus is coming soon!
Leader:	Rejoice! Rejoice!
Group 1:	Get ready! Get ready!
Group 2:	Jesus is coming soon!

If your group is really into this you might improvise some additional statements John would have said—such as "No more lying!"—before concluding with the "rejoice!" verse. The reading starts quietly and gets louder and louder.

Starting the Advent Calendar Chain

Discuss ways we can do what John asked. Gather ideas about what children can do to share love at home and school. Point out that sharing love is not always easy. Then show the children one of the chain calendars. Explain that each link contains instructions that help us prepare the way of the Lord on that day. Show children how to tie the chain to a doorknob and encourage them to have an adult open a link with them and do what it says each day. Open the bottom link and share ideas about what you will draw in your thank you pictures and to whom you will give them.

At the tables, help the children use crayons or watercolor sets to make pictures of the Thanksgiving meal they ate last week. As children recall who was there and what was served, they may want to draw the whole table and everyone around it or just their favorite food at the meal and the person who fixed it. Be sensitive to children who for a variety of reasons may not have had a happy family feast to report. As children draw or paint, leaders move among them writing their one sentence thank you notes on each picture—such as, "Thank you for the pumpkin pie, Grandma." As each child finishes his or her drawing, help put it in a bag with an Advent chain. Write each child's name on his or her bag—with a purple marker, of course!

Lighting the Wreath and
"O Come, O Come, Emmanuel"

Introduce and explain the Advent wreath. Set up one for your group together. Take time to talk about the purple candles and the four weeks before Christmas. Compare it to the wreath in the sanctuary if the children have seen one there. Act as though you are going to light the first candle, then stop and tell the children that you need a song to sing as you light the first candle of waiting.

Introduce the song "O Come, O Come, Emmanuel" as one people have sung while they waited for Christmas for hundreds of years. Sing the first verse through, asking the children to listen for the feeling of the music. (The words are too difficult for kindergarteners, but they can easily identify the sad wistful sound of the music.) As they talk, point out that we often feel sad and trapped. Use some examples—like two brothers who mean to get along but always get into fusses in the back seat of the car. Have the children hold out their hands as if they were handcuffed together. Explain that we, like those brothers, though we want to change and be better, feel like we are handcuffed to our bad ways. No matter how hard we try, we can't be better. This song is good for those times. It starts with, "O come, O come Emmanuel," which means "Please, God, come be with us"—especially when we feel handcuffed to our bad ways. Practice singing the first line together with your hands held out as if in handcuffs. Then announce that the song has a happy ending. Sing the chorus to them with joy, emphasizing that Emmanuel *shall* come. Point out the promise that God *will* help us and be with us. Discuss the meaning and feeling of *rejoice* (it may be a new word to many children). Invite the children to sing the "rejoices" with you and to break their hands apart and raise them over their heads as they sing. Try it a time or two. Then light one candle of the Advent wreath; sing the song with the motions, asking children to sing the first line and the "rejoices"; and follow with a short prayer, asking God to be with you as you prepare to share Christmas love.

As They Leave

Be sure one leader is at the door to remind parents of the Advent calendar in the sack and to encourage them to use it with their children.

Looking Ahead

Next week you will need a variety of things that you can gather from home. Cleaning supplies and makings for a gorp-like snack need to be gathered. You also need to locate an unbreakable nativity set that can be used every week between now and Christmas.

ADVENT CALENDAR CHAIN DIRECTIONS

1. Make a copy of the next three pages of links for each child. Include extras for visitors. If possible, copy them onto heavy purple paper, using a copy machine, *or* print them in purple ink on white paper (ditto machine?) *or* if all else fails print them in black ink on regular white paper.

2. Cut the pages into separate strips. Keep up with the first link on this page to use as the final link on the chain, but do not worry about the order of the others.

3. The number of days in Advent varies from twenty-two to twenty-eight, depending on the day of the week Christmas falls. Count the fourth Sunday as day twenty-two, then keep counting through Christmas Eve. (If Christmas Eve falls on the fourth Sunday, Advent is twenty-two days long.) So consult a calendar, then discard extra links.

4. Curl the first strip on Thanksgiving into loop with the print face in and staple it in place. Thread another strip through it and staple it into a loop to form the second loop in the chain and so on until all strips are used and the chain is completed.

5. Through the link away from the Thanksgiving link, thread a 12″ piece of purple yarn or ribbon for tying the chain onto a doorknob at home. Put each chain in a separate sack for the trip home.

Draw a picture to say thank you to the person who fixed your Thanksgiving dinner.

Say a special thank you to the person who drives you to school today.

Give out smiles today. Watch for people who look like they need a smile.

Be sure everyone in your family gets a hug from you today.

Tell all the members of your family one thing you like about them today.

Tell the person who fixes your lunch something you like about the food.

Tell the person who fixes your breakfast something you like about the food.

Tell the person who fixes your dinner something you like about the food.

Draw a picture and give it to someone as a loving surprise.

Tell your teacher something you like about her or him.

Make a Christmas picture and get help to mail it as a surprise to someone.

Surprise someone in your family by doing one of his or her jobs today.

Find someone to sing "Away in a Manger" with you. Give that person a thank you hug.

Read the story about the shepherds coming to see Jesus from Luke 2:16-20 or a storybook.

Read the story about the wise men coming to see Jesus in Matthew 2:1-12 or a storybook.

Draw a picture of when Jesus was born. Give it to someone and tell that person the story.

Find out one Christmas song each person in your family likes. Sing the song with them.

Tell a friend one thing you really like about him or her.

Think of a person who is hard to get along with. Say something nice to that person today.

Think of two nice things that happened today. Tell God about them tonight.

Make "I Love You" hearts. Put one under the pillow of each person in your family.

Give out thank yous today. Count how many you can give to people who help you.

Get someone to help you make a phone call to say "I love you" to a special person.

Practice giving compliments today.

Be a helper today. Watch for people who need your help and give it to them.

Work on sharing today. Share toys with your friends and brothers and sisters.

Sing your favorite Christmas song for someone. Maybe he or she will sing with you.

Don't talk about what you want for Christmas at all today. Ask others what they want.

Session 14: The Second Sunday of Advent

Worship Focus: Waiting is never easy. Children are very aware of that fact during this season of waiting for gifts and friends and special events. Advent insists that we not simply wait patiently but that we fill the world around us with love while we wait. In so doing we prepare the way for the Lord. Today we will compare two biblical stories about waiting. We will confess our sins related to waiting, and we will serve and sing while we wait.

Time	Worship Activity	Materials/Resources
5 min.	1. Add patch to calendar Unwrap box	calendar and patch
10 min.	2. Hear "Prepare Ye . . ." "Get Ready" chant light Advent wreath	*Godspell* record wreath and match
5 min.	3. Learn "Waiting Song"	
10 min.	4. "People Wait for Moses" Waiting Confession "Mary Waits for Jesus"	
10 min.	5. Clean the room	cleaning supplies rags or paper towels
10 min.	6. (optional) Make snacks for homeless	snack makings ziplock bags ribbon
2 min.	7. Add pictures to board	pictures maybe camera
10 min.	8. Sing—"O Come, O Come, Emmanuel" "O Come, All Ye Faithful"	

GATEWAYS TO WORSHIP

Getting Ready

Put a small nativity set (one that can stay throughout Advent beside your Advent wreath) in a box. Cover the box with a long single strand of red yarn or ribbon. Use approximately 2' of yarn or ribbon for each child as your measuring standard.

Getting Started

While one leader welcomes the children at the door, the other gathers them on the rug for conversation about your Advent wreath and the calendar chains. Share stories of what students did to prepare the way of the Lord by using the chain. Add a purple patch to the church year calendar for today. When most of the group has gathered, if no one has asked about the ribbon wrapped box, point it out. Tell them that it is for the class and that they must unwrap it together by passing it around the circle. Each person wraps the ribbon *loosely* around a finger or wrist or arm, then passes the box to the next person. Pass the box until all the ribbon is unwrapped. When the box is unwrapped, laugh briefly together at all the different ways you have tied yourselves together, then shake off the ribbon and put them aside.

Open the box and arrange the nativity set together, identifying each person and animal as you work. Point out that each of the people had to wait for Jesus to be born. Then invite the children to listen to "Prepare Ye the Way of the Lord." Together do the "Get Ready" choral reading from last week. Then light two candles on the wreath.

Songs and Stories About Waiting

Learn the song "Wait, Wait, Wait." Talk about how hard it is to wait. Sing the song, showing your feelings with your faces.

WAIT, WAIT, WAIT!

Words and Music by **Mary Catherine Carter, S.C.L.**

1. Wait, wait, wait! I re—ally hate to wait.
2. Wait, wait, wait! I wait—ed for a friend.
3. Wait, wait, wait! I know God waits for me.

1. I wait at school, I wait at home. Wait, wait, wait!
2. I wait—ed and he didn't come. Wait, wait, wait!
3. He waits to hold me close to Him. Wait, wait, wait!

Tell the story of people who did not wait well. (Present a teaching picture of the people with the golden calf, if possible.)

God's People Refuse to Wait

God promised the people a very special gift, the Ten Commandments. The people were excited and waited at the bottom of the mountain as Moses went up the mountain to get the Ten Commandments from God. But

Moses was gone a long time. They got tired of waiting. They wondered whether he would ever come back with the gift from God. Finally, they stopped waiting. They gathered all their gold and asked Aaron to make them a big golden cow statue. They prayed to that statue as if it were God. When Moses finally did come back down the mountain with the Ten Commandments, he was very, very angry. He broke up the statue and punished the people.

Ask: What were the people waiting for? What did they do while they waited? Invite children to think about times they have gotten tired of waiting as you share in the litany prayer. Teach them the response, "I am sorry, Lord" to repeat after you say each sentence below.

For the times I wouldn't wait to let someone else have his or her way, but wanted my own way right then,

I am sorry, Lord.

For the times I did not wait, but tried to do by myself what I was supposed to wait for someone to do with me,

I am sorry, Lord.

For the times I fussed because I had to wait for my parents,

I am sorry, Lord.

For the times I wanted my parents to do or get something for me and pouted when I had to wait,

I am sorry, Lord.

For the times I yelled because I had to wait for my brothers and sisters,

I am sorry, Lord.

For the times when I was mean because I had to wait,

I am sorry, Lord.

For the times I was too busy when someone else needed my help,

I am sorry, Lord.

For the times I have made others wait,

I am sorry, Lord.

God, thank you for waiting for us. Thank you for loving us and forgiving us when we do not wait for others. Help us to be better at waiting happily and helping other people. Amen.

Present a teaching picture of Mary waiting for Jesus and tell the children a story from the Bible about another way of waiting.

Mary had to wait, too. It was nine long months from the time the angel told her that she would have a baby to the day Jesus was born. While she waited, she went to visit her cousin Elizabeth to see if she could help her.

Ask: What was Mary waiting for? What did she do while she waited?

Serving While We Wait

Invite the children to be like Mary by helping clean up the room for Christmas. Provide dust cloths, window cleaner, paper towels, and other cleaning supplies for children to use in teams to clean the room. Play the *Godspell* music as background music as you work.

If you have extra time, prepare snack bags to be delivered to a shelter for homeless people. Children mix peanuts, raisins, candy, and other goodies in big bowls as a gorp-like mixture. Spoon the mix into ziplock bags and tie red ribbons around each bag. Take pictures with an instant camera to add to your bulletin board.

Singing While We Wait

Spend the remainder of your time together singing favorite songs. Then sing "O Come, O Come, Emmanuel" using the motions you learned last week.

Begin learning the chorus to "O Come, All Ye Faithful" with motions. Motion for people to come toward you as you sing "O come," then rock the baby gently in your arms as you sing "let us adore him." Raise your hands over your heads as you sing "Christ, the Lord." Sing the chorus several times to learn and enjoy. Also sing other Christmas songs about Jesus that the children know.

Looking Ahead

Next week you will need a recording of Handel's *Messiah*. There are some simple preparations requiring standard craft materials.

Session 15: The Third Sunday of Advent

Worship Focus: During Advent we are waiting for Jesus. Our carols are full of names and titles ascribed to Jesus that remind us of who Jesus is and why he is so important.

Kindergarteners are interested in names. They are aware of family names, nicknames, and titles. We will use this interest as the entry point to explore several carols or choruses of carols. We will listen to "For Unto Us a Child Is Born" to introduce children to classical church Christmas music.

Time	Worship Activity	Materials/Resources
5 min.	1. Conversation Add calendar color	church year calendar
10 min.	2. Listen to "Prepare" . . . "Get Ready" litany Light three candles "Is It Time?" game	*Godspell* record Advent wreath message package
5 min.	3. Discussion about names	
15 min.	4. Make name ornaments for a name tree	stiff paper circles glue glitter hangers or tape
5 min.	5. Confession about name- calling	
20 min.	7. "O Come, O Come, Emmanuel" with game "Away in a Manger" with rocking "O Come, All Ye Faithful" "For Unto Us a Child Is Born"	Jesus' name stars ready to hang "For Unto Us . . ." record or tape
1 min.	Closing	

Getting Ready

1. Write the words of Isaiah 9:6 on a sheet of paper and gift-wrap it in a box for the "Is It Time?" game. You will need a timer for this game.

2. For the name tree or name display, find a small tree or branch to set in a stand or put a large paper tree on a door, wall, or bulletin board. For each child cut out one round stiff paper ornament (trace around the top of a cereal bowl to get a good size). Punch a hole in each ornament if you will hang them on a tree. Gather tree ornament hangers or unbend paper clips to serve as hangers. Make four ornaments out of gold paper. On each one write with glitter one of the following names for Jesus: Jesus, Emmanuel, Lord, and Christ.

3. Find a recording of Handel's *Messiah*. The choir director may have one, or check your public library.

Getting Started

As children arrive play the record "For Unto Us a Child Is Born" as background music. While one leader greets the children at the door, the other gathers them on the rug for conversation about their Christmas preparations. Again give them a chance to share stories about the use of their Advent chains. Put a purple patch in the proper place on the calendar.

"Prepare Ye the Way of the Lord," "Get Ready," and Lighting the Wreath

Listen to "Prepare Ye the Way of the Lord." Say the "Get Ready" chant together. Light three candles of the Advent wreath.

Play "Is It Time?" Present a wrapped box and tell the children that it has a message inside for them, but they must wait to open it. While they wait, they must stand in a circle and pass the package around. Set a timer for several minutes just before play starts. The first player hands the box to the second player saying, "Merry Christmas." The second responds with a question, "Is it time yet?" The giver replies, "No, not yet." The second player then hands the package to the third, and so forth until the timer goes off and the whole group yells, "It's time!" If enthusiasm for the game is high, reset the timer and play the game one more time. Then open the package and read the message aloud.

Discussing Names

Point to all the names your message gave Jesus. Then talk about your own names. Tell your full name and any nicknames people call you. If there is special significance to any of your names, share it. Then ask each child to share all their names and any nicknames they have. Without getting bogged down in too many details, note what it means to have "Jr." in your name or to be named "after someone." Let children tell short stories about their names. Be sure that all the children get a chance at least to say their names.

Name Ornaments

Each child writes one of his or her names on a name ornament and draws decorations on it. Then children trace their names with glue and cover them with glitter. (The easiest way to glitter is to purchase tube or shaker jars. Have children place their ornaments in a shallow box and shake the glitter over the ornaments in the box. Shake excess glitter off of the ornament. When the tube is empty, an adult tips the box up to slide the glitter into a corner of the box and from there into the tubes or jars. You will need one glitter box for each eight children with an adult to oversee each box.) Let glittered ornaments dry for a few minutes on the table.

When the children have cleaned up and the ornaments have set a little, help the children to hang their ornaments on the name tree or tape them on the name board. Read each name aloud with appreciation in your voice.

Confessing

Immediately point out to the children that though we can enjoy names, we can also use names to hurt people. Say one of the children's name with sharp anger in your voice. Ask the children to tell how it makes that person feel. Then say another child's name with snooty condescension and discuss the feeling it evokes. Then call someone "Dumb!" and discuss that. Avoid getting into stories about "what she called me" but take time to discuss the feelings. Then invite the children to bow their heads, close their eyes, and tell God about ways they have used names to hurt. Pray the following prayer aloud, pausing in appropriate places.

> Dear God, we are sorry to tell you that we have used names to hurt people. We even use them to hurt people we love. We say someone's name with hate in our voices. We call people names like "Stupid!" and _____(fill in with names used in your group). Forgive us, God, and help us do better. Help us say names kindly. Amen.
> Remember, no matter what others may say to us, God will only call us by our names with love. God calls _____(say lovingly the names of the children whose names you spoke meanly to make your point). And God stays close to us, making us strong enough to keep from name-calling.

Jesus' Names

Tell the children that Jesus has several names just like we do. One of them is "Jesus." Give the "Jesus" ornament to a child to add to the name display.

Remind them that there is another name for Jesus in a song they have been learning. Sing a little of "O Come, O Come, Emmanuel" and ask what name of Jesus is there. They may need help to identify "Emmanuel." Remind them that *Emmanuel* means "God is with us." Hang the "Emmanuel" ornament on the display, commenting that you are glad that Jesus' name is "God is with us" and that you wish everyone knew that.

Play a game that starts when you gently squeeze the hand of the person next to you and say "God is with us." That person turns, gently squeezes the hand of the next person and repeats the phrase, and so on. Go around the circle several times—once whisper the message, once shout it, and the last time say "Emmanuel" instead of the phrase. Then sing "O Come, O Come, Emmanuel."

Next sing "Away in a Manger" and ask the children to listen for a name for Jesus as they sing. Discuss what a lord is and why we call Jesus "Lord." Add the ornament to the display. Ask children to show you how to hold a baby to rock it to sleep. Then invite them to sing the song with you, imagining that they are rocking the little Lord Jesus to sleep.

Finally sing the chorus to "O Come, All Ye Faithful" together. Find the name for Jesus in it: Christ the Lord. Explain that some lords are good and others are not. But "Christ" is the name for the special lord that God would send. Christ would be all loving and would take care of everyone. Christ is the very best lord the world will ever have. There is only one Christ: Jesus. Add the "Christ" ornament. Sing the chorus again.

If you have time, introduce "For Unto Us a Child Is Born" as Christmas music that includes many of Jesus' names. Play a little of it to give the children a feel for it after reading Isaiah 9:6 again to alert them to the words. Then assign small groups to listen to the song and find one of Jesus' names and stand up each time they hear it. Assign one group each to Wonderful Counselor, Almighty God, Everlasting Father, and Prince of Peace. Play the whole song and help groups by pointing to them at the appropriate time. (It may help you to put the name of each group on the floor in front of them.)

Closing

Close with a prayer to thank God for sending Jesus, who is "God with us" and "Lord" and "Christ."

Looking Ahead

Next week is an important one in the church and a busy one in our lives. So look ahead now at the plans. You need to make some advance decisions, but there are not many things to prepare.

Session 16: The Fourth Sunday of Advent

Worship Focus: Today is the Sunday before Christmas. It may even be Christmas Eve. In many churches it is one the most festive Sundays of the year with full Christmas decorations and lots of choir music. This is a Sunday for the children to spend at least a little time in the sanctuary if at all possible. If you cannot arrange for them to participate in the first part of the service with their families, plan a class visit to hear the choir sing. Children need to feel the extra excitement of Sunday before Christmas worship. You cannot reproduce it in your room.

Once back in your room focus on the excitement by exploring the three G's of Christmas—good news; go tell it; and glory to God in the highest! All three are related to the story of the shepherds.

Time	*Worship Activity*	*Materials/Resources*

10 min.	1. Conversation
	   Add purple to calendar
	   Light Advent wreath
		calendar and patch
		wreath and match

10 min.	2. Good News game
	   Learn chorus of "Go, Tell
	     It on the Mountain"	

10 min.	3. Shepherds' story "Glory to God" rhythm	nativity set rhythm instruments
15 min.	4. Angel Wash pictures	manila paper crayons blue paint wide paint brushes
5 min.	5. Closing litany	Advent wreath

Getting Ready

1. If the children will be in the sanctuary for part of this session, look carefully at the plan and eliminate some activities so that you will have a full, but not frantic, time.

2. The key preparation for this session is learning the chorus of "Go, Tell It on the Mountain" well enough to be able to "really rock out" with the children and to learn the clapping pattern for "Glory to God in the Highest."

3. Decide how to paint the angels. If your children are likely to arrive decked out in their best

Christmas finery, think wisely about two alternatives. Either plan for one of the adults to do the painting while the children watch, or provide plastic bag smocks and one adult to oversee each two painters working at a painter's table. Children are fascinated by the way the paint beads off the crayon pictures and love the resulting night picture. Enlist extra helpers if needed.

Select the colors from the crayon box for use in drawing the angels. Mix up *thin,* dark blue water paint and locate several large soft brushes. (A little liquid soap in the paint will make it more washable.)

4. If you have rhythm instruments, get them out.

Getting Started

Be set up well in advance so that one leader can be at the door to greet children. There will probably be a crowd that will include visitors. So have extra name necklaces handy. The second leader gathers children on the rug for conversation about Christmas plans. When most of the children have arrived, add the purple patch to the church year calendar, light all four candles of the Advent wreath, and sing some Christmas carols of the children's choice. (Decline suggestions of nonreligious songs, saying simply that today you are going to specialize in songs about Jesus.)

Good News Game

Whisper a message to the child next to you. That child whispers it to the next one and so on until it has gone all the way around the circle. When it comes back to you, if it is correct (or close enough to it), say, "Go, tell it on the mountain!" as a call for everyone to say the message aloud together. If the message has gotten garbled, start it again, encouraging players to listen carefully. Messages are "Good News!"; "Jesus' birthday is almost here!"; and "Go, tell it on the mountain!"

The last message leads you into learning the chorus of "Go, Tell It on the Mountain." Say the words together a time or two. Then sing them. Then stand in a circle to sing them. Sing them again, changing the first word each time you sing. For example, sing "Skip to tell it . . ." while skipping in a circle. Then "Hop to tell . . ." while hopping in a circle. Try several action rounds, then close with "Tiptoe to tell it . . ." while tiptoeing until you sit down before the final round of "Whisper to tell it on the mountain" (whispering, of course.)

The Shepherds' Story

Read or tell in your own words the story of the shepherds in Luke 2:8-20.

Get the children to tell the story back to you, using the figures in your nativity set. Ask questions about what happened next and who was there to help them get the details straight. Finally ask what the angels sang to the shepherds. They will probably need help to say, "Glory to God in the highest." Ask what this means. Use Luke 2:20 to explain it in concrete terms.

Clap the rhythm for the words below

Glo — ry to God in the high — est!

Once the children have learned the rhythm, hand out rhythm instruments if they are available. Mark the same rhythm with the instruments, saying the words as you play. With instruments or clapping, get the feel of the growing host of angels by starting with one person saying and clapping the words and adding one more person each time they are said until everyone in the circle is saying them. Then start saying the words softer and softer until they are just a whisper. One leader can serve as angel choir director to point out who is to come in next and to indicate when to get louder and softer. After a brief silence, repeat quietly, "And the angels went away from them back to heaven."

Angel Wash Pictures

While the children are still quiet in the circle, introduce the idea of drawing pictures of the angels coming to the shepherds. Explain the wash process and tell them they must use only bright colors and must press hard. The children will draw pictures of the angels, shepherds around their campfires, the sheep, and so on. When the pictures are finished the children or an adult will apply one coat of very thin dark blue paint over the whole paper. This makes the drawn figures stand out brightly in a night sky. White angel robes and gold halos and shepherd campfires are especially effective. Leave papers out to dry flat on the table (thin paint runs). Pat any puddles dry with paper towels so that the pictures will be dry enough to take home.

Closing

Relight your Advent wreath. With the children, compose a Christmas litany. Invite each child to say one thing about Jesus' birth. The group response to each statement is, "Glory to God in the highest." Close with a brief prayer.

Looking Ahead

Next Sunday you will change your room from purple to white. Preparations are simple and not too time consuming.

Session 17: The Sunday After Christmas

Worship Focus: Our task in the days after December 25 is to keep the joy to carry into all the world every day. As children relax after the holiday excitement, they may be more ready than ever to think about joy and love. So today we take advantage of the after Christmas mood to enjoy again much of what we did during Advent and to dedicate ourselves to keeping the love and joy growing in the coming year.

We also move into a new season and a new color for the church year. White is the color for Christmas, Epiphany, Easter, and special events like weddings and funerals. Most churches also use white on Sundays when the Lord's Supper is celebrated. White is the happiest color of the church year. It is the color of purity, shining lights, and joy. Today we will decorate with white and think of its joy. Next week we will think about the white shining star that the wise men followed to find Jesus.

Time	Worship Activity	Materials/Resources
5 min.	1. Conversation	
30 min.	2. Remove purple and add white to the room Draw "joy" center Change worship pictures	boxes for purple white paper, colored paper frames, crayons white tablecloth
10 min.	3. Light the Christ candle Retell story using the nativity set "Glory to God" claps Sing favorite carols "Go, Tell It on the Mountain"	Christ candle and match nativity set, bag rhythm instruments
5 min.	4. Confession time	
5 min.	5. Story: "It Is Just the Beginning"	
5 min.	6. Closing: Go Tell It!	

Getting Ready

Merry Christmas! This session requires limited preparation. Gather from home one grocery bag, a large box, and a square of white cloth to cover your worship center. You need white paper to cover the door and/or bulletin board, white drawing paper and colored paper a little larger than the white paper (to serve as frames), and crayons.

Getting Started

As one leader greets children and their parents at the door, the other gathers children on the rug for conversation about Christmas. If new toys have been brought, hear about each one briefly. Then put them all on a designated shelf out of the way for the session.

Once most children have arrived, explain that we are now in a new season and a new color. Introduce Christmastide briefly and add the white color to the church year calendar. Think about reasons white is a good color for Christmas (angel robes, stars, sheep the shepherds brought) and suggest that it is a happy, shining color.

Make a game of changing your room from Advent purple to Christmas white by allowing children to identify purple items in the room and put them in a box one at a time in the center of your circle. Each suggestion begins with a child saying, "Advent is over. We do not need. . . . " The leader gives permission to put the item in the box or explains why the item needs to stay out.

When all the purple is in the box, begin decorating with white. Cover your door and bulletin board with white paper. Add a sign to each that says "Christmas Is for Joy." Each child draws on white paper a picture of a happy time during Christmas this year. Mount each drawing on a slightly bigger piece of colored paper before putting it on the white bulletin board.

Back in your circle, put a white cloth on your worship center. Light the white Christ candle. Then ask children, one at a time, to pull a nativity set figure out of a paper bag without looking. As each child pulls out a figure, he or she places it in an appropriate place on the worship table and tells why that person or animal was happy to be in the barn when Jesus was born. (You may have to empty the bag and refill it if all the children want a turn.) As the figures are placed, sing songs about them or redo one of your Advent activities from past sessions.

Children may suggest songs to sing. End with the chorus from "Go, Tell It on the Mountain." (Hop it, skip it, and so forth as in session 16.)

Confession

Remind the children that it is easier to sing about sharing God's love and joy than it is to really do the sharing at home and with our friends. Invite them to think about what they do and do not do as you pray together.

Dear God, we really *do* want to go tell it on the mountain about Jesus and his love *(throw arms up wide over your head)*, but it is harder to share your love with people right here *(drop hands in your lap)*.

We hold our Christmas toys close *(clutch hands as if hiding something against your chest)* instead of sharing them *(open hands in gesture of offering what is in them)*.

We say, "Not me!" or "I'll do it later" when someone asks us to help at home *(fold arms across your chest)* instead of asking, "What can I do to help?" *(arms out, palms up)*.

We point our fingers and laugh at people who look different *(point your finger with a derisive look on your face)* instead of reaching out to meet them as new friends *(put out your hand to shake)*.

When a friend hits us or calls us a name, we hit back or call even meaner names *(stick out your lower lip, looking fierce)*, instead of finding a way to make peace *(extend hand to shake again)*.

We're sorry. We want to do better. Please help us to share love better with our families, with our friends, and with everyone we meet. Amen.

God promises us that even when we are mean and selfish instead of loving, God still loves us. And when we tell God we are sorry about what we have done, God will help us to do better. So right now God says, "I love you, _____(child's name)."

Say this assurance of pardon to each child around the circle. If possible, give each child a hug. Then ask the children to show God that they want to share Christmas love and joy by shaking the hands of the people on each side of them.

"It Is Just the Beginning"

Point to the nativity set and ask if children know what happened during the days just after Jesus was born. Then tell this story.

After they had seen Jesus, the shepherds went back to the fields to take care of their sheep. But as they went they sang happy songs and told everyone they met about the angels and the baby in the manger. They said, "God is doing something wonderful. Just you wait! This is just the beginning! Jesus is the Christ!"

After they gave gifts to Jesus, the wise men went back to their far away homes. Everywhere they stopped, they told people about the star they had followed to see the baby born in a barn. "Just you wait!" they said. "This is the beginning of something very wonderful that God is doing. That baby will be the Savior of the whole world."

When Jesus was eight days old, Mary and Joseph took him to the Temple. There at the door was a man named Simeon. God had promised Simeon that he would not die until he had seen the Christ. So Simeon was always watching. When he saw Mary and Joseph and Jesus, he knew that Jesus was the one he was waiting for. He took Jesus in his arms and hugged him tight and thanked God, "You have kept your promise, O God. With my own eyes I have seen the Christ. It's just beginning, but I know that through this child you will give your love to the whole world!" Then he gave Jesus back to Mary and said, "This is just the beginning. God has chosen this child to love each one of us. He will bring joy, but his life will not always be happy. Some of the things that will happen to him will make you very, very sad."

Anna was eighty-four years old when Jesus was born. She never left the Temple but stayed there to worship God day and night. She, too, saw Jesus. She told everyone. "I have seen the Christ! It's just the beginning, but it has started. God has come to save us!"

And they were all right. It was just the beginning. Jesus was a tiny baby. He had to eat and sleep and grow and learn just like you and I do. When he grew to be a man, he did show everyone how much God loves us. He told stories about God's love. He made friends with people no one else would love. He even loved the people who hated him. And he asked people to share that love with one another. One of the last things he said was, "This is just the beginning. Tell everyone about God's love and love one another. Spread God's love throughout the whole earth."

Closing: Go Tell It!

Sing "Go, Tell It on the Mountain" once through. Then sing some variations, such as: "Go, tell it to your family"; "Go, tell it on the playground"; "Go, tell it to your school friends"; and so forth. The children may suggest some verses to try. After singing about several places children can share God's love, offer a brief prayer to thank God for Jesus and to ask God to help us spread Christmas love everywhere we go this week.

Looking Ahead

Next week you will be staging a trip with the wise men that will require several leader-made props and a collection of gift boxes or bottles so that each child has a pretend gift to present at the manger. Think ahead!

Session 18: Epiphany Sunday

Worship Focus: On Epiphany we remember the wise men and the star they followed.

Time	Worship Activity	Materials/Resources
5 min.	1. Conversation Add white to calendar Light Christ candle	calendar and patch candle and match
25 min.	2. Traveling with wise men Crown making Visit Herod Leave gifts at manger Tiptoe past Herod	pre-cut crowns stapler and staples sequins and stickers gifts to carry
20 min.	3. Making window stars	paper crayons cooking oil paper towels
10 min.	4. Closing	pre-cut paper frames

Getting Ready

The majority of your session will be an imaginary trip with the three wise men, for which you will need some props.

1. From a 12″ × 18″ sheet of gold construction paper make two crowns by cutting peaks and valleys across the length of the page.

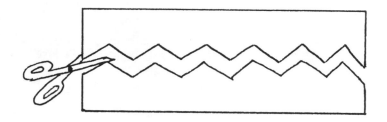 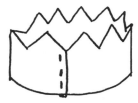

Cut enough crowns for each child and leader. Gather gummed stars, stickers, and other odds and ends (even torn pieces of colored paper) for the children to glue onto the crowns as decorative jewels. Get a stapler and a supply of staples to hold the crowns in shape to fit each head.

2. From the side of a large cardboard box or from a piece of poster board cut a big star. Cover it with white and gold glitter on one side. Tape it onto one end of a yardstick or broom handle to make a star banner to follow. After class tape it to your white door or bulletin board.

3. Set up a manger (if you are lucky, there will still be hay in it left over from the Christmas plays) with a doll baby Jesus in it in a quiet room some distance from your regular meeting room. If you do not have a manger, use a cardboard box.

4. Gather boxes and plastic bottles of all sizes to serve as pretend gifts for Jesus. Find one for each child.

5. Copy one pattern of the star for each child. Gather crayons, a bottle of cooking oil, and a supply of paper towels. Then cut construction paper frames that will fit the stars. Make a sample star to show the children and try out the process for yourself.

Getting Started

As one leader greets children, the other gathers them on the rug for conversation about lights. Talk about the different kinds of lights people put on their Christmas trees. Talk about how it feels to be outside at night with and without a flashlight. Find out what kinds of nightlights children may have in their bedrooms. Identify white as the color of light. Add a white patch to today's square on the church year calendar. Light the white Christ candle one more time. Sing some Christmas songs of praise and such songs as the doxology and "Praise Him, All Ye Little Children" to celebrate Christmas. Then read the story of the wise men who followed the light from a star (Matthew 2:1-12, using the *Good News Bible* or another simple language version).

Traveling with the Wise Men

Invite the children to act out the wise men's journey with you. Remind them that it took the kings a while to get ready for this long trip. They had to pack clothes and get the gifts they wanted to take to Jesus. To be ready for the trip, each child needs to make a crown and to select a pretend gift package to take.

When all are ready gather in one line at the door. Imagine how long the line was when the kings and their camels and servants got ready to leave on their trip. Ask how the wise men knew where to go. Then produce the star banner to follow. Lead the procession off, slowly swaying gently back and forth as if riding a camel.

Outside "Herod's Palace" stop and announce that the star has stopped moving but you do not see a king. Suggest that you all go to the palace to ask where the new king is. Have the second leader or another adult helper stand in another room wearing a crown (and even full costume). As you enter the room, Herod haughtily says, "Welcome. You may each come one at a time and bow before me. Then go sit over there quietly. You may come first *(point to the leader, who does as Herod says, then to each child in turn)*." Herod sourly asks why you are there. The leader with the children's group explains that you have been following a star to find the new king. Herod looks very suspicious but volunteers to consult his advisors, leaves the room for a minute and returns, with the message in Matthew 2:8. Thanking him, the leader guides the children out of the room, picks up the star to follow, and leads the way to where the manger has been set up. Invite the children to kneel quietly around the manger after placing their pretend gifts around it. Start singing "Away in a Manger" and other familiar carols. Then get up, signaling the others to follow you. Before you get back to the palace room, stop to tell the children about your dream (Matt. 2:12). Together tiptoe past the palace so that Herod will not notice you. Go back to your room.

Making Window Stars

Invite children to make window stars to hang at home to remind them of the light of the Christmas star. Show them the finished product. Tell them to press hard on their crayons as they work and to leave some places blank.

As they finish, an adult uses a paper towel to spread cooking oil over the surface of the picture until the blank paper becomes translucent. Gently pat it dry to avoid smearing the crayon. With a very small group that is calm, the children may be able to take turns doing this step.

Center the star in a paper picture frame and tape it in place. After writing the artist's name on the back of the frame, tape it on or set it in the window until time to go home.

Closing

If your congregation lights two candles at the front of the church, bring a photograph of those burning candles. Explain that the reason for these candles is that Jesus said, "I am the light of the world" and "You are the light of the world." Put into your own words what Jesus meant. Point to one candle for Jesus' light and one for your own. (If your congregation does not burn two candles in the front, simply introduce Jesus' statements about light.)

Think together of ways we can light up the lives of people we know. Start by thinking of things children can do to light up the lives of their mothers, then focus on other persons in their homes, and move out into the community. Close with a prayer to ask for God's help in bringing love light to people around us. Use some of the ideas discussed with the children.

LENT AND THE LORD'S PRAYER

Lent begins with Ash Wednesday and lasts for forty weekdays and six Sundays until sunrise on Easter morning. It is the season in which we prepare ourselves for Easter.

Lent is like Advent in many ways. Both are seasons in which we wait and prepare for a holy day that celebrates a central fact of our faith. Purple is the color for both Advent and Lent because in both seasons we wait for the coming of the King. During Advent we await his birth while during Lent we await the coming of his kingdom in the resurrection. During both seasons we focus our attention on all in this world that is less than it should be. We begin Advent remembering all the hopes and dreams of the Old Testament prophets. We begin Lent on Ash Wednesday remembering the failings of our best intentions. Roman Catholic Christians mark their foreheads with the ashes of Palm Sunday's palm branches to remind themselves that each of us, though we may welcome Jesus as Lord with the crowd on Palm Sunday, has in our own ways also called for his crucifixion.

Lent is a season for reevaluation, rededication, and discipline. It is a good time to devote ourselves to a discipline of spiritual growth and service. Many churches offer special study courses for adults during Lent. Preachers present sermon series related to our needs to grow as disciples. Many denominations schedule events related to international missions and hunger relief for Lent as opportunities for people to develop their discipleship. The old tradition of giving something up for Lent is growing into a tradition of giving ourselves up to something for Lent. It is a time to stretch our spiritual wings.

For kindergarten children, Lent is a time to prepare for Easter by working on a specific task that will enrich their relationship with God. In this course that task is to learn and to explore the meaning of the Lord's Prayer. We will explore prayer as a way to communicate with God and to share our lives with God every day.

Before you begin planning, be sure you know what your congregation will be doing to keep Lent this year. Will purple be prominently used in the sanctuary? Will any special symbols be present? What Lenten worship events are planned? Will there be a Lenten service or outreach project in which the children can participate? Incorporate all of these.

Look ahead to Palm Sunday and Easter. Kindergarten children need to be in the sanctuary for at least part of worship on Palm Sunday and Easter. The sense of excitement, the special events, and the decorations introduce them more effectively to these days than anything you can do in a classroom. On Palm Sunday many congregations begin worship with a processional of children waving palm branches or of choirs carrying palms while the congregation sings a Palm Sunday hymn. If a children's choir is going to sing often it will do so early in the service. That makes it natural for children to be in the sanctuary for the first ten or fifteen minutes. *If the children are leading a palm processional,* seat them together on the front pew (or floor if pews are at a premium) after they have processed. Be sure that plenty of adults are walking with the children in the processional to keep them moving and to sit with them to keep them attentive. *If they are not in a processional,* have the children sit with their parents. With the minister, plan a point at which they can exit (possibly during the singing of a hymn). Even in a large sanctuary children will go to the front to join a familiar adult leader. As a last resort, visit the sanctuary as a class, sitting just outside a side door to watch the beginning of the service.

Read the introduction to the chapter on Easter to begin planning the children's presence in the sanctuary on that day, too.

Dear ___:

Lent is the season in which we are encouraged to stretch our spiritual wings in preparation for Easter. During the worship hour our children will keep Lent by learning the Lord's Prayer. Each Sunday we will sing the prayer, pray the prayer, and explore the meaning of one phrase of the prayer.

We invite you to join your child in this discipline. Help your child learn the prayer, and pray it together. Try:

 * praying the prayer together each day;

 * playing games, in the car and at home, in which you say a phrase and pause for your child
   to fill in the next word or phrase (keep this fun, not threatening); and

 * using phrases in specific situations to which they apply so that your child
   understands their meaning more fully. For example, use ''give us this day our daily
   bread'' at mealtime or ''forgive us our sins as we forgive those who sin against us''
   when helping children resolve a squabble. (NOTE: It is easier for young children to
   understand the meaning of the phrases of the prayer than it is to understand the
   meaning of each of the ''big'' words.)

Next Sunday your child will bring home a purple finger-painted cross. Mount it on your refrigerator door or in another visible place as a reminder to both you and your child of your lenten prayer discipline.

We are looking forward to sharing the discipline and privilege of prayer with the children and hope that Lent will become a golden opportunity for you and your child.

                              Faithfully,

Session 19: A Time for Prayer

Worship Focus: Lent is a time to wait for Easter by finding ways to be closer to God.

Introduce Lent, with its purple color, theme of waiting for Easter and growing closer to God, and discipline of prayer. Unlike Advent, Lent includes no special songs, stories, or rituals that are obvious to children. Therefore, our goals are simply that children recognize Lent as the time when we wait for Easter and know its color to be purple. Deeper understanding of this season will come later.

Children are already familiar with a variety of prayers we use in congregational worship and they should be grasping the concept that we can worship and pray at any time and in any place. In this unit we will develop that idea further by focusing on the possibility of prayer every day. We will also work on learning the Lord's Prayer, which children may pray in both individual and group worship. Today focus on generalities and set the stage for the rest of the unit.

Time	Worship Activity	Materials/Resources
10 min.	1. Talk about Easter Sing praise songs	
10 min.	2. Decorate room and display board for Lent	purple display paper pre-cut letters-LENT purple cloth Bible purple bookmark portraits of Jesus
10 min.	3. Finger-paint paper purple	finger-paint paper with cross outline purple finger paint paint aprons clean up supplies

5 min.	4. "Prepare . . ." and "Get Ready"
	   Jesus teaches us to pray
	   Challenge: learn the
	   Lord's Prayer
		Godspell recording
		   and player

5 min.	5. Learn "Kum Bah Yah"	
15 min.	6. Make praying hands and cut out crosses	crayons colored marking pens scissors stapler, staples tacks
5 min.	7. Closing	

Getting Ready

1. Gather materials for decorating your room for Lent. You will need purple paper to cover a bulletin board or your door as a background for displays, purple cloth to cover your worship table, a Bible, a purple bookmark to put in the Bible, and a collection of portraits of Jesus. Find the portraits in a file of teaching pictures or in old Sunday school books. Look for a variety of ideas about what Jesus looked like. Cut large block letters spelling LENT in white paper to use as a title for your display space.

Check storage rooms near the sanctuary for a freestanding cross to keep on your worship table during Lent.

2. On the back side (the non-slick side) of sheets of finger paint paper, draw a cross that takes up most of the paper. Draw with a thick black pen or with a black crayon. Gather purple finger paint, paint smocks (see the Craft Patterns section), and needed clean-up supplies.

3. Draw around your own hands with the middle fingers touching, as below, to make a praying hands drawing sheet for each child.

Getting Started

As children arrive and get their things settled with the help of one leader, the other leader gathers the children on the rug to talk about Easter. Ask what Easter is and what we do at Easter time. Listen to stories about "what we did at Easter." Use the time as an information gathering time and as time to aim the children's thinking toward the coming holy day. This is not the time to correct misinformation. If conversation is strictly about the Easter Bunny, ask "What do we do for Easter at church?"

When most of the children have arrived, sing several favorite praise songs.

Decorating for Lent

Explain that today is the first Sunday of the season of Lent. Briefly describe Lent as the time we prepare for Easter. Then see if children can guess what color goes with Lent. (Your box of purple things will be a hint.) If they have been in the sanctuary for part of congregational worship, identify where they saw purple. If children point out that purple was also the color for Advent, congratulate them. If no one makes the connection, remind them of it.

Working together as a whole or in small groups, use the materials in your box to cover a bulletin board and/or a door with purple paper. Add the pre-cut letters spelling LENT. Put a purple cloth on your worship center. Add a Bible with a purple bookmark. If the Bible has pictures of people praying, open it to one of those pictures. Ask the children to select a portrait of Jesus from several teaching pictures to mount on the display board. (Encourage children to discuss their selection to learn what they are feeling and thinking about Jesus.) Add a purple square to your church year calendar.

When all have regathered, add a cross to your worship center and comment briefly that the cross is an important part of Lent. (Save explanations of its importance for later. For now it is enough for children to know the name of the figure and to associate it with Lent.)

To make purple crosses to decorate your homes (refrigerator doors?) for Lent, each child finger-paints one of the prepared sheets of paper. Limit the amount of paint children use so that papers can dry during the session. Set the papers aside to dry.

Preparing for Easter

Gather around the worship center. Listen to the recording of "Prepare Ye the Way of the Lord." Relearn the "Get Ready" chant from session 13. Recall some of the things you did to get ready for Christmas. Then explain that to get ready for Easter you are going to work on getting to know God better by learning to pray.

As a group identify different times to pray—at church, at mealtime, at bedtime, and at other times named by the children. Then tell the following story.

Jesus Prays

Long ago, when Jesus was born and grew up to be a man, people thought that praying was very difficult. They had special prayers for every situation. Boys and girls worked hard to learn those prayers exactly right and to learn just when to say each one. Families were very careful to say each prayer at the right time and place. On big holidays the leaders read beautiful prayers with lots of big important-sounding words. Some of the words were hard to understand. Men and boys wore a special scarf called a *tallit* when they prayed. People worked so hard at praying and were so careful because they knew that God was the powerful Lord of the universe. They did not want to say anything that would make God unhappy with them.

When Jesus was growing up, he learned all the prayers and wore a tallit just like everyone else. But Jesus knew something the others did not think about. Jesus knew that God loves us. God wants to be our friend and to share everything we think and do. God is not watching to see if we make a mistake, but is waiting to help us when we need help.

So Jesus would pray anytime he wanted to be close to God. When he was happy or saw something beautiful, Jesus shared his feelings with God right then, in his own words. When he was making hard decisions, Jesus told God about them and asked for God's help. When he was tired, Jesus told God about that, too. Most mornings he got up early and went off by himself to pray.

His friends watched Jesus and asked him to teach them how to pray. Jesus told them that they could pray any time about anything. He explained that just as you do not use special words to talk to your friend, you don't have to plan out special words to talk to God. It's easy. You can pray like this, *(say the Lord's Prayer).*

Find out who has heard that prayer before. Talk about where it is used. If any children know it by heart, ask them to say it for the group. Challenge each child to learn it before Easter. Tell them about the letter you sent to their parents. Promise that you will start learning it together next week.

Learning "Kum Ba Yah"

Introduce the African folk song "Kum Ba Yah" (Come By Here) on page 205 as one way of remembering what Jesus told us about prayer. Some of the children will know the song from singing it in camp and school. Learn the motions to use with the song. Make up verses to reflect other situations in which we can pray.

Conclude with a brief prayer to thank God for loving us so that we can share anything that is important to us, at any time we need to share it and in our own words.

Cutting Out Praying Hands and Crosses

1. For your bulletin board, the children make sets of praying hands by writing their names on one side of a praying hands sheet and drawing a picture of themselves doing something they enjoy and can share with God. Fold the hands at the fingertip to form praying hands. Fold and staple the extended "arms" to give the hands depth. Thumbtack the hands to the bulletin board as a border.

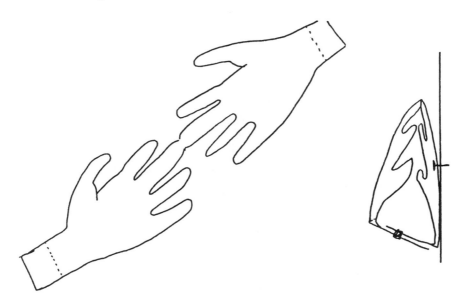

2. When their hands are finished, children cut out their finger-painted crosses following the outline on the back of their paper. (Show them a picture of your refrigerator at home with a finger-painted cross on it to encourage them to mount theirs in the same way.)

Closing

Regather to chant "Get Ready" and to sing "Kum Ba Yah." Close with an adult-led prayer to thank God for loving us enough to be our friend in prayer.

Looking Ahead

To begin a mural for the choir next week, you need to gather painting supplies and talk with the choir director.

Session 20: The Second Sunday of Lent

Worship Focus: "Our Father, who art in heaven, Hallowed be thy name" (Matt. 6:9 RSV).

As we begin learning the Lord's Prayer today, we will focus on God and speaking to God. We will translate the archaic *art* into plain *is* and explore what *hallowed* and *holy* mean. The message for the children is that we begin this prayer by speaking to a holy, special God who is different from anyone else.

As you explore the meaning of these words, avoid discussions about where God or heaven is. No answer will entirely satisfy the concrete thought processes of the kindergarten child. This is a question they will simply have to live with until they mature enough to understand the abstract truth that God is omnipresent. Instead of talking about where God is, focus on who God is and what God is like.

Who is God? God is our Father. What is God like? God is "hallowed." *Hallowed* is one of those words that cannot be precisely defined. Its meaning grows and is shaped by our experiences of God. In today's story, DeLise hears a man explain the holiness of God by pointing to God's ability to create a daisy from a small, hard seed. An older woman speaks of God's comforting presence when she is alone and frightened. A teenager speaks of God's holy laws, which take priority in her life. Each of these definitions points to a part of what makes God holy.

One way we respond to the holiness of God is in song. Each of us can sing our praises every day. The choir sings of the glory and holiness of God in a unique way on Sunday mornings. This week we will explore the choir's singing and begin a mural for them. Next week we will finish the mural and present it to the choir to thank them. This is one way of living out the prayer "Thy will be done" by loving one another.

Time	Worship Activity	Materials/Resources
15 min.	(?) Observe choir and visit choir room	
5 min.	1. "Kum Ba Yah" and add purple to calendar	calendar and purple patch
5 min.	2. Learn lines of prayer Learn "Hallowed . . . Name"	
10 min.	3. Story and discussion	
20 min.	4. Start choir mural	prepared mural paper paints, brushes smocks, paint dishes clean-up supplies
5 min.	5. Closing	

Getting Ready

1. Today your group will begin a mural for the choir, to be completed and delivered next Sunday. To introduce children to the choir and its work, do two things this week.

First, plan for the children to listen to the choir singing in the sanctuary. If children attend the beginning of worship with their parents each week, that will be sufficient. If the children do not regularly see and hear the choir at work, plan to visit the sanctuary today to hear the choir. If the choir processes into the sanctuary, be where the children can watch as well as listen. Find out from the choir director what the choir will sing this week and plan to be in the sanctuary at the most appropriate time.

Second, clear with the choir director your plans to visit the choir room to see where the robes and music are kept, to sit in the chairs the choir sits in to rehearse, and to rehearse one of your songs there.

2. Prepare to make a mural of the choir. Have available for all the children tempera paints and shallow dishes, large brushes, paint smocks, and clean-up supplies. Cut a large piece of chart paper (about 2′ × 3′) for each child. Today each child will paint one big choir member. Next week these figures will be cut out and presented to the choir.

Before class draw with a pencil a basic outline of a choir member. If the choir wears robes, draw in the shapes of the robes. The children then paint on top of the outline. This ensures that the pictures are all nearly the same size.

Getting Started

If the children begin worship with their parents, meet them as they leave the sanctuary and go to the choir room to talk about the work of choirs. See where the robes and music are kept and sit in the chairs the choir sits in to rehearse. Rehearse one of your songs there. If the children do not go to the sanctuary, gather in your room to talk about choirs. Then visit the choir room and listen to the choir sing in the sanctuary.

Introducing "Our Father . . . Hallowed be thy name"

Back in your room, sing "Kum Ba Yah" with the motions and add the purple square to your church year calendar. Briefly look at your display board to recall the name of the season of Lent and remind the children that they are going to begin learning the Lord's Prayer today.

Line out the first three phrases one phrase at a time several times. Then divide into three groups. Assign the first group "Our Father," the second group "Who art in heaven," and the third group "Hallowed be thy name." Playing prayer choir director, point to each group to say its phrase. (You will have to say it with them at first.

After doing this several times, point to the "Who art in heaven" group. Ask them what their part means. Briefly explain that *art* is an old word that means "is."

To practice the words of the Lord's Prayer, begin learning the song that is sung to a West Indies tune (see page 204). Today teach the refrain, "Hallowed be thy name." When the children know it, one of the leaders sings all the words of the prayer, pausing for the children and the other leader to sing the refrain.

Story

Ask the children what "Hallowed be thy name" means. Explain that this is a really hard question. Hear their ideas. Share with them the funny misunderstanding of one little boy who thought the phrase was "Harold be thy name" and, therefore, that God's name must be Harold. Point out that *hallowed* is not God's name but a word that describes God. Then urge them to listen to the following story for ideas of what *hallowed* means.

Hallowed Means . . .

DeLise jumped on the first square in the sidewalk. "Our Father," she said.

Landing on one foot in the next square, she said, "Who . . . *(pause for group to add* "art in heaven"*).*

Then with both feet in the third square, she said, "Hallowed be . . . "*(pause for the group to add* "thy name"*).*

"Hallowed be thy name," she said as she landed in another square.

"Hallowed be thy name!" and another.

"What's that, DeLise?" asked Mr. Debs.

"Hallowed be thy name," said DeLise. "It's a prayer we are learning at church."

"Oh, that prayer. I know that prayer. 'Our Father, which art in heaven, Hallowed be thy name,' " smiled Mr. Debs as he leaned on the hoe in his garden.

DeLise waited a minute. "Mr. Debs, how come God is hallowed?"

Mr. Debs squinted his eyes to think, then he smiled down at his flowers. "DeLise, put out your hand." DeLise did, and Mr. Debs dug a tiny black speck out of a package in his pocket. "It's a seed, DeLise—a daisy seed. When I plant it in my garden, it grows into a plant like this. And," Mr. Debs picked a daisy and handed it to DeLise, "makes a flower like this. Only God knows how to do that. That's why God is hallowed."

DeLise smiled and tucked the daisy in her top buttonhole. "Thank you, Mr. Debs." And she jumped onto the next square, "Hallowed be thy name."

On the fourteenth square, Delise looked up. Mrs. Roney was sitting on the steps in the sun. "You're learning the Lord's Prayer, DeLise. Good for you!"

"Did you know that God is hallowed?" asked DeLise.

"Do I ever!" exclaimed Mrs. Roney. "Last night in that thunder storm I was really scared. The wind was so-o-o-o strong and the lightning so-o-o-o bright and the thunder so-o-o-o-o loud. I was all alone—at first. Then I began to feel God close all around me. God was taking care of me. That's why God is hallowed. God is with me when I am frightened."

Hop, hop, hop. Hallowed, hallowed, *bump.* DeLise hopped straight into Andrea, who turned thirteen-years-old last week.

"Sorry, DeLise," muttered Andrea. "I guess I wasn't watching where I was going."

DeLise could see big tears splashing down Andrea's cheeks. "What's wrong? Why are you crying?" asked DeLise, peering up into Andrea's unhappy face.

"Oh, I'll be okay." Andrea sighed a big, heavy sigh. "My friends called me some names because I didn't help them play a mean trick. But it's God's holy law to love one another. No way was what they were going to do loving."

DeLise pulled the daisy out of her buttonhole and handed it to Andrea. "I love you, Andrea."

Andrea smiled a very small smile. "Thanks, DeLise."

Then DeLise hopped on home. "Hallowed be thy name. Hallowed be thy name. Hallowed be thy name."

Discuss what DeLise learned about the meaning of *hallowed* from her three friends.

Starting a Mural for the Choir

Recall what you saw when you visited the choir room and watched the choir sing in the sanctuary. Point out that we can all sing for God every day. Then note that the choir sings for God every Sunday.

They work hard to sing their best songs for God and to sing to us about how hallowed God is. Introduce the making of a mural as a thank you gift to the choir.

Today each child will paint a picture of one member of the choir on separate pieces of chart paper. While they paint, talk about what the choir does. A small group may even want to sing some familiar songs informally as they paint. Be sure there is time for cleanup and a closing.

Be sure to write each artist's name on his or her paper so that it can be identified for cutting out next Sunday.

Closing

Sing "Kum Ba Yah" and "Hallowed Be Thy Name" if you have time. Then line out the whole of the Lord's Prayer as your closing prayer for the day.

Looking Ahead

While the paint is still available, paint a few extra choir people for children who may have missed today's session.

Session 21: The Third Sunday of Lent

Worship Focus: "Thy kingdom come, Thy will be done, On earth as it is in heaven" (Matt. 6:10 RSV).

To understand this verse, children need to understand the words *king, kingdom,* and *thy will be done.* Some of this should be familiar from children's stories. Once the children understand the basic meaning of these words, they are ready to explore the ways we do God's will by serving one another and by loving God. Finish your thank you mural for the choir.

Time	Worship Activity	Materials/Resources
5 min.	1. Share feelings Sing "Kum Ba Yah"	
10 min.	2. Review the Lord's Prayer with game and song Add purple to calendar	purple patch for church calendar glue stick
10 min.	3. Talk about kings Play "Thy Will Be Done"	
5 min.	4. Learn this part of the Lord's Prayer with puppet story	two sock puppets
25 min.	5. Finish choir mural	choir figures prepared background scissors, tape
5 min.	6. Closing	

Getting Ready

1. Prepare puppets to help the children distinguish between the two sons in the story today. Puppets can be elaborate works of art or simple as socks. For today, dig two socks of different colors out of your drawer. Each sock will be one of the sons. They need no ornaments or eyes or anything else. Simply pull the socks over your hands and forearms. Hold your fingers straight and high to express a proud, positive response. Wad your sock-covered hand into a fist to express an angry, closed response. March off to work or slink off to hide as the sons in the story do. Practice telling the story using the puppets.

2. Before cutting the background paper for your mural, visit the choir room and decide where and how you will mount your masterpiece. Then figure in your mind the arrangement of the choir figures on the paper. Title the sheet "Thank You, Choir" and "Sing for God." Place the titles wherever they fit best. (You may also want to write a personal note to the choir, telling them about why your class made them the mural. This will make them feel especially loved and will help them to see your group as an important part of the worshiping congregation.)

Gather enough scissors so that all the children can work at the same time. Also get whatever you need to mount the figures on the mural.

Getting Started

One leader greets the children and helps them get their belongings settled while the other gathers the children on the rug to talk about their morning. Discuss what has made them happy or sad or even angry today. When most of the children have arrived, sing together "Kum Ba Yah," using verses about feelings.

Reviewing the Lord's Prayer

Add a purple square to your church year calendar and note that you are halfway through Lent, waiting for Easter. Recall your task of learning the Lord's Prayer before Easter. To review, first line out the phrases of the Lord's Prayer that you learned last week. Then have all the children stand in a circle. An adult becomes the choir director as was done last week. This week, point to individuals to say the next word in the prayer. Begin by saying several words, then point to a player to add an obvious word—"who art in. . . . " As children miss fewer of the words, begin omitting more and more of them until the children are saying all of the words. The first time the children say all the words, go around the circle and have each child say one word, in order, after the preceding child. If your group is doing really well at this, begin to point to children randomly around the circle.

Sing "Hallowed Be Thy Name" (the Lord's Prayer song). Challenge the children to sing with you on the phrases you have learned together and to sing the refrain on the other parts.

Defining the "King" Words and Playing a Game

Ask the children to tell you what a king is. The important facts for them to know are that kings rule and that they are the leaders of their countries. If none of the children mentions it, ask what a kingdom is. Finally ask what it means to say "Obey the will of the king!" If they have no idea, explain to them that the will of the king is what the king wants done. Give examples like: "If the king says, 'Tonight we *will* have roast beef for supper,' his will is to eat roast beef." Offer other examples about making laws about how people treat one another or taxes they must pay to the king.

Once they have the idea of what a king is, reinforce it with a game based on "Mother, May I." One of the adults is the King. All of the children stand against a wall. The King stands against the opposite wall to call out commands to groups of players or to individual players. Commands include such directions as, "My will is that all of you take five baby steps forward" or "My will is that Carla and John and Pete hop three times backwards." Before following the command, the players must say "Thy will be done." If they do not, they must go back to the wall. The first player to reach the King is the winner. Stop the game before that occurs by commanding the whole group to sit in a circle on the rug. (**Note:** The game is most fun when it moves rapidly, so use an adult rather than a child for the King.)

Praying "Thy Kingdom Come, Thy Will Be Done . . . "

Back in your circle, the King commands everyone to put their hands in their laps, close their eyes, take a slow deep breath to relax, and then to quietly open their eyes. Open on your lap the Bible from your worship center to Matthew 21. Then tell the following story.

>One day when Jesus and his friends were sitting around together, just like we are, Jesus said, "Now what do you think? There was once a man who had two sons. He went to the older one *(present one of your puppets)* and said, 'Son, go and work in the garden today.'
>
>'I don't want to,' he answered. *(Scrunch up your sock face into a tight closed fist-face as you say his words with feeling.)* But later he changed his mind and went. *(Relax your sock face and march it off obediently to your knee.)*
>
>Then the father went to the other son *(present the other sock puppet)* and said the same thing. 'Yes, sir,' the second son answered *(say it with your sock at alert attention),* but he did not go. *(Sulk your sock puppet off to the other side.)*
>
>Which one of the two *(look from one puppet to the other)* did his father's will?"
>
>*(Let the children answer the question and tell why they gave those answers. When talk is centered on one son, raise that puppet and let it react in character.)*
>
>Jesus told his friends that they should do God's will, too. We know what God's will is. God wants us to love God and to take care of one another. When we pray "Thy kingdom come, Thy will be done, On earth as it is in heaven," we are promising God that we will look for ways to show our love.

Use this story as the lead in to working on the choir mural, which says that you all love the people in the choir.

Finishing the "Thank You" Mural for the Choir

Each child cuts out a choir figure. Children who were not present in last week's session will cut out one of the teacher-painted figures. Help the children mount the pictures on the mural. When all the figures have been mounted, take the mural to the choir room and mount it on a wall.

Closing

Sit in the choir chairs to sing praise songs for a few minutes. Say a prayer using the phrases of the Lord's Prayer you have learned so far. Continue to pray, thanking God for the choir that sings songs that show how hallowed God's name is. Ask God to help you know and do God's will. Then return to your room to meet parents. (If you have a few extra minutes, play "Thy Will Be Done" until the parents arrive.)

Looking Ahead

Next Sunday we explore "Give us this day our daily bread. You will need a tray of bite-sized pieces of a variety of fruits and vegetables and materials with which to make no-bake cookies. It may be wise to enlist a parent or two to be present as extra hands.

Session 22: The Fourth Sunday of Lent

Worship Focus: "Give us this day our daily bread" (Matt. 6:11 RSV).

For adults, "bread" can mean all that is needed for survival, but such thinking is beyond kindergarteners. For children, this is a trusting prayer for food for ourselves and for all the people of the world. As such, it becomes a prayer that unites the whole hungry world before God, who feeds us all.

Time	Worship Activity	Materials/Resources
10 min.	1. Foods we like Conversation and praise Songs	tray of fruit pieces
20 min.	2. Make cookies	sealable plastic bags
20 min.	3. Make "Give Us This Day" place mats	prepared place mats pre-cut Contact paper covering food pictures scissors, glue
5 min.	4. Share the food with others	bigger bag or box for packing
5 min.	5. Closing: Eat cookies Sing and pray Add purple to calendar	cookie for each one prayer worksheet purple square for calendar glue stick

Getting Ready

1. Prepare a tray of bite-sized pieces of fruit. Include a variety of fruits the children will recognize and one or two that they may be a little less familiar with.

2. Prepare to make no-bake cookies in this session. Gather enough plastic sherbet or margarine tubs for each child to use as a mixing bowl. Before class, measure into each bowl the peanut butter, powdered sugar, and dry milk. Put 1½ graham cracker squares in a plastic sealable sandwich bag for each child. Have the other ingredients ready to add. Most important, plan for cleanup. Have lots of paper towels ready for hand washing.

RECIPE

¼ cup crunchy peanut butter
¼ cup powdered sugar
⅛ cup instant nonfat dry milk
2½ graham cracker squares
1 tbsp. water
1 generous handful of miniature marshmallows, raisins, M&Ms, chocolate chips, or other treats
  of your choice

Each recipe makes about six 1″ cookies.

Before class, make up a double or triple recipe to see how it works and to have ready one cookie each for the children to eat during the session closing. Also write each child's name on a label on a cookie bag after the cookies are made.

3. Rip out pages of pictures of food from magazines and have the children cut out the pictures. Have enough so that all can work at the same time. Be sure you have plenty of scissors and glue.

For each child you expect, print "Give us this day our daily bread" in the center of a large (approximately 12″ × 14″) sheet of construction paper, which will be the background for a place mat. Cut out in advance sheets of clear Contact paper (available in the shelf paper section of most stores) about 2″ wider and longer than the place mat. Cut a diagonal across each corner as in the sketch on page 96.

Getting Started

As one leader greets the children and helps them settle their belongings, the other gathers children on the rug around a tray of small pieces of fruit. Talk together about which fruits the children like. If they are interested, talk about where each fruit comes from—trees, bushes, or vines. Discuss different ways of fixing them—apple jelly, slices of apple, apple pie, apple salads, and so on. When most of the group has arrived, offer each child his or her choice of one piece of fruit on the tray.

Sing the doxology, noting that food is one of the blessings that flow from God. Continue singing praise songs of the children's choice for a few minutes.

Making Cookies to Eat and Take Home

Invite the children to help you make some cookies that include several foods almost everyone likes. Name the ingredients slowly to enjoy each one.

Before going to the tables to work, tell the children the four steps required to make these cookies.

1. Crush the crackers *in the sealed bag* before putting them in the bowl.
2. With clean hands, mix all the ingredients in the bowl plus those the teacher adds (1 tbsp. water and a handful of the treat).
3. Roll dough into small balls.
4. Crush one more graham cracker *in the sealed bag*, add the balls, reseal the bag, and shake the bag to coat the balls with graham cracker crumbs.

Send the children to the tables (by way of the sink if hand washing is needed) with bagged crackers set at each place. While the children crush the crackers, hand out the bowls of pre-measured ingredients. When the children have their dough well mixed, add marshmallows, raisins, or chocolate chips. Urge the children to mix these in gently before they make their balls. Have the children wash their hands after they roll the dough into balls, but before they crush the second graham cracker, so that they will not get the outside of the bag sticky. When their cookies are complete, instruct the children to leave them in the bag to take home.

Learning the Prayer and Making a Place Mat

Gather on the rug. While one leader completes the cleanup and readies the tables for the next activity, the other leader reviews the phrases of the Lord's Prayer you have already learned using the "Choir Directing Game." Then introduce today's phrase. Say it several times for the children to repeat. Ask the children what it means.

Suggest that this could be a mealtime prayer. Talk about mealtime prayer practices in the children's families. If children know blessings that their families say at meals, ask them to share these with the group.

Show the children a place mat background and read its message. Suggest that a place mat like this could go on their tables at home to remind them to pray when they eat. Challenge them to mount pictures of foods they like around the words on their place mats. As they finish their mats, the children take them to an adult, who will cover the mats with Contact paper. (Instructions for using Contact paper are included in each package.

Fold the extra Contact paper over the back of the place mat. With a pencil, write each child's name on the back of his or her place mat. Send the child to another table to gently press the Contact paper in place on the front of the mat with the bowl of a spoon. As contact is made, the cloudy film of the Contact paper will disappear.

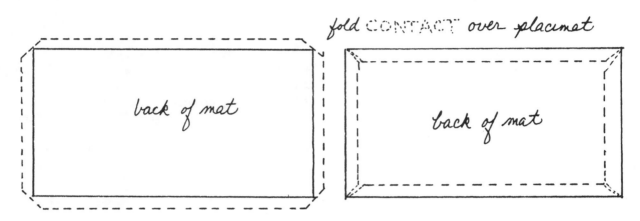

Sharing Cookies with Others

Regather on the rug. Repeat the prayer phrase on the place mats together. Begin to offer each child one of the cookies, but stop dramatically. Repeat the prayer phrase and thoughtfully point out that Jesus did not say "Give *me* this day *my* daily bread." He was concerned that everyone have bread, and he wanted us to be concerned about that, too. Briefly tell the children about people in your community who do not have enough daily bread and have to go to a soup kitchen or other feeding program your church supports. Suggest that if you each put one cookie in a box or bag, you would have a fine treat to share with a person at one of those centers. Have the children donate one cookie from their bags to share.

Closing

When the donated cookies are all packed, regather on the rug. Place the packed cookies on a place mat in the center of the circle. Then offer each child one of the cookies you made in advance. Enjoy them together. When all have finished eating, invite them to sing the doxology together, then pray together. Add a purple square to your calendar and note your progress in getting ready for Easter by learning the Lord's Prayer.

If you have extra time, play the game to review the Lord's Prayer and include today's phrase. You might also ask individual children to try repeating it alone. Be generous with praise for successes and help in getting through the rough spots.

Looking Ahead

Easter *is* coming. Be sure you have complete plans for the children to participate in parts of the Palm Sunday and Easter services.

For next Sunday you will need to prepare simple paper mobile forms for the children to use and a large peek box to use for at least two weeks.

Session 23: The Fifth Sunday of Lent

Worship Focus: We will look ahead to Palm Sunday and Easter and will explore "Forgive us our debts [trespasses] as we forgive our debtors [those who trespass against us]. And lead us not into temptation, but deliver us from evil" (Matt. 6:12-13 KJV).

Today we will learn Easter songs and use a peek box to peek ahead to the coming week. We will also continue learning the Lord's Prayer. Today's phrases are difficult. They use unfamiliar words and speak of abstract realities that are just beyond the understanding of most kindergarten children. Our aims are limited by this. Therefore, we will define *debt*, or trespasses, by connecting it to the more familiar vocabulary of *sin* or *wrongs*. The children will make Forgive Mobiles to connect our forgiveness of others with God's forgiveness of us. We will take an introductory stab at offering examples of temptation.

Time	Worship Activity	Materials/Resources
10 min.	1. Getting ready for Easter Add purple to calendar "Get Ready" chant Sing Alleluia songs	calendar and purple glue stick bowl of temptation
20 min.	2. "Forgive Us . . ." Slap or "Trespass" story Sing "Forgive Me, God . . ." Make "Forgive Mobiles"	prepared mobiles yarn and crayons
10 min.	3. Review the Lord's Prayer	
10 min.	4. "Lead us not . . ." Define *temptation* using story litany and experiment	
5 min.	5. Review the Lord's Prayer	"hot" potato
5 min.	6. Closing: look in peek box	

Getting Ready

1. If you have not already made plans for the children's participation in Palm Sunday and Easter worship in the sanctuary, *do so immediately*. These are high holy days with worship traditions that children respond to at an early age. Once your plans are set, let the parents know by letter or phone what they and their children are offered. Also see that appropriate notes about the children's departure from these services are printed in the order of worship.

2. Be sure that you know which liturgical colors your church will use on Palm Sunday. Some congregations use purple; others use red.

3. Make a peek box that will be used this week to look ahead to Palm Sunday and next week to look ahead to Easter. This can be as simple or as elaborate as you choose to make it. In its simplest form, it is a large box with the top shaped to look like a tent and a small hole cut in one side (see below). Children take turns peeking into the hole to see an object or two that will be important on the coming Sunday.

The light to illuminate the objects is that which comes through the open space left in the tent on the side of the box opposite the peek hole. Cover the opening on the peek hole side with cardboard or a piece of paper. Face the back of the box toward a window or another light source.

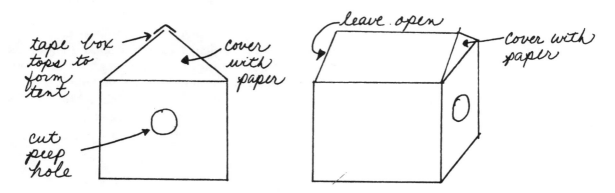

For this week's session, place several palm branches in a vase or spread them on the bottom of the box. If your congregation gives palms to everyone on Palm Sunday, secure one or two early, or ask your local florist for some.

4. To prepare the "Forgive Mobiles," you need two different colored sheets of construction paper for the children, one to draw on and a second color for the title hanger. Any color will work. (If you have access to a good art supply or paper store, try to get paper with a different color on each side. The different colors will emphasize the difference in the before and after forgiveness drawings. This is nice, but not necessary.)

To make the title hangers, fold a piece of construction paper as shown below. Cut off the extra paper, then cut the two triangles apart at the fold. Staple each triangle to the long side of a sheet of construction paper. Punch a hole in the upper corner of each triangle. On each triangle, print with a marking pen "Forgive us our debts, as we forgive our debtors."

Cut a 12″ piece of yarn for each child.

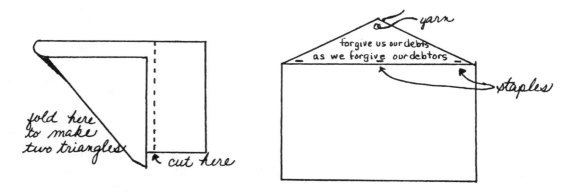

5. Prepare a bowl of "temptation," such as a bowl full of wrapped candies, to display in the room throughout the session. Keep an eye on the children to lead them away from temptation if necessary.

Getting Started

While one leader welcomes the children and helps them get their belongings settled, the other gathers them on the rug to talk about Easter preparations. Spend time looking at your Christian year calendar. Add the purple patch for today. Add a sticker or a small picture of a palm leaf to next Sunday's square and a flower or another Easter sticker or picture to the following Sunday. (Remember, Easter and Palm Sunday may be new holidays for many children whose families are only nominally involved in the church.)

Do the "Get Ready" chant again. To get ready for Easter, introduce *alleluia* as an Easter word. Whisper "alleluia" to the person next to you. Tell that person to whisper it to the next person and so on around the circle. Explain that *alleluia* means "Hurray!" and "Glory to God" and "What a happy day!" all at the same time. We say it because of God's big Easter surprise. Because the surprise of Easter is still a secret, we can only whisper "alleluia" until Easter morning.

Sing "Praise Ye the Lord, Alleluia" and other praise songs the children know that include the word *alleluia*, whispering the word *alleluia* in each song. Then introduce "Jesus Christ Is Risen Today" as a song you will sing in church on Easter. Sing the first verse and ask the children to stand up each time they hear the word *alleluia*. Sing it again. This time one leader sings the verses and the other sings the *alleluia*. Ask the children to join the leader singing the *alleluias*.

"Forgive Us . . . "

1. If your congregation says "Forgive us our debts . . . " work through the following exercise from *Let All the People* by Agnes Junkin Peery.

> I'd like to play a game with you!
> (To one child) Hold out your hand. (Slap hand.) Now you owe me a slap. That's a debt. Pay me back. (Child slaps your hand.)
> Now I owe you a slap. That's a debt. Now you pay me back. (The game goes back and forth with the same conversation for a little while.)
> We could go on like this forever! We'd finally forget who started this hitting game. But I want to stop it, so I'm going to say, "Let's forget it. I'm going to forgive your debt and you can forgive mine. We don't have to pay back slaps anymore. Everything is forgiven."
> When Jesus taught us to pray, "Forgive us our debts as we forgive our debtors," he was talking about this kind of game played out every day in lots of different ways: Somebody hits you. You "pay him back" by hitting him and he "pays you back" again with another hit, and soon you are in a fight. Someone says something mean about you. You "pay her back" by saying something mean about her. Pretty soon you are so mad at each other that you won't speak. And so it goes.
> How can you stop this "paying back" game? (Help children realize that we can say "Let's forget it. Let's forgive each other's debts.")

If your congregation says "Forgive us our trespasses . . ." tell and discuss the following story.

> Sara Jane and Susan shared a room. Well, actually they really didn't *share* it. Each lived in her half of it.
> When Susan borrowed one of the books on Sara Jane's bookshelf, Sara Jane would yell, "Susan's trespassing. She has *my* book."
> When Sara Jane borrowed the bride's dress for Betsy, Susan's doll, Susan screamed at her. "That's Betsy's dress! You're trespassing!"
> When Susan left her wet raincoat on the rug beside Sara Jane's bed, which made the rug cold and icky when Sara Jane's bare feet hit it that night, Sara Jane jumped back on her bed. "Somebody and her raincoat have been trespassing again!"
> When Sara Jane had a friend over and Susan found them sitting on her bed talking, she whined, "Now who is trespassing? Sit on your own bed, Sara Jane."
> Finally, Sara Jane drew a line on the floor with a red crayon and put up a sign that said "No Trespassing."
> *No trespassing.* What did Sara Jane's sign mean? (*Discuss what was wrong between the sisters.*)
> When Jesus taught us to pray "Forgive us our trespasses as we forgive those who trespass against us," he was thinking of all the ways we all get into one another's things and make life difficult for one another. He was thinking about how we want our own way and do not want to share anything we have. And he was thinking sadly about how unhappy all that trespassing makes us.
> When we pray "Forgive us our trespasses as we forgive those who trespass against us," we are telling God that we are sorry about the trespassing we have done, *and* we are promising God that we will forgive those who trespass against us. We are saying that we do not want to act like Sara Jane and Susan.

2. Sing the first verse of "Forgive Me, God . . ." in two sections.

3. To make Forgive Mobiles, the children draw a picture of some angry, unhappy children who need forgiveness on one side of their paper. They will draw a second picture of happy children who have been forgiven on the other side. Emphasize the difference in feelings and facial expressions before and after forgiving. Use the stories you have told during the session as examples. As a group, think of some debt or trespassing situations they might draw. Then go to work. When the pictures are complete, each child ties one end of a piece of yarn through the hole in the hanger. The other end is left free to tie to a window latch or a ceiling light fixture as a mobile.

Review the Lord's Prayer

Regather on the rug to sing "Hallowed Be Thy Name." Point to different children to sing each phrase with the adult leader. The whole class sings the refrain.

"Lead Us Not Into Temptation . . ."

To introduce the concept of temptation, tell a few stories about temptation. Conclude each with the phrase, "That's temptation." Then ask the group why that is tempting and why the tempting act should not be done.

> The piano is open. The rule is that no one plays the piano during Sunday school. But it's open and you *do* like to play it and you do not have a piano to play at home. That's a temptation. *(You may substitute some other infringement of class rules to fit your group.)*

> Your friend got a _____ *(fill in the name of a currently popular toy)* for her birthday. She has been playing with it all morning. You really want to play with it. It does not look like she will ever give you a turn with it. The only way you'll get it is to grab it. That's a temptation.

> There is a big bowl of _____ *(whatever you prepared)* sitting right in the middle of our classroom. You really love them. There are so many in the bowl that if you took just one, no one would notice. That's a temptation.

After discussing several examples of temptations, say the verse together several times. Explain that when we pray "Lead us not into temptation, but deliver us from evil," we are asking God to help us when we want to do wrong things. Do not take too much time on this discussion. The aim is to make the verse familiar. Repeat the verse several times together. Pass an object around the circle. Each player says a word of the verse when receiving the object before passing it to the next player, who will say the next word. After going all the way around the circle several times, add the option of changing the direction of the object by passing it the other way.

Review the Lord's Prayer

Expand the game to include the whole Lord's Prayer, but concentrate on the verse just learned.

Closing

Sing "Hallowed Be Thy Name" and "Kum Ba Yah."
Present the peek box and explain that in it is something that the children will see next Sunday in worship. Give each child a turn to look in the box, but tell no one what they will see. After they all have peeked, ask what they saw. It may take a while to clarify what the object is. You may have to tell the children that the object is palm leaves. Tell them about how the leaves will be used in church next Sunday. As parents arrive, remind them of any schedule changes for the next two weeks.

Looking Ahead

Next Sunday, Palm Sunday, the children will begin the morning in the sanctuary. Be sure plans are set and known by parents. You need to gather materials for a simple craft project and obtain an Easter lily for your peek box.

Session 24: Palm Sunday

Worship Focus: As we celebrate Palm Sunday, we will explore the conclusion of the Lord's Prayer, "Thine is the kingdom, and the power, and the glory for ever. Amen" (Matt. 6:13 KJV).

The Lord's Prayer concludes with the recognition that God is the supreme King of life. Holy Week begins with our recognizing Jesus as the Messiah (God's King). So the power, the glory, and the kingship of God are the focus of our worship with the children today as we conclude our work on the Lord's Prayer and celebrate Palm Sunday.

The best way for children to celebrate Palm Sunday is to be in the sanctuary during the Palm Sunday processional. The feelings of excitement communicate to them most effectively that your church does indeed welcome Jesus as King. In Sunday school, the children will hear the story of Palm Sunday, so in children's church we will focus less on the story and more on exploring the image of Jesus as our King.

The final verse of the Lord's Prayer will reinforce the Palm Sunday theme of God's kingship. The crown making activity will help the children recall the prayer verse and will set the stage for a time of confession based on our preference to be the rulers of own worlds.

Time	Worship Activity	Materials/Resources
15 min.	1. Participate in the palm processional in the sanctuary	
5 min.	2. Conversation about Palm Sunday Story and branches	
5 min.	3. Sing: "Hosanna" Praise songs Whisper practice Easter song	
5 min.	4. Review the Lord's Prayer with song and game	"hot" object
10 min.	5. Make "Kingdom, Power, and Glory" crowns	prepared crown forms decorative jewels glue, paste, scissors
15 min.	6. Closing: confession Peek box Whispered Easter song	peek box and lily

Getting Ready

1. The children should be in church for the opening of worship this morning. They may be with their parents, participating in a palm processional themselves (maybe with you as their leader), or

observing with you from the wings. Be sure all parents know what the plans are. Signs on the door, notes in the church bulletin or newsletter, or phone calls to parents are in order.

2. Prepare stiff paper crowns and gather jewels for children to mount on them. Cut crown shapes from long strips of poster board or very heavy stiff paper. Cut them at least 22" long so that they will *not* fit the children's heads when the crowns are stapled end to end. Gather "jewels" for the children to mount on the crown. To make decorative jewels, provide gummed stars, stickers, and small scraps of brightly colored paper. (Old wrapping paper is great to tear into jewels!) Gather scissors and glue sticks or paste to mount the jewels.

3. This week, hide an Easter lily or a similar flower in your peek box. Set the box out of the way so that the children will not be tempted to peek too soon.

Getting Started

As you leave the sanctuary together talk about what you saw and heard and did. Get the children's belongings settled in your room. If the children have palm branches, have them place the branches in a big vase on your worship table or spread them on your table and assure the children that they will get them back before they leave. Then gather in a circle on the rug.

Ask the children to tell you the story about the parade of palm branches that was held for Jesus. If they have been in Sunday school, they will probably be able to tell the basic story. If they cannot, the story from Matthew 21:7-9 (use the Revised Standard Version so that its *hosanna* will open the way for the next song).

Sing

Learn and enjoy the simple song that sets to music what the people shouted to Jesus.

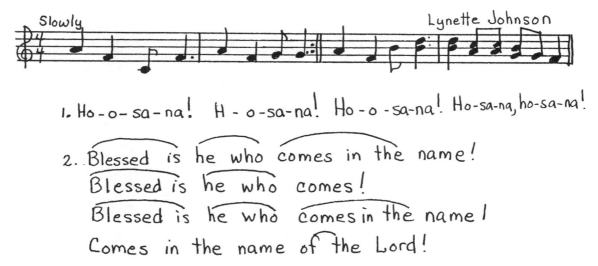

Go on to sing other praise songs the children know, such as "Praise Him, All Ye Little Children," "Praise Ye the Lord, Alleluia," and even the doxology.

Review the Lord's Prayer

Make your last song "Hallowed Be Thy Name" (The Lord's Prayer Song). Point to different children or groups of children to sing with you different lines in the Lord's Prayer, with the whole group singing the refrains.

Briefly play the "Hot Potato Game" to review the verses you have already covered. (Directions for the game are in session 23.)

"Thine is the kingdom . . ."

Introduce the final verse of the prayer as a good one for Palm Sunday. Line it out for the children, stopping to define the big words and to assign each word an arm motion.

For thine is *(point up)*
the kingdom, *(bow from the waist)*
and the power, *(flex arm muscles)*
and the glory *(throw arms up and out with open hands turned up)*
for ever. Amen. *(fold hands)*

Say the lines with the motions several times. Then ask the children to tell you why this is such a good prayer for Palm Sunday. Discuss their ideas briefly.

Give each child a prepared crown form and a page of the Lord's Prayer jewels. Then staple the crowns, being careful to keep them too big for the children's heads.

Closing

Gather the children on the rug with their crowns placed on the floor in front of them. Have a crown in front of you, too. Take a moment to admire their handiwork. If the children have not already noticed, point out now that the crowns are too big for them because none of them is the king of the world. God is. Remind the children that we get into trouble when we pretend that we are the king. We end up fighting with one another. As you pray the following prayer of confession together, all children and leaders pick up their crowns and hold them over their own heads while the leader describes a way we try to be king of the world. Then put the crowns on the floor in front of you to say the refrain.

Leader: God, sometimes I act like I am the king of the world. I try to make all the rules and break the ones I do not like, but

All: Thine is the kingdom, and the power, and the glory.

Leader: Lord, sometimes I act like I am the king of the world. I want to be the strongest so that I can get *my* way all the time, but

All: Thine is the kingdom, and the power, and the glory.

Leader: God, sometimes I act like I am the king of the world. I want everyone to listen to me and watch me and pay attention to me and tell me that I am wonderful, but

All: Thine is the kingdom, and the power, and the glory.

Leader: *(place a crown in front of you and push it a little away, folding your hands in your lap)* Forgive us, Lord. Help us to remember that you are the King, not us. Help us to serve you as our King. Help us to love one another, for

All: Thine is the kingdom, and the power, and the glory.

Leader: For ever and ever. Amen.

Say the "As High as the Sky" assurance of pardon with motions (see page 202). Then sing again the "Hosanna" song you learned at the beginning of the session in happy response.

Let each child take a look into the peek box without saying anything about what he or she sees in it until all have had a turn. Help the children identify the flower as an Easter lily and tell them how the flower will be used to decorate the sanctuary next Sunday. If possible, show pictures of how the sanctuary has been decorated in the past. Tell the children about other special features of the Easter celebration they will share in next Sunday. Practice singing (still in whispers) the *alleluias* in "Jesus Christ Is Risen Today" as you did last week. Spend any remaining minutes in general discussion of Easter plans the children's families may have.

EASTER

Easter is more than one day. It is a season of fifty days that begins at sunrise on Easter morning and lasts until Pentecost Sunday. The color of Easter—like that of Christmas, Epiphany, and the Lord's Supper—is white. It is a season of joy, celebrating the resurrection and our new life in Christ.

The season parallels the experience of the disciples. On Easter morning, the tomb was found to be empty. For forty days thereafter Jesus appeared to his disciples in a variety of settings to explain the significance of his death and resurrection and to prepare them to undertake the work of the church. It was a time of very mixed emotions. The disciples were excited by what they had seen, but they were also frightened by it and were riveted with curiosity about the future. Once Pentecost came, empowered by God's Spirit they began building the church.

Easter is also a very adult season. For young children, the details of the story are difficult to understand. What children can understand is that God is always with us and that not even death can beat God's love.

We will devote two Sundays to this season. On Easter Sunday, the children will experience the feelings and music of Easter in the sanctuary and in their own room. The following Sunday, they will bake Easter bread and recall stories about Jesus' life as they eat the bread together. Plan carefully the sessions you will use between the second Sunday of Easter and Pentecost. For Mother's Day, consider using session 46, "Thank You, God, for Families." "Praise God Who Makes Spring" is appropriate as well. Keep your worship center covered with the white cloth. Include flowers in the center each week, if possible.

Note: At this point in the year, kindergarten children are ready and able to spend more time in the sanctuary. If they do not already do so, plan for the children to attend the beginning of the service with their parents every Sunday. Notify parents of your plans.

Session 25: Easter Sunday

Worship Focus: God's Easter surprises.

On Easter we celebrate God's biggest surprise of all—the resurrection. Kindergarten children are just beginning to grasp the meaning and finality of death, so it is difficult for them to grasp the significance of the empty tomb story. What they can understand is the feeling of joy with which we respond to the all-time big surprise God pulled off on Easter. Everyone thought that Jesus was dead. They had killed and buried him on Friday, but God would not let Jesus remain dead. Jesus rose on Sunday.

The best place to experience that joy is in the sanctuary. So be sure the children participate in part of

Easter worship. They should sit with their families for the first ten or fifteen minutes, then depart as a group at a designated time. If special music will be used at the end of the service, plan to return to the sanctuary to hear it. Parents can meet their children at the front of the sanctuary after the service.

During your time as a group, explore the sense of happy surprise and the new life of Easter.

Time	Worship Activity	Materials/Resources
15 min.	1. Children in worship	
10 min.	2. Return trip	recorded Easter music
10 min.	3. Learning from darkened room and story of colors about Jesus' life	black crêpe paper dark cross poster freestanding cross color book/filmstrip
15 min.	4. Redecorating the room for Easter	white cloth for worship table white crêpe paper streamers Easter Lily or other flowers white patch for calendar pre-cut flower petals, centers glue, thumbtacks
10 min.	5. Chants and songs	

Getting Ready

1. Be sure that parents know the plans for the day. Remember to get in touch with those families you normally see only at holiday times. Enlist extra "helpers" and prepare name necklaces for visitors.

2. To decorate your room for Good Friday, darken it by closing the curtains, pulling the shades, or taping paper or garbage bags over the windows so that the room is dim, but not frighteningly dark. Remove all purple trimmings and displays. Place only the cross and a Bible on the worship center. Drape a piece of black cloth or crêpe paper around the arms of the cross. Cover a bulletin board or other wall display space with white background paper. Mount in the center of it a large cross cut from dark poster board or cardboard. Around the edge staple black crêpe paper streamers.

Prepare supplies to make flowers. Cut out flower centers from gold and yellow construction paper. Cut petals from a variety of colors of tissue paper. Gather glue bottles for the children to use. Have colorful thumbtacks on hand for mounting the flowers on the cross.

3. Using the directions and "pages" at the end of this session, make your own "A Story About Jesus" book.

4. Find a recording of Easter music, maybe the "Hallelujah Chorus," or light, happy music.

Getting Started

Gather the children as they leave the worship service by the designated door. As quietly as possible, walk together to an open room or to the hallway near your class, but away from the sanctuary.

If the children's energy levels are high after their visit to the sanctuary, fueled with Easter candy, play some upbeat music and ask the children to fly like butterflies until the music stops. Play the music for two or three minutes or until in your judgment it's time to quiet down. Direct the "butterflies" to land around you very quietly. When all have landed, tell them that you are going to go to your room but that there will be some surprises and changes there. They are to get in a line, walk without saying a word to the room, sit down in a circle on the rug, and look around them for everything that is different. If possible, stop at a water fountain on your way to the room so that everyone can get a sip of water. (If the children are quiet as they leave the sanctuary, skip the flying activity.)

Learning from the Darkened Room

Quietly seat the group on the rug. One adult leader needs to help the children set aside their belongings while the other focuses the group's attention on the dark room by asking them to identify all the changes they see. When all the dark changes have been noted, introduce the color storybook and promise that it will explain the changes.

Read through the dark purple page. Then pause to discuss why the black drape is on the cross and connect other dark things in the room with the story. Then finish the story.

Redecorating the Room for Easter

Invite the children to help you redecorate so that the room looks like God's Easter surprise. Send children to raise the shades or open the curtains. Then have other children remove the black drape from the cross and add the white cloth to your worship table. Next, have a child place the Easter lily, or other flowers you have hidden, on the worship center. Ask another child to replace the black crêpe paper from around the bulletin board with white streamers. Add a white square to your Christian year calendar.

Finally, direct everyone's attention to the dark cross on the bulletin board. Point out that when Jesus was killed on a cross, the cross looked terrible, but with the Easter surprise God made the cross beautiful. Invite the children to cover the cross completely with tissue paper flowers.

Each flower requires two centers. Lay one on the table. Glue colored tissue paper petals to it. Then place the second flower center on top of the first with the ends of the petals still glued in between. One thumb tack will hold the flower in place on the cross. If you end up with extra flowers, use them to decorate the board around the flower-covered cross.

petals

2 centers

glue petals to 1 center

glue second center on top

tack to board

Easter Chants and Songs

When your cross is covered with flowers and your mess cleaned up, gather on the rug to finish redecorating your room by filling it with happy Easter words and songs. Start singing "Jesus Christ Is Risen Today," pausing meaningfully before the first *alleluia*. Sing through the first verse. If it was sung in church, let the children who recognize it tell about hearing it.

Remind the children that *alleluia* means "Hurray for God!" Today it also means "He is risen." Divide into two groups. Have one group say "alleluia" with you in the chant pattern below. The second leader has the other group say "He is risen" to the same pattern.

Ale-le-lu-ia!   He is ri-sen!

Begin the chant in a whisper, alternating groups and getting slowly louder then softer again. Just for Easter fun, tell them that now they are to say what the leader in front of them says in the way the leader has said it. The two adult leaders then lead their groups in what they have been saying. Keeping the chant going, the leaders change sides so that the children must say the other words. Change back and forth several more times, trying to trip the children up. Finally slow the chant down and quiet it down. Leaders stay in one place and bring it to a whispered end.

Closing

Close with a brief prayer to thank God for the Easter surprise.

Looking Ahead

Next Sunday, your group will bake Easter bread (hot cross buns). Read the recipe to gather ingredients and equipment. You will also need an unsliced loaf of bread to eat together.

A Story About Jesus

To make a copy of this book, gather sheets of poster board or construction paper. (The poster board makes a great flip chart for larger groups, while the construction paper book may be easier to use with smaller groups.) You need one sheet each of red, pink, green, blue, gray (you may have to settle for black), dark purple, white, yellow, and orange. Choose one other colored sheet to use for a cover and write the title on it with a marking pen. Arrange the sheets in the order below. Punch holes in the sides and thread metal binder rings or tie yarn loops through the holes.

Copy the text of the story. Cut your copy into sections. Glue each section of the story to the back of the preceding sheet of construction paper or poster board so that you may read the story while showing the correct color to the children.

Introduction:
I am going to read a beautiful story today,
I am going to read it from a very strange book,
It is a strange book because the pages you will see have no pictures . . . no words . . . just pages of color:
(flip through)
The way to read this book is to look and think
Look at the color and then
   Think about what it reminds you of
     and how it makes you feel.
Some colors are gay and happy colors.
Some are scary.
Some are sad.
Not all colors make all people feel the same way.
I will read to you what the colors in this book said to the lady who made this book.

Now we will begin the story. It is A STORY ABOUT JESUS.

(turn to RED)

The first color we see is RED.
Red makes me think . . . Christmas!
God has always loved this world and the people in it.
God wants us to know and feel that love.
The person who helped us feel God's love best was . . . Jesus.
Jesus started in this world as a tiny baby, just as you and
   I started.
But he was born in an unusual place,
  In a stable,
    Because there was no room for his mother
      in the Inn.

(turn to PINK)

Here we see PINK.
I think pink is a fun color.
Pink makes me remember that the baby Jesus grew
To be a boy just your size . . .
  A boy who liked to laugh . . .
    Who liked to have fun . . .
      Who liked to be happy.
I wonder what he liked to do best of all
When he was your size.
Maybe he had a pet goat he liked to play with.
Maybe he liked to help his father in the carpenter shop.
Maybe he liked to go exploring in the country.

(turn to GREEN)

When Jesus grew up he thought a lot about God.
He thought a lot about people . . .

especially people who weren't able to feel God's love.
He chose twelve men to be his helpers and they went from
Little town to little town talking and teaching.
They didn't have classes in a school, or services in a
Building: but they talked with people outdoors . . .
     out on the GREEN hillsides.
The people sat on rocks or in the grass and Jesus walked among them and talked with them.

(turn to BLUE)

Everywhere Jesus went he told people
God's love was meant for each of them.
Just as the BLUE sky is there for each and every
Person to look up at and enjoy.
Jesus cared about everyone. He cared about the sick,
And the lonely and the sad.
He cared about rich people and poor people.
He cared about grown-ups and
He cared about little children.
Many people heard Jesus and were glad about the things he told them.

(turn to GRAY)

Some people did not understand him.
They thought his caring for everyone was foolish.
They said, "Jesus talks only about big rules like
'Love one another' and 'Love God all the time.' "
"Those rules are too big to obey. Why should we even try?"
They also said,
"We wouldn't be so uncomfortable if Jesus were not around.
Maybe we could get rid of him somehow."
These complaining people talked to the ruler about
Getting rid of Jesus.
The ruler was not sure what to do.

(turn to DARK PURPLE)

Finally the ruler decided to do as the people asked.
He ordered his soldiers to kill Jesus on a cross of wood
Which is the way criminals were put to death in those days.
As Jesus was dying, he talked again of loving
And forgiving one another.
People wondered how he could go on loving when those he
Was trying to love hated him so much.
People were very confused and very sad.
Many of those who had wanted Jesus killed became frightened
At what a terrible thing they had done.
People who had believed Jesus were sad and frightened too.
They thought,
"Jesus is dead now. He must have been wrong about God's love."

(turn to WHITE)

But Jesus was not wrong:
Through the power of God's love
A most wonderful thing happened:

After being dead for three days,
   Jesus became alive again.
When Jesus came to life again it was God's way of saying
That his love is more powerful than pain . . .
   or sadness . . .
     or even death.
It was a beautiful gift for all those sad and lonely people
Who had seen Jesus killed.
But it was not a gift for them alone,
It was a gift for all of us.

(turn to YELLOW)

Jesus left his world soon after this.
But before he left,
He told his helpers, the disciples,
That his love and power would be with them
And with all of us . . . forever.
After Jesus left,
The disciples thought about the things Jesus had told them.
They thought about his dying and coming alive again.
They began to tell other people the story of Jesus.
Some of it they wrote down in books.
In a few years a great many people had heard the story of Jesus.
Churches were being built so even more people
Could hear and believe.

(turn to ORANGE)

Today you and I and many other people around the world
Are Jesus' disciples.
When we gather together on Sunday to sing our happy songs
It is because we are thankful for his promise
That his love will be with all of us forever.
We go and tell others,
   And they tell others.
     And they tell other people,
And this is the way the church grows.

Session 26: The Sunday After Easter

Worship Focus: We celebrate God's Easter surprise when we eat bread together and remember Jesus.

The six Sundays after Easter celebrate the season of Easter with their white color and scripture readings about the resurrection appearances of Jesus. Today we will explore the story of the travelers to Emmaus, who recognized the risen Jesus as he broke the bread. The story is connected to Jesus' request that the disciples remember him by breaking bread together.

By making and eating bread together, we will be exposing the children to one of the foundations of the Lord's Supper. However, the Easter Bread Picnic is *not* in any way a form of the sacrament. Do not use grape juice or any of the words of consecration. Avoid mentioning the sacrament unless the children do. Instead simply talk about eating bread and remembering Jesus. In this way we are offering the children what they need to begin building an understanding of communion and continuing the Easter celebration of new life in Christ.

Time	Worship Activity	Materials/Resources
10 min.	1. Children in sanctuary	
5 min.	2. Praising God	
15 min.	3. Making Easter bread	prepared bread dough, raisins, floured table, name sticks, pans
5 min.	4. "The Easter bread Surprise" Story	
15 min.	5. Easter Bread Picnic	big loaf of bread teaching pictures of Jesus
5 min.	6. Add crosses to bread	powdered sugar icing paintbrushes bags, notes about bread
5 min.	7. Closing song and prayer	

Getting Ready

1. Get ready to make bread with the children. Clean the tables or cover them with paper so that the children can knead small loaves of bread on them. Just before class, mix up the dough and store it in a covered bowl. Also prepare a small bowl of stiff white powdered sugar icing. Gather several cookie sheets for baking, a cooling rack, and a few clean paint brushes (for icing the crosses on the bread), and paper bags for taking the bread home.

EASTER BREAD RECIPE

Stir together:
   1 cup prepared baking mix
   1 tsp. sugar
   ½ tsp. cinnamon

Add and mix to form a stiff dough:
   ⅓ cup milk

If needed, add a little more baking mix for dough that can be kneaded without sticking to your hands.

Sprinkle a small amount of baking mix on the table at each child's place. Give each child a lump of dough a little bigger than an adult fist. As children knead their dough, add a spoonful of raisins for them to knead into the bread. Form bread into round loafs. Place on ungreased cookie sheets. Flatten each loaf to about ½″ thick. There should be 2″ between the flattened loaves. Bake at 450 degrees for fifteen minutes or until brown on top. This makes enough for four small loaves.

2. Get a large loaf of unsliced bread (cinnamon raisin would be great!) for the children to eat together. Place it in a basket or on a tray in your worship center.

3. From the teaching picture files or from old curriculum resources, gather six to eight big pictures of stories about Jesus that the children know. Include birth stories, healings, feeding the crowds, teaching, blessing the children, eating with friends, and the like.

4. Make copies of the note to parents at the end of this session. One note will be packed with each loaf of bread to help parents keep the discussions about Jesus going as the family eats the bread at home.

Getting Ready

As the children come in from the sanctuary together, help them set their belongings aside and gather together on the rug. Wish them all a happy Easter and discuss the fact that Easter is more than one day. Add a white square to your calendar and identify the signs of Easter you saw and heard in the sanctuary. Sing "Jesus Christ Is Risen Today" and other praise songs. Do the Easter chant "He Is Risen/Alleluia" from last week.

Making Easter Bread

Invite the children to celebrate Easter with you by making Easter bread together. Send them to prepared tables (by way of the sink to wash hands if needed). Each child kneads his or her own dough. A leader adds the raisins. Put a craft stick with each child's initials written on it under the loaves on the cookie sheet to identify them. When all the loaves are on the cookie sheets, an adult takes them to bake while the children move on to other activities.

"The Easter Bread Surprise"

Gather back on the rug to hear the story of the travelers on the road to Emmaus. If your group is small, read *The Story of Emmaus* (Little People's Paperbacks, Seabury Press) or tell the story below.

On Easter Sunday, two friends walked from Jerusalem to Emmaus. They were sad. Their friend Jesus had been killed on Friday. They were also frightened. They were afraid that Jesus' enemies would kill them, too. As they walked along, a stranger caught up with them and asked what they were talking about.

"Are you the only person in Jerusalem who has not heard about Jesus?" asked one of the travelers. "What about Jesus?" the stranger asked.

So the travelers told the stranger all about Jesus. They told how Jesus had been born. They told how kind and good he had been. They told some of the wonderful stories Jesus had told them and some of the important things Jesus had taught them. They told about the way Jesus healed sick people and made friends with lonely people. They told about the last supper with Jesus, when he took a loaf of bread, broke it, and gave it to them, asking them to share bread to remember him. Then they told how Jesus had been killed on a cross and buried in a cave. The stranger listened. Somehow the travelers knew that the stranger understood.

Soon it was dinner time. The travelers invited the stranger to have dinner with them, and he did. As they sat down to supper, the stranger picked up the bread and said the blessing. Then he broke the bread and gave it to them. Suddenly the travelers recognized the stranger. He wasn't a stranger at all. He was Jesus! Jesus was not dead. He was alive! He was with them—or he had been. As soon as they recognized him, Jesus disappeared. The surprised travelers were amazed and happy and excited. They hurried all the way back to Jerusalem to tell the others, "Jesus is alive! We have seen him. He gave us bread to eat. We are not alone anymore."

Ask the children how the travelers recognized Jesus and what Jesus asked his friends to do to remember him. Then invite them to join you in doing just that.

Easter Bread Picnic

Pass around the big loaf of bread on your worship table so that each child can break off a big chunk. As you eat, show the children the pictures of Jesus one at a time. Ask the children to tell you the story in each picture. If no one can tell the story, one of the adults tells it. The children may think of other stories to tell about Jesus. Hear them out. After talking about these stories, remember a prayer that Jesus taught us: the Lord's Prayer. Pray it together.

Adding Crosses to the Bread

Taking turns, the children paint an icing cross on their bread. After letting the icing dry a minute, put each child's loaf and the note explaining the Easter Bread Picnic in a bag for the child to take home. (Since the bread will still be warm, a paper lunch bag might work better than a plastic one.)

Closing

The children set their bags in front of them as they sit in a circle on the rug. Show the children a copy of the note you have put in each bag and encourage them to share their bread with the people at their house and to tell the stories about Jesus when they do. Sing "Jesus Christ Is Risen Today" and say a brief prayer to thank God for bread that helps us remember Jesus. Ask God to remind us that God is with us always.

```
Have an Easter Bread Picnic

   Today in children's church your child heard the story of the travelers on the road to
Emmaus (Luke 24:13-35) and baked a loaf of Easter bread with a cross on it. We also sat
around eating bread and telling all the stories about Jesus we could think of. You can
continue this process at home. As you share the little loaf of bread your child baked, tell
each other stories about Jesus. Have fun and share God's love with each other.
```

PENTECOST

Pentecost is not the most familiar holiday in mainline Protestant churches. Therefore, a big part of your time will be spent introducing children to this holy day.

For forty days after Easter Sunday, Jesus appeared to the disciples to explain his death and resurrection. On the fortieth day he ascended, leaving them with the Great Commission: "Go ye into all the world . . . " (Mark 16:15 KJV) and instructions to wait in Jerusalem for God's gift. For the next ten days, the disciples met together to worship and pray and talk and hide out in fear. On the tenth day they received the gift of the Holy Spirit. (Read Acts 2 for details.) Empowered by the Spirit, they came out of hiding and preached about Jesus to anyone who would listen. The church had begun.

The Holy Spirit was God's life-giving gift to the disciples. Without it they were a well-intended crowd with wavering commitments. With it, they became bold people with a vision and the commitment to give their lives to it—that is, they became the fathers and mothers of the Christian church. The Holy Spirit is the mark of the church today. Without it, we are as lost as the disciples were before Pentecost. With it, we become God's agents at work in the world today.

On Pentecost we celebrate the presence of the Spirit. The color is red for the flames of fire that came upon the disciples and for the fire of God's Spirit in our own lives.

Children can participate in Pentecost in two ways. They can hold a birthday party for the church, complete with cake and candles, and hear the story of the day the church was born. On Pentecost Sunday you will have such a party.

Second, they are alerted to God's presence in their own lives. We need to help them recognize that the moments of peace and the warm feelings of closeness to the whole world are signs of God's presence. Children have these experiences. It is our task to help them interpret these experiences. That will be the focus of the second Sunday.

If your congregation celebrates Pentecost in a way the children can understand and participate in, plan for them to be in the sanctuary during this event. Also be sure that you know what colors your congregation uses during the season of Pentecost, which lasts until Advent. Some congregations use red only on Pentecost Sunday and green on the remaining Sundays of the season. Others use red longer. Find out what your congregation does.

Session 27: Pentecost Sunday

Worship Focus: The birthday of the church and the story of Pentecost.

Today's session will be less clearly identifiable as worship than some others. It is a birthday party for the church in which we will tell the story of Pentecost. Because the story is complex, we cannot expect the children to be able to grasp the details of the story or even to be able to tell it back to us. For now it is enough for them to hear it (probably for the first time) and to gather from the story and the birthday party that God started the church and is the "Power behind the church." It is also an opportunity to celebrate the existence of the church. The worship mood in all of this is praise.

Time	Worship Activity	Materials/Resources
15 min.	1. Children in sanctuary	
5 min.	2. Respond to decorated room	iced birthday cake Bible with red bookmark red cloth red streamers and balloons
10 min.	3. Hear "The Pentecost Story" Add red patch to calendar	red patch and glue
10 min.	4. Make tablecloth	white paper pictures of church people red crayons flame "stickers"
10 min.	5. Sing "Happy Birthday" Eat cake and talk about the church	birthday cake with candles and match red napkins
10 min.	6. Birthday prayer and "Go, Tell It on the Mountain" chorus	

Getting Ready

1. Decorate your room for a birthday party. Put a red tablecloth on the worship center with a Bible and a cake with white icing and red birthday candles. Red streamers and balloons are appropriate for bulletin boards or hanging from lights. If you want to go all out, write "Happy Birthday, Church" on enough balloons for each child to take one home after the session.

2. Gather supplies for making a large paper tablecloth, around which the children will eat their cake. You will need a piece of chart paper or a white paper tablecloth big enough for your group to sit around on the floor. You will also need pictures of people they know around their church. Include ministers, worship leaders, church school teachers, and one or two parents. Find flame stickers or cut flames out of bright red paper (see the Craft Patterns section) and have some glue sticks handy.

Getting Started

On your way from the sanctuary to your room, stop and ask whether anyone noticed anything different in the sanctuary today. If they did, congratulate the keen observers for seeing the red and recognizing any other signs of Pentecost. If they did not, tell them that they will see some changes in their room. In either case, instruct the children to enter the room quietly. Have them put aside in a proper place anything they brought with them and sit on the rug without saying a word.

When all are settled, ask what new and different things they see. After hearing about what they see, ask them what the room looks like it is ready for. Then see if anyone knows whose birthday it is. (If someone does have a birthday today, hear about the birthday, but point out that you do not usually have birthday parties in children's worship and that this is not a party for any person.) Since they probably will not know that Pentecost is the birthday of the church, urge the children to listen to your story to learn whose birthday it is. Then tell "The Pentecost Story."

The Pentecost Story*

When Jesus was killed on the cross, most of his friends ran away to hide. They were afraid that the soldiers might kill them, too.

When the women came back from Jesus' empty grave saying that Jesus was alive again, his friends were surprised and happy, but mostly they were confused. They just did not understand what was happening.

Then for forty days Jesus kept surprising them. Jesus came through a locked door to talk to them one night. He walked on a road with two of them one day. He fixed breakfast on the beach with some of the others. Every time he was with them, Jesus talked. He talked about how much God loved them, and he talked about sharing God's love with others. When Jesus was with them, his friends felt brave and strong and happy. Something new and exciting was happening, and they were going to be part of it. But when Jesus was not with them, they would remember the soldiers and feel scared and weak and uncertain.

When Jesus left them the last time, he said two things. First he said, "Go into all the world. Tell everyone about me and teach them to be my disciples." Then he said, "Wait in Jerusalem. God has a special gift for you." Well, the first job sounded big and important *and* scary. So they were glad to wait for the gift.

What do you think they did while they waited? Well, they hid out together. Every day each one would come by a secret route to the hideout. They would knock quietly on the door. Someone inside would open it just a crack to see who was knocking. Then, the friend would be let in *fast* and would be asked, "Did anyone follow you?" All day they stayed in that room and remembered what Jesus said and did. And they prayed. They prayed and prayed and prayed. Do you know what happened at the end of the first day? *(pause)* Nothing.

So they all went home by their secret paths and came back the next day. And they prayed all day. And do you know what happened? *(pause again)* Nothing. *(repeat this several more times)*

On the tenth day, they were beginning to wonder whether God was ever going to give them that special gift. But they carefully came to the hideout using their secret paths. And they began praying again. And that day something *did* happen!

They had hardly started praying when a strong wind came through the hideout. The wind wrapped itself around each person there *(reach out and wrap your arms around one or two nearby children),* and it felt like the wind was God's loving arms holding them close, hugging them tight. They felt happy and loved and loving. Then bright fire came through the air, and little flames of fire licked each one of them on the head *(with your finger, trace a flame in the air over the heads of several children).* It felt as if God's courage and bravery were burning in their hearts, and they knew that with God's courage they could do things they couldn't do before.

God's love in the wind and God's courage in the fire were the special gifts they had been waiting for. They were so excited about their gifts that they could not keep them secret. They ran out of their hideout and started telling everyone they met. Their hiding days were over. They even told some soldiers. In fact, that day three thousand people heard, were baptized, and became the very first members of the first church.

That night as they went home, they did not go secret ways. They knew that people were staring at them, saying, "There goes one of them now, you know—a follower of Jesus." But they did not care at all. They could still feel God's love all around them and God's courage burning in their hearts. And they knew that they would feel that way all the rest of their lives. And they were right.

After the story, discuss what began on that day. This will take some work because the story is complex. But lead the children to realize that the church was born that day when the disciples received

---

* Adapted from a story by Mark DeVries. Used by permission.

God's gift and started telling others about Jesus. Add a red patch to your calendar and introduce the word *Pentecost* as the special name of the church's birthday.

Preparing for the Party

To finish preparations for a birthday party for the church, ask the children to make a big tablecloth for the group to eat around. Spread your "cloth" on the floor. Explain that this will be a special tablecloth that will show some people who are part of the church. Present one at a time your pictures of people the children know in your church and ask whether they are part of the church. When the children agree that they are, place the pictures in the middle of the tablecloth. When all of the pictures are in place, point to one of the children and ask the others whether that child is part of the church. Once they agree that the child is, point to another child and so on until the group concludes that each is a part of the church. Explain that they will have their handprints on the church tablecloth. Assign children to a partner and give each pair one red crayon. The pairs are to trace around each other's hands to make a border around the tablecloth. Children may write their names in their hands or color them as they wish. When the hands are finished and the crayons have been collected, pass out flame stickers to be added beside each hand and each picture to remind us that God's Spirit is with that person.

Sing and Eat Cake

When the tablecloth is ready and the art supplies have been put away, call the children to gather in a circle around the cake. Light the candles and sing "Happy Birthday" to the church. Then all blow the candles out together. (This is easier to manage with the cake on a table than in the center of your tablecloth on the floor.)

Cut a small piece of cake for each person to eat. Serve the cake on red napkins if possible. You may provide a small cup of red punch for them to drink. While you eat, talk about the things the children like to do at church and what they like about the church. Enjoy and accept the variety of the children's thoughts about the church. As children finish eating, you may want to begin creating the birthday prayer around the table as a continuation of your conversation, or you may want to clean up the cake mess and move to another area of the room. Decide what is best for your group.

Closing with a Birthday Prayer and a Song

Introduce the children to the idea of a birthday prayer in which we thank God for all the things we love about birthdays. Invite the children to create a birthday prayer for the church. You will start it by thanking God for one thing you especially like about the church. Children may then take turns thanking God for something they like about the church. When all who want to speak have had a turn, voice a prayer to ask God to take care of the church.

Close by singing the chorus to "Go, Tell It on the Mountain." First sing it with the usual words and relate it to the disciples' going out to tell everyone about Jesus. Then add some different last lines—such as, "That God's own church is born"; "God's Spirit makes us brave"; or "God's Spirit is with us today"—to express the good news of Pentecost. If you have time, enjoy favorite praise songs together.

Session 28: The Second Sunday of Pentecost

Worship Focus: God's gift to the church on its birthday was the Holy Spirit. God's Spirit is with us every day, empowering us to sing, pray, and serve.

The Holy Spirit is God's presence with us. God's Spirit can bring peace in the midst of troubles and can urge us into doing what we really would prefer to avoid. We encounter God's Spirit in the beauty of nature, as we are caught up with others in meaningful worship, when we have our sleeves rolled up for service to others, and in the middle of everyday life when we least expect it. That presence is one of the greatest mysteries of the Christian life.

Today we will explore that presence by singing, praying, and serving together, alert for the sense of God's presence with us. The discussion/story "God's Spirit Is Like . . ." aims to give children ways to identify and to recognize God's Spirit at work. A prayer of confession will honestly expose the children to the truth that at times we all would prefer to turn our backs on God's Spirit. This whole session is obviously just an introduction to what we hope will be a lifelong experience and mystery.

Time	Worship Activity	Materials/Resources
	1. Children in sanctuary	
	2. Pentecost Story and "Go, Tell It on the Mountain"	Bible
10 min.	3. Make pinwheels	prepared paper forms red pens scissors long straight pins pencils with erasers
5 min.	4. "God's Spirit Is Like . . ."	teaching pictures
5 min.	5. Singing when the Spirit . . .	
15 min.	6. Serving when the Spirit . . . emptying garbage cans	prepared note for usual can emptier
5 min.	7. Praying when the Spirit . . . "Kum Ba Yah" and prayer of confession	

Getting Ready

1. Copy a pinwheel pattern (page 119) on stiff paper for each child. Gather long straight pins on which to mount the pinwheels and pencils with erasers, in which to stick the pins. Gather red pens to decorate the pinwheels and scissors to cut along the diagonal lines of the pinwheels.

2. Read "God's Spirit Is Like. . . ." Then gather the needed pictures from your teaching picture file or from old curriculum resources.

3. Find out who empties the garbage cans in the Sunday school classrooms and into what the cans are emptied. Be sure you have all the keys and equipment needed for your group to empty the cans during this session. On a large piece of drawing paper that all the children can sign, write a sample note to thank the person who usually does this work.

Getting Started

As you walk back from the sanctuary together, discuss whatever is uppermost in the children's minds. When you get to the room, one leader helps the children settle their belongings while the other continues the conversation with the children as they gather on the rug. When everyone is on the rug, ask who can remember last week's activities. After hearing their versions of the birthday party, remind them of the story of the day the church was born. Pick up the Bible in your worship center to read Acts 2:1-4*a*, 41. Put it into a child's language as you "read." Sing "Go, Tell It on the Mountain" using some of the Pentecost lines from last Sunday.

Making Pinwheels

Introduce the pinwheel as a Pentecost toy. If pinwheels are not familiar to the children, show them how they work. Then invite them to make one of their own.

Give each child a square pinwheel form to decorate with red marking pens; suggest drawing Pentecost flames. When the children are satisfied with their decorating, show them how to cut *only* on the lines from each corner. An adult will have to poke a straight pin through each of the corners, the center, and then into a pencil eraser. Shape the pinwheel on the pin according to the sketch.

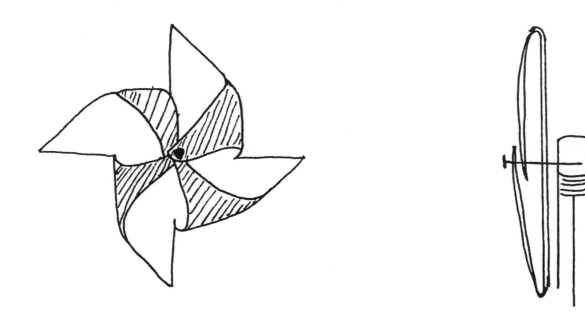

Children will enjoy blowing on their pinwheels to make them spin. When all are ready, gather on the rug.

God's Birthday Gift to the Church

Tell the following discussion/story.

God's Spirit Is Like. . . *

(Blow on your pinwheels to make them all spin at once. Then ask the following questions.)
    What makes the wheel go around? *(wait for response)*
    Wind? I didn't see any wind? Where was it? *(wait for response)*
    Oh, you can't see the wind! Well, it is here, let us catch some. Moving air is wind. Let's stir some wind up.
(wave your hand vigorously in the air, inviting the children to help you) I can feel it! Can you?
    It must be here. Close your hand and hold it tight! *(close hand and lead the children to do the same)* Now,

---

*Adapted from "Pinwheels and Pentecost" in *Let All the People* by Agnes Junkin Peery. Used by permission.

let's look at it! *(wait for response)*

You can't see anything? No, you cannot. But we could feel it.

What happens to people's hair when the wind blows? *(wait for response)*

What happens to people's coats when the wind blows hard? *(wait for response)*

What happens to the rain when the wind blows? *(wait for response)*

What makes the clouds move across the sky? *(wait for response)*

Hmmm, even though you cannot see the wind, you know when it is here because you see what it does. You can tell when and where it is by noticing what it is doing.

Jesus said that God's Holy Spirit is like the wind. We do not know where it comes from or where it is going. But we do know that when we see people doing the kinds of things Jesus did God's Spirit is working right there!

(show a picture of Jesus feeding people) What did Jesus do here? *(wait for response)* Do you think that God's Spirit was working in us when we . . . ? *(describe something the children have done to feed hungry people)*

(show a picture of Jesus befriending someone) What is Jesus doing here? *(wait for response)* Yes, Jesus made friends with lonely people. Do you think God's Spirit was working when . . . ? *(describe the one way the children have shared love with lonely people through a class project)*

(repeat the process with other appropriate pictures of Jesus or pictures of people doing loving acts)

You cannot see God's Spirit. But if you look very carefully at what people do, you can sometimes see the Spirit working. Whenever you see people being loving and kind, you are seeing the Spirit of God at work.

When the Spirit Says Sing

Celebrate what you've learned about God's Spirit by singing the old spiritual "I'm Gonna Sing When the Spirit Says Sing.) Make up verses. Try "I'm Gonna . . . clap, smile, smile, hop, dance," and so on, doing each thing you sing about. After doing several action verses, settle down with "I'm gonna praise, love, and serve." As you finish singing about serving, ask how the children are going to serve to lead into the next activity.

When the Spirit Says Serve

Do something to serve. Surprise the person who usually empties the garbage cans in the church school classrooms by doing the job. Leave a note on the cleaning supply closet door or wherever it will be found, thanking that person for doing the job and telling that person that you love him or her. Let everyone in the class sign the note. Then go back to your room and sing "I'm Gonna Serve When the Spirit Says Serve."

When the Spirit Says Pray

Sing one verse of "Kum Ba Yah." Explain to the children that when we pray we often feel God's Spirit very close to us. Discuss some times when we want God's Spirit very near.

After pointing out to the children that sometimes we do not want God's Spirit near us, line out this prayer of confession together.

God, we sing "Kum Ba Yah" *(do motions for "Kum Ba Yah")*
And sometimes we mean it. *(throw arms open wide)*
We feel your fire in our hearts, and *(hold fists over hearts)*
We want to sing. *(hands by mouth)*
We feel your courage, and *(sit very straight and tall)*
We want to serve. *(mime emptying cans)*
But sometimes, God, *(look up)*
We don't want your Spirit. *(hang your head)*
We want to close you out. *(draw up like a closing flower)*
We don't want to love *(hands out to push others away)*
Anyone but ourselves. *(hug yourself)*

We don't want to take care of *(hands out palms up)*
Anyone but ourselves. *(fold arms across chest)*
Forgive us, Lord. *(hang your head)*
Send your Spirit to open us again. *(peek up tentatively)*
Send your Spirit to help us pray *(clasp hands in prayer)*
And sing, *(hands around mouth)*
And serve. *(mime emptying cans)*
Even when we don't want you,
Please come by here. Amen. *(motions to "Kum Ba Yah")*

As an assurance of pardon, remind the children that God's Spirit is God's gift to us every day. God is always near us. In response, sing some praise songs.

SACRAMENTS

UNIT INTRODUCTION

Sacraments lie at the heart of our worship. In the sacraments, we celebrate the most fundamental parts of our faith and experience. Sacraments are mysterious, and we never fully understand them. The church has been discussing the nature and practice of the sacraments since its beginning. Catholics identify seven sacraments. Protestants identify two. Some Christians baptize children as infants. Others wait until a person can request baptism with at least some understanding of its significance. Theologians argue about Christ's presence in the Lord's Supper in terms of transubstantiation, consubstantiation, and signs or seals.

But if you were to ask most Christians to explain the importance of one of the sacraments, you would be told about their personal experiences. They will describe their own baptisms or those of their children. They will talk about communion experiences in which they found themselves deeply in God's presence and in which their lives were profoundly shaped. And they will tell about the cumulative effects of more "everyday" experiences with the sacraments.

Young children do not need instruction about the significance of the sacraments. They do not even need to learn the term *sacrament* at this point. What they do need is the facts about what is happening so that they may begin to participate in the sacraments in their own way. It is time for them to begin building their storehouse of experiences with the sacraments. For that reason, each session calls for time in the sanctuary to observe, and possibly participate, in the particular sacrament. Schedule these sessions to coincide with the celebration of the sacraments. The sessions have been planned to stand alone so that you can do each one at the appropriate time rather than as a unit.

For young children, *baptism* has two basic meanings: one, we belong to God, and two, we are part of God's family. In this unit there is one session on each of these. Each session suits both infant and believer's baptism.

Communion has many layers of meanings. Basic to all of them are the facts that as we eat bread and drink wine, (1) we remember Jesus, as he asked when instituting the sacrament; (2) we celebrate that we are part of God's worldwide family by coming to the family dinner table of God; and (3) we recognize that we are loved and forgiven by God.

This unit includes one session on the meals Jesus ate with his friends. During the session we will go on a picnic prepared by the group, praise God for mealtimes, and hear some stories about Jesus, After hearing the story of the Last Supper, you will observe the sacrament in the sanctuary. In the process, the children will encounter the first two truths listed above.

In the second session, emphasis is on the third truth. The bread and wine of communion remind us that God loves us "always, no matter what, forever."

Note: All of the sessions on the sacraments deal with such basic understandings that they should be appropriate in most Protestant congregations. Be sure that you know the details of what is done in your church so that you can answer specific questions.

BAPTISM

Session 29: Welcome to God's Family

Worship Focus: We are part of God's family.

Baptism is the sacrament of belonging to God's family. When we baptize infants, we welcome them into God's family and promise to love and care for them, helping them to grow toward loving God and becoming disciples of Jesus Christ. When older children, youth, or adults are baptized, they are casting their lot with God's family. Today we will celebrate that family and explore baptism as one way we show that we are part of that family.

Time	Worship Activity	Materials/Resources
10 min.	Observe a baptism	
5 min.	1. Look at pictures of God's family and of people praying	pictures of members of your church
5 min.	2. Sing praise songs about God's family	
5 min.	3. Confession and pardon	
10 min.	4. Act out the baptism and discuss it	props for baptism
15 min.	5. Make a gift for the baptized person	material and paints for selected gift
5 min.	7. "God's Family" game	pictures of God's family
5 min.	8. Closing	pictures from game

Getting Ready

1. Schedule this session for a Sunday on which there will be a baptism. Make the necessary preparations for the children to visit the congregation for the baptism. Plan with your minister where the children will stand so that they can see.

2. Collect eight or nine pictures of people in your congregation whom your children will recognize doing tasks for which they are known. If you do not already have such pictures in your growing file, make photographs or cut them out of church directories.

3. Gather the needed props to act out a baptism. Use a doll for infant baptism. Let children take the role of the baptized youth or adult. Have pretend water, a font, a pool (upside down table with chart paper taped across the front), a candle, and anything else that is used.

4. Decide which of the described baptismal gifts you want to make with your group and gather the necessary supplies.

5. Gather from old curriculum resources or the teaching picture file pictures of people singing, praying, working, eating, and taking care of one another as God's family.

Getting Started

While one leader greets the children and helps them put aside their belongings, the other leader gathers the children on the rug to talk about a collection of pictures of people in your congregation. Talk about the people and what they do in your church and community. When all of the children have arrived and you have talked about all of the pictures, show the children each picture and invite them to join you in praying, "Thank you, God, for ————." The leader adds one sentence to thank God for one thing about the person you have discussed. The adult leader closes the prayer with: "Thank you, God, for making us each a part of your family. Thank you for all the love and work and play that we share together. In Jesus' name, amen."

Singing Songs of God's Family

Invite the children to sing some of the songs of God's family. Sing favorite praise songs including "Jesus Loves the Little Children," "We Are the Church Together," the doxology, and Gloria Patri (if you have learned it).

Confessing Our Sins (Even in God's Family)

Stand up and form a circle holding hands. Ask the children to listen to you and do what you do as you pray together as God's family.

Thank you, God, for friends *(hold hands in circle)*
Who are more than friends,
Who are our brothers and sisters in your big family.
Thank you for all the happy times we spend together. *(swing arms together)*
Most of the time we love and take care of one another. *(smile at each other)*
But, God, sometimes we do not. *(stop swinging arms)*
Sometimes we do not want to be friends. *(drop hands to side)*
We do not want to take care of one another *(fold arms across chest)*
Or even be kind. *(frown hard)*
We feel mean and act mean.
We are selfish.
We fight and scream and shout.
Forgive us, God. *(turn hands and faces upward)*
In Jesus' name, amen.
(assurance of pardon)
When we apologize, God promises to forgive us *(smile)*
And help us to forgive one another. *(shake hands with neighbor)*
And become friends again *(hold hands)*
So we can still be God's family! *(swing arms together)*

Acting Out and Discussing Baptism

After observing a baptism in the sanctuary, lay all the props before the children and challenge them to act out a baptism. Begin by asking what people we need in order to have a baptism. Assign parts and set the stage. Get the children to tell you who stands where with which props. Correct misinformation gently as you go along. Once everyone and everything is in place, ask what happens first and proceed to act and talk your way through the ritual. Do not expect much detail but a sense of the action and flow of events. As you go, emphasize the use of the child's name and the questions that point to saying this child is part of the family of God. Then try to go through it without many stops to get the flow of the whole event. If interest is high, children may want to switch parts and go through "the play" a few more times.

Making a Welcome Gift for the Baptized Person

As a class, make a welcome sign to which each child adds his or her handprint and name. The gift may be one of the following.

1. A crib sheet for a baby or a pillowcase for an older child. Before class, an adult writes "Welcome to God's Family, ———(*child's name*)" in the center of the gift using waterproof paint pens. The children each press one hand onto a paint pad—paper towels soaked in fabric paint—and make a handprint on the sheet (Stretch the sheet over a tabletop covered with a pad of newspaper. Pull the pillowcase over a piece of cardboard.) They also put their handprints on a piece of paper (titled "I am part of God's family") for themselves. Have soapy water ready beside this operation for immediate cleanup! An adult writes each child's name beside his or her handprint with a paint pen. After they have made their prints, the children will use marking pens to decorate their paper handprints to take home.

Perhaps you can persuade an artistic church member to head up this project, preparing the sheet, writing the central message, gathering supplies, and serving as extra hands during the group session.

2. A Welcome Poster. This is made the same way as the crib sheet, but is done on a big piece of poster paper. Instead of fabric paints, use tempera paints. Plan to deliver the gift during the week and to use your camera to take a picture of the delivery of the gift.

"God's Family" Game

Set chairs in a circle facing outward. Put a picture of God's family in action on each of the chairs, with one chair and one picture for each child. You may also set the pictures against the furniture and on the wall around the edge of the room. Play soft music while the children walk around, passing the pictures. When the music stops, the children put a hand on a picture, with only one child to a picture. Ask one or more players to tell the others what God's family is doing in that picture. Then start the music again. Try to give different children a chance to describe different pictures.

Closing

Gather the game pictures as the children sit down on the rug. Sitting with the children, pray a litany of praise. One leader shows the group one of the pictures, saying "Hurray for ———" (*describe what's going on in the picture),* to which the children and the other leader reply, "Hurray for God's family!" Pray for six or seven of the pictures. Then close with an adult-led prayer to thank God for being part of the family of God and for the person who was baptized this morning.

Session 30: We Belong to God

Worship Focus: We belong to God. Baptism is one way we celebrate that.

God made us, creating each one of us as a unique individual. God has a plan for us join in the work of loving the world. In baptism, we accept this situation. When we baptize an infant, we acknowledge that the child belongs to God, and we promise to do our part to raise that child accordingly. When an older child, youth, or adult is baptized, that person declares first loyalty to God.

Time	Worship Activity	Materials/Resources
10 min.	1. Comparing ourselves and praising God	paper and marker for measuring heights
5 min	2. Story: "Belonging to God"	
15 min.	3. Observe a baptism	
15 min.	4. Paint baptism pictures and discuss baptism	tempera paints medium brushes paint aprons clean-up supplies
5 min.	5. Story: "We Belong to God"	
5 min.	6. "God Made You" game	
5 min.	7. Closing: Psalm 100 "Take My Life and Let It Be Consecrated"	Bible "Take My Life" song chart

Getting Ready

1. Schedule this session for a Sunday on which there will be a baptism. Make the necessary preparations for the children to witness a baptism.

2. Gather large sheets of paper, tempera paints (mixed with a squirt of liquid detergent), and medium-sized brushes for painting baptism pictures. To enable all the children to paint at once, pour small amounts of several colors of paint into the bowls of egg cartons. Make extra painting space by spreading plastic tablecloths or plastic garbage bags on the floor. Be sure to have plastic painting aprons on hand for each child and sponges and water for cleaning up.

3. Prepare a story about how the person being baptized today has come to be part of God's family. If it is a baby, tell how the parents and the rest of the family prepared for the baby to be born. Tell about choosing the child's name. Tell a story about something that has already happened to the baby, and tell about preparations for the baby's baptism. If the person to be baptized is older, tell appropriate things about that person's life and how he or she decided to be baptized. Obviously, you will have to talk personally to the parents of the baby or to the person to be baptized to get the information you need for the story. Most folks will be delighted to talk with you and will feel that they really are part of the church family to be included in this way.

As you tell the story, present it in terms of God's having made this person unique and special. Be sure you indicate that God has always loved this person very much. Present this baptism as a way of saying that this person belongs to God. If a baby is being baptized, talk about the parents' love and their promise to help the baby know God's love and to love God. If the baptized person is older, describe his or her belief in being created by and belonging to God.

Getting Started

While one leader greets the children and their parents at the door and puts aside their belongings, the other leader gathers the children on the rug to talk about their similarities and differences. Find out who has which color of eyes and hair. Compare the size of people's hands and feet (keeping shoes on). Look at their hands and talk about fingerprints and the fact that no two people have the same fingerprint. Compare heights either by having them stand back to back or by marking each child's height on a strip of paper mounted on the wall. Also identify different things each child does well and likes to do. Let each child name one thing he or she likes to do. Enjoy and emphasize the variety. Conclude your conversation by praying a praise prayer together. Each child in turn says, "God, you made me . . . " mentioning something about their appearance or what they like to do. The group then adds the prayer, "Thank you, God."

Then sing some praise songs for the God who made each one of us. Include "Jesus Loves Me" and, if you learned it at Thanksgiving, "Now Thank We All Our God" as well as the children's favorites.

Hear a Story and Observe a Baptism

Before going to the sanctuary to observe the baptism or while sitting outside the door of the sanctuary as you wait to go in to observe the baptism, tell your story about the person who is being baptized. Then observe the sacrament.

Painting a Baptism

Upon returning to your room, challenge each child to paint a picture of the baptism. Leave directions open enough that the children can paint what most impressed them and can include their interpretations. As the children paint, talk informally about what they are painting as a way of discussing what they saw and heard. Clarify facts and talk about your interpretations. Avoid judging what a child painted as "not right." As the children finish and clean up, one leader oversees the last of the painters while the other gathers the children on the rug to continue the discussion of baptism or to sing for a few minutes. When all are through, go on a tour of the paintings as they dry. Stop at each painting and let the artist tell you about it. If your group is large, divide into two tour groups with one adult leading each tour of the paintings of the artists in that group.

Hear the Story "We Belong to God"

Gather back on the rug for a story.

We Belong to God

"Bo, can I go with you?" Derrick called after his brother as he ran down the steps.

"Course, not," Bo yelled over his shoulder. "You don't belong to the team. This party is for people on the ball team."

"Oh," said Derrick, sadly watching Bo disappear around the corner.

Just then Shantelle bounced down the stairs two at a time. "Where ya goin', Shantelle?" Derrick asked hopefully.

"Girls' Club."

"Can I go with you?"

"No way! You don't belong to the Girls' Club. You aren't a girl AND you don't know how to sew," Shantelle said, and the door slammed behind her.

"Oh," said Derrick. The house was empty except for Gran in the kitchen. Derrick went out the back door and sat on the bottom step. Smokey and Snowball were playing tug of war with an old rag. Derrick was too big to get under the house and play with them. He didn't even belong with the puppies.

Gran came out on the back porch with a big bowl of apples to peel and a bowl of nuts to crack. Derrick sat beside her.

"Gran, Bo belongs to the ball team so he gets to go to practices and games and ball team parties. And Shantelle belongs to the Girls' Club, so she gets to learn to sew and do stuff at the Girls' Club. I don't belong to anything!"

"Oh, don't you?" said Gran. Then she handed him a bowl of nuts. "You belong to this family. So why don't you shell some nuts for our apple salad tonight?"

Gran and Derrick worked quietly for a few minutes, then Gran said, "Everybody wants to belong, Derrick. You already belong to lots of things. And as you grow older you will belong to more. Right now you belong to this family. We all love one another and take care of one another. We work hard and play together. That's good. And you belong to this neighborhood. Remember when you fell off the monkey bars at the playground? Everyone there came running. Mrs. Jones picked you up and held you in her lap. Donna ran to call me and your mom. Old Mr. Ed brought ice to put on the lump on your head. That's because we all belong to this neighborhood."

Derrick smiled and rubbed his head. "I remember that," he said. "And remember Shantelle used her last quarters to buy me an ice cream cone that afternoon."

"Yep," smiled Gran. "Belonging is good. It's good to belong to a family and a neighborhood. But you belong one more place that is even better than that."

Derrick looked up with a big question on his face.

"You belong to God, Derrick. Before you were born, God decided what you would look like. God planned your curly hair and the way you can stand on your toes. God planned that you would be a fast jumper and a good singer. And God smiled at all those plans. God planned you, so you belong to God. God is watching you grow up. God smiles when you run faster and faster and when you sing in the choir at church. God laughs at your silly jokes. And God is proud when you do kind loving things, like shelling all those nuts for me. Belonging to God is good! The Bible says: 'Never forget that the Lord is God! He made us, and we belong to him. We are his people and the sheep of his pastures.' "

Derrick stood up and dusted the nutshells off his shirt. "How about I take some of these nuts over to Mr. Ed? He likes to sit on the steps and eat nuts."

Play the "We Belong to God" Game

Explain that just as Derrick belongs to God, each one of us belongs to God as well. God planned us and depends on us. Then teach the song below—sung to the tune of "Are You Sleeping, Brother John?"—for the game.

God made ———*(child's name)*.
God made ———*(child's name)*.
He/She is God's.
He/She is God's.
———*(child's name)* likes to *(fill in a motion, such as whistling, hopping, clapping, for the group to do)*.
———*(child's name)* likes to *(repeat)*.
(On the last line, say what you are doing three times; for example, "hop, hop, hop.")

Play until all of the children have had turns or interest wanes.

Closing

Use the word chart you made in a previous session to sing a verse of "Take My Life and Let It Be Consecrated." Relate its meaning to belonging to God. Close by lining out Psalm 100, noting that it is the psalm Gran said to Derrick.

COMMUNION

Session 31: Remembering Jesus with Bread and Wine

Worship Focus: When we celebrate the Lord's Supper, we remember Jesus.

As he instituted the Lord's Supper, Jesus said, "Do this in remembrance of me" (Luke 22:19 RSV). So today we will remember Jesus. On a picnic of your own, tell stories about meals Jesus shared with his friends. Back in the room, gather around a worship table set with filled communion ware to tell the story of the Last Supper and to introduce communion as a way we remember Jesus. The group will then go to the sanctuary to observe and participate in the sacrament with the congregation.

Note: In this session, "grape wine" is mentioned in stories to avoid the giggles plain "wine" might elicit while still being true to scripture. Use whatever terminology fits your congregation's celebration.

Time	Worship Activity	Materials/Resources
5 min.	1. Conversation about meals	
10 min.	2. Prepare for picnic	crackers spreaders peanut butter or cheese spread
20 min.	3. Picnic: "Jesus Eats" story Praise songs Enjoy food	picnic blanket box or basket prepared snacks
5 min.	4. Follow the Leader	
5 min.	5. Look at communnion ware Hear "Last Supper" story	communion ware with bread and wine
10 min.	6. Observe communion in sanctuary	
5 min.	7. Closing	

GATEWAYS TO WORSHIP

Getting Ready

1. Schedule this session for a Sunday when your congregation will observe the Lord's Supper. Begin by planning the children's visit to the sanctuary with your minister. Decide whether or not the children will participate based on your congregation's practices. Plan for the children to stand or sit where they can see well. Know when they will enter and when they will leave. (Some ministers might be willing to invite the children to stand around the table while the minister explains the sacrament. The children then move to the side with their leaders to watch the sacrament.)

Even if the observance of communion is at the end of your congregation's worship service, plan to return to your room so that the children can discuss briefly what they saw, share a closing prayer, and gather their belongings.

2. Prepare for a class picnic. Find a blanket big enough for the whole class to sit on in a circle and a box or basket in which to carry your snack to your picnic spot.

Gather what you need for the children to prepare their picnic snack. For cracker sandwiches, bring crackers, peanut butter or cheese spread, spreaders, and a serving plate. If you plan to make snack bags, bring granola cereal, raisins, nuts, seeds, and the like to be mixed by the children in a large bowl and then spooned into plastic bags, one for each member of the group. Gather ingredients for mixing a powdered drink. Remember cups and napkins!

3. Borrow communion ware and obtain whatever form of bread your congregation uses. Fill the cups and set them on your worship center. (Clear your plans with the person who prepares the communion elements so you do not borrow what will be needed in the sanctuary.)

Getting Started

As one leader greets the children at the door and helps them set their belongings aside, the second leader gathers the children on the rug to talk about meals. Ask the children to describe special meals, such as birthdays, holidays, picnics, and celebrations in restaurants. Talk about what they ate, who ate with them, and anything else that made the meal special. Try to give each child an opportunity to tell about one such meal. When all of the children have arrived, point out that Jesus enjoyed happy meals, too, and that we are going to remember some of those meals by going on a picnic together.

Preparing for the Picnic

Divide into groups. One group makes the plate of cracker sandwiches. A second group prepares the drink. If your group is large, assign a third group to prepare individual snack bags.

When everything is ready, pack a big basket or a box and have a picnic either outside or (in inclement weather) in another room in the building, but do not go too far. This is a full session, so you will want to spend as little time in travel as possible.

The Picnic

When you arrive at your picnic place, spread out your blanket and sit on it in a big circle. Leave the food in the basket while you tell the story "Jesus Liked to Eat with Friends" and sing several songs about Jesus. Sing the doxology last as your blessing for your picnic and note that food is one of the blessings that flow from God.

Jesus Liked to Eat with Friends

Jesus liked to eat. He liked the warm softness of bread fresh from the oven. He liked to chew slowly on raisins and dates until he could taste them with his whole mouth. He liked the squirt of cool juice that filled his mouth when he bit into a grape. There really were not many foods he did not like to eat. He liked cheese and figs and fish and bread and onions and milk and honey.

But more than eating good food, Jesus liked to eat good food with other people. One day a whole crowd of people were listening to Jesus teach. When lunch time came, his disciples told Jesus that it was time to stop teaching so that everyone could go home for lunch. Jesus decided it would be more fun to have a picnic right there, and that is what they did. A little boy gave Jesus his lunch. Jesus broke it and passed it out, and there was more than enough for everyone there. That was amazing! It was also amazing that everyone spent the whole afternoon talking to one another and listening to Jesus. It was a very happy day.

Jesus especially liked to eat with lonely people. Another day, he saw lonely, mean old Zacchaeus sitting way up in a tree, trying to see and hear Jesus. Jesus walked right up under the tree, looked straight up at Zacchaeus, and said, "Zacchaeus, may I have dinner with you?" During dinner, Jesus and Zacchaeus talked about all sorts of things. By the end of dinner, Zacchaeus had changed. He became friendly, kind Zacchaeus. It was another very happy day.

Jesus ate snacks as he walked around with his friends. He ate fancy dinners at weddings. He cooked the fish for a fish fry on the beach with his friends one morning. And sometimes he just sat down with a few close friends to eat and talk and laugh and be happy together.

Enjoy your picnic snacks together.

Follow the Leader

When everyone has finished eating, invite them to play "Follow the Leader" with you. Pick up your trash and put it in a garbage bag held by the other leader, signaling for the children to do the same. If the group is small, each child should pick up an edge of the blanket and shake it together. Then fold it up. Pick up the basket and start leading a line back to the room. Hop, skip, go around trees, even go down the slide or over some climbing equipment if they are handy, back to your room. As you enter the room, lead the line to form a circle on the rug, still standing up. Do a few more motions there, stretching, clapping, touching your toes, and so on until you finally sit down and fold your hands in your laps.

Exploring Communion

Call attention to the communion elements on your worship center. Ask the children to tell you what they are and how they are used. Based on their responses, talk together about how your church celebrates communion.

After talking about the "hows," tell the story below to explain the "whys" of communion.

Jesus Eats a Last Supper with His Friends

It had been a busy, exciting week for Jesus and his friends. Everyone in Jerusalem was talking about Jesus. Jesus and his friends were tired and excited about what was going on.

One night they got together in a quiet room away from the crowds. They ate dinner together. As they ate they talked about what they had been doing together. They remembered things Jesus had done. They told some of the stories Jesus had told them. They remembered what he had been teaching them. At the end of dinner, while they were still sitting around the table, Jesus picked up a loaf of bread. He broke it and gave it to his friends, asking them each to eat a piece. He told them that his body was going to be broken for them just like the bread was broken. Then he passed around a cup and asked everyone to take a drink from it. He told them that just as the grape wine was poured into the cup, his blood was going to be poured out for them. Then he looked straight at them and told them to eat bread and drink grape wine together to remember him.

Later that night, Jesus was arrested. He was killed by his enemies. But on Easter Sunday morning he was alive again. Then his friends understood what Jesus meant about the bread and the grape wine.

Ever since then Christians have eaten bread and drunk grape wine together to remember Jesus. We will do it in our church this morning. *(Describe what will happen and explain your visit.)*

Observe the Sacrament

Go to the sanctuary to observe and possibly participate in the sacrament according to your plans. On the way back to your room talk informally with the children about what they saw.

Closing

Once back in your room, let the children tell you what they saw and answer any questions about what happened. Close with an adult-led prayer to thank God for giving us bread and grape wine as a way of remembering Jesus.

Session 32: Communion Reminds Us That God Loves Us Always

Worship Focus: Communion reminds us that God loves us and forgives us.

Communion helps us remember all of Jesus' life, but most especially it recalls his willingness to die for the forgiveness of our sins. Until about the age of seven or eight, children are not ready to understand fully sin, guilt, and God's forgiveness. Before that time, they need to know that God will always love them, even when they do things they should not. (You may want to review the introductory material in the unit on confession as you prepare this session.)

While symbolic thinking is also beyond the capabilities of young children, they are learning to recognize traffic signs, souvenirs, and photographs as reminders of important truths or events. So we will explore communion as a reminder that God loves us always.

Time	Worship Activity	Materials/Resources
5 min.	1. Conversation about reminders	reminder examples communion ware
5 min.	2. "Jesus Gives His Friends a Reminder" story and discussion of communion story	
20 min.	3. Making reminders of God's love	prepared patterns glue and brushes seeds shallow trays paint and sponge stamps stapler and staples
3 min.	4. "Peter Needs a Reminder"	
2 min.	5. Thanking God for reminders of God's love	
10 min.	6. Observe the sacrament	
5 min.	7. Children add stickers to "Reminder Sheets" and sing	Jesus and heart stickers

Getting Ready

1. Schedule this session for a Sunday when your congregation will observe the Lord's Supper. Begin by planning the children's visit to the sanctuary with your minister. If your minister wants to invite

the children to stand around the table for an explanation of the sacrament, suggest that the pastor tell the story "Peter Needs a Reminder."

Plan your session around this visit, rearranging activities as necessary. Even if the observance of communion is at the end of your congregation's worship service, plan to return to your room during the singing of the final hymn so that the children can discuss briefly what they saw, add stickers to their reminder sheets, and gather their belongings.

2. Gather the needed examples of "reminders" that you have and get out the most important reminder of the morning: the communion set. Be sure that you do not borrow a bread tray, chalice, or set of cups that will be needed in the sanctuary this morning.

3. Copy one page of the Last Supper patterns for each child on thick beige colored paper. Gather fine seeds—such as sesame or alfalfa—to glue onto loaf designs, white glue, paint brushes for spreading glue on the loaf design, and shallow boxes or cookie sheets in which to work.

Cut a sponge into approximately 1" cubes for the children to dab purple paint on the goblet design. Prepare paper towel pads soaked in purple tempera paint and gather clean-up supplies.

Set up two work areas, one for each project. In each center provide extra paper for children who want to continue painting. Staple the bread and chalice pictures back to back after they have dried.

4. Get out two stickers of Jesus and two red heart stickers for each child to add to each of the pictures.

Getting Started

While one leader greets the children and gets their belongings settled, the other gathers the children on the rug for conversation about several "reminders," little things we keep to remind us of important things. Show and discuss some of the following.

* a photo of a happy time (maybe Christmas)
* a note on a calendar about something to do
* a souvenir from a trip

Each of these items will probably lead to stories about similar items the children have at home. Hear brief descriptions of them, trying to give as many children as possible a chance to talk.

The Reminder Jesus Gave Us: Communion

When all the children have arrived, direct their attention to the communion service on the worship center. Ask the children to tell you what it is and how it is used. Through conversation, build a picture of how your congregation celebrates communion. To explore communion as a reminder, tell this story.

Jesus Gives His Friends a Reminder

Jesus had been with his friends for three years, and oh, how he loved them. He wished that they would always remember how much he loved them. So he told them stories about love. He showed them by loving them every day. But he was still worried that they would forget.

So one night when they were eating dinner together Jesus gave them a reminder. He picked up a loaf of bread and passed it to his friends, asking each of them to break off a piece and eat it. He told them that he loved them so much that he would let his own body be broken for them, just as the bread was broken. Then he asked them each to drink grape wine from a cup he passed to them. He told them that he loved them so much that he would pour out his blood for them, just like the grape wine was poured out. Then he looked straight at them and told them that eating bread and drinking grape wine together was to be a reminder to them of how much he loved them. They were to remember that he loved them *always, no matter what, forever.*

Later that night, soldiers came to arrest Jesus. The next day, they killed him. But on Easter Sunday Jesus was alive again. His friends understood about the reminder. Ever since then, Christians have eaten bread and drunk grape wine together as a reminder of how very much Jesus loves us. Today in our church we will eat bread and drink grape wine. *(Explain the communion celebration and note that you will visit the sanctuary to observe and possibly participate.)*

Making a Reminder

Show the children the background sheets and explain the process for making a reminder. Send half of the group to the seed table and the other half to the sponge print area to begin work. Write, or ask them to write, their names on the backs of their pattern sheets. As the children finish their work in one area, they move on to the other. (Remember to offer them extra paper to "play with the medium" before they do their reminder page.) As the children finish both centers, gather them on the rug to visit and sing while the others finish their work.

While one of the leaders moves to the next activity with the children, the other cleans up the mess and staples each child's pictures together back to back.

Peter Needs a Reminder of Jesus' Love

When all of the children have finished, tell the following story.

Peter Needs a Reminder of Jesus' Love

Peter was one of Jesus' twelve special friends. For three years, Peter went everywhere Jesus went. He listened to Jesus tell stories. He watched how Jesus loved people. He ate with Jesus. Peter loved Jesus more than he loved any other person in the world.

Peter was there the night Jesus gave them bread and grape wine. He ate the bread and drank the grape wine and heard Jesus say that they were to remember that he loved them *always, no matter what, forever.*

Later that night, soldiers came and took Jesus away. Peter was very frightened. He was frightened about what would happen to Jesus, and he was frightened about what might happen to himself. All night he waited outside the place where they took Jesus.

When one man said, "Aren't you a friend of Jesus?" frightened Peter told the first lie *(hold up one finger).* "No, I don't know him." Peter felt awful inside.

Then someone else asked him, "Didn't I see you with Jesus today?"

"Not me," Peter lied a second time *(hold up a second finger),* feeling even worse.

The third time he lied about knowing Jesus *(hold up a third finger),* he looked up and saw Jesus being led out the door. Jesus' hands were tied up tight, and he looked very sad. Peter felt even sadder. He had lied three times about knowing the best friend he had ever had. Peter ran away and hid and cried.

The soldiers killed Jesus. But Jesus did not stay dead. Three days later he was alive again. And Peter was happy and ashamed at the same time. He was happy that Jesus was alive. But he was ashamed to see Jesus after his three lies. He was afraid that Jesus would not want to be his friend ever again.

Then Jesus came to Peter and said, "Peter, I have a job for you to do. Will you do it?" *(Hold up one finger on the other hand.)*

"Oh, yes, Jesus, I'll do it," said Peter, happy that Jesus still wanted him around.

Jesus said again, "I have a job for you to do Peter. Will you do it?" *(Hold up a second finger.)*

"Sure," said Peter, worrying about why Jesus had asked him a second time.

(Hold up a third finger.) "Peter, will you really do the job?"

Peter remembered the three lies. He looked at Jesus' face. Then he remembered the bread and the grape wine. Jesus had said that he would love them *always, no matter what, forever.* Maybe Jesus would love him—even if he told those three terrible lies. Jesus was smiling.

Deep inside, Peter started feeling very happy. "Yes, Jesus," he said, smiling for the first time in days. "Yes, I really will do the job." And he loved Jesus more than ever.

Ask the children how Peter felt after he told those three lies. Then discuss how we feel when we have done something wrong. Finally, point to the communion ware if it is nearby and ask what Peter remembered. Point out that every time we eat the bread and drink the grape wine in communion we remember that Jesus loves us, just as he loved Peter, *always, no matter what, forever.* Just as there is nothing Peter could do that was so bad that Jesus would not love him, there is nothing we can do that is so bad that we cannot tell God about it and still be loved by God.

Tell the children that this makes you so happy that you want to thank God. Invite them to bow their heads while you pray.

Thank you, God, for loving us always, no matter what, forever. And thank you for giving us bread and grape wine to remind us of your love. Amen.

If you have time, sing songs about God's love ("Jesus Loves Me," "Jesus Loves the Little Children," the doxology). Point out that bread and grape wine are reminders of our blessings.

Closing

Give the children their dried, stapled reminder sheets. Ask what it is that the bread and grape wine remind us of. Then give each child stickers of Jesus and a heart to put on each page to help them remember that bread and grape wine remind us that Jesus loves us *always, no matter what, forever.*

INDIVIDUAL SESSIONS

PREPARING TO WORSHIP IN THE SANCTUARY

Session 33: Dedicating Our Work to God (Officer Installation Sunday)

Worship Focus: We dedicate church officers to do God's work in our church.

A church is like a family. It takes everyone working together to get things done. Each member has a special job to do. The church asks some people to serve as officers to direct the overall work of the church.

In our varying denominations, we call our officers by different names and install them with different rites, but all of us promise the officers and God that we will follow these leaders, and we pray for them. Introduce the children to your particular titles for officers and the installation service, but also be sure that they get involved in praying for the new officers.

Time	Worship Activity	Materials/Resources
5 min.	1. "Who does it at your house?" conversation and litany	
5 min.	2. Singing	
5 min.	3. Confession and pardon	
10 min.	4. "They Do God's Work" pictures and game	pictures of people working at church
10 min.	5. "Church Officers" story	
10 min.	6. Visit sanctuary to watch officer installation	
10 min.	7. Drawings and prayer for new officers	paper and crayons chart paper, marker glue, paste, or staples
5 min.	8. Closing: "Take My Life . . . "	song chart

Getting Ready

1. Find or take pictures of four to six people doing a variety of jobs around your church. Be sure to include some of the paid staff and some volunteers. (Possibilities: the minister preaching in the pulpit, the organist playing, members of the choir in their robes singing, whoever cleans the building or mows the lawn, a Sunday school teacher with a class of children, and someone doing mission work the children would recognize.) Mount the pictures on individual pieces of stiff poster board and plan to save them; you will need them again.

2. Find out about the officers and installation of officers in your church. Be sure you know the names of the offices; what the rite of installation, ordination, or commissioning is called; how officers are selected, elected, or appointed; what happens in the installation rite; what questions are asked of the officers and the congregation; whether officers kneel; if there is laying on of hands; and who the new officers to be installed are.

3. Plan your visit to the sanctuary. Talk to your minister about your visit to decide where the children should stand or sit, when you should enter and leave the service, and at what time you need to have the children ready. The easiest place for the children to see well and enter and leave without disruption is a side door near the front, to get to the front pews. Be sure the ushers save the pews for you.

Rearrange the session plan as necessary to be sure that you arrive at the sanctuary at the right time and that the children are aware of what is to go on there.

4. For the prayer poster, gather drawing paper and crayons, a large sheet of chart paper of poster board, a broad-tipped marking pen, and paste, glue, or staples to mount the children's drawings on the poster.

5. You will also need your song book for "Take My Life and Let It Be Consecrated" (see page 47).

Getting Started

While one leader greets the children at the door and helps them get their belongings settled, the other leader gathers the children on the rug to talk about who does what tasks around their homes. Be sure to affirm the way work is done in every household. Talk about such things as who takes out the garbage, fixes breakfast, makes the beds, vacuums, and so on. Conclude the discussion with a brief adult-led prayer of praise and thanksgiving for families that work together.

Singing

Sing together some favorite praise songs.

Confession and Pardon

Recall the good feelings about families that work together. Then point out, perhaps referring to comments from your discussion, that no matter how hard we try, we sometimes do not work well together. We get lazy or selfish or too busy to think about others in our families. We need to tell God about these times.

Pray this confession litany with an adult leader reading each line and the children responding, "God, forgive us."

> Dear God, we really do love our families. But sometimes it is hard, especially when there is work to be done. Sometimes we want to hide or forget what we have to do. We need your forgiveness.
> When we say, "I won't do it!"
>
> **God, forgive us.**
>
> When we say, "It is not my job!"
>
> **God, forgive us.**

When we say, "Not me!"

God, forgive us.

When we say, "But I do it *every* time!"

God, forgive us.

When we say, "He never does *anything*!"

God, forgive us.

Please, God, forgive us and love us. In Jesus' name, amen.

As the assurance of pardon, say to the person next to you, "God *does* forgive us and love us." Instruct that person to say it to the next and so on around the circle. When it has gone all the way around the circle, say the phrase together and add a firm, "Amen."

Who Does What in Our Church Family

Explain that just as we all have to work together in our families at home, we all have to work together to get God's work done at church. Show a picture of a person who works at the church and identify the work. Together decide on a motion for that work. For example, to represent a nursery keeper, mime rocking a baby in your arms. Repeat the process for a second pictured person. Then ask, "And what does _____ (first person) do?" The children will answer by doing the correct motion. As you add each new picture, review the old ones. Once the children appear to be sure of what different people do, call on one or two children, instead of the whole group, to respond. (This should move fairly rapidly, like a game.)

Now play a variation of "Simon Says" in which everyone stands up facing the adult leader. The leader flashes one of the pictures and says, "Show me what this person does for God at church." The children respond by doing the correct motion. The leader points out who was first to give the correct motion and recognizes anyone who does the wrong motion. Then flash the next picture. Keep it light and fast.

Church Officers Story

Open your Bible to Acts 6 and set it on your lap as you tell this story.

The Bible tells us that when the church was very new, everyone worked together very hard. Each woman did what she thought God wanted her to do. Each man did what he thought God wanted him to do. The children helped, too. But there was so much to do! Sometimes important jobs just did not get done. People were starting to grumble.

They called a meeting to figure out what to do. At that meeting, they came up with a wonderful plan. "What we need is officers," they decided. "We need people to decide what needs to be done and to be sure that someone is doing it. That way, we always know what we need to do and who is responsible for doing it." Everyone agreed that it was a great plan.

So they selected officers. They picked the very wisest, strongest, and most loving people in the church. They had a special worship time for the new officers. The officers promised to do their jobs well, and everyone promised to follow them. Then everyone prayed. They asked God to help the officers know what needed to be done. They asked God to make them wise and strong and faithful to make good decisions for the church. And they asked God to be with the whole church as they lived and worked together. There was a lot of happy hugging after that worship service. Then everyone got to work.

You know what? Having officers *was* a great idea! All the work went better. People stopped grumbling. It worked so well that we still have officers in our church today. In fact, our church is having a worship service for new officers today. We have asked _____ (*name officers, pointing out their relationships to any in your group*) to be our officers. (*Describe simply your order of worship, especially mentioning promises to serve and follow and prayers for guidance.*)

Observe Officer Installation

One leader waits with the children just outside the sanctuary while the other listens for the appropriate time to enter. If this is one of your first trips to the sanctuary, the leader with the children should review expectations about not talking or waving or moving away from the group. Enter the sanctuary quietly. Watch the service of installation. Then leave at the planned time. As you walk back to the room, comment on the children's behavior with as many compliments as possible and corrections as needed.

A Gift and Prayer for Our New Officers

Give each child a sheet of paper and crayons to draw what they remember of the officer installation service. Each is to give his or her drawing to one of the officers. As they draw, talk with them about what they saw.

As they finish, tape, staple, or paste their pictures around the edges of a large sheet of poster board or chart paper, leaving plenty of space in the center for a group composed prayer. When all are finished, gather on the rug. Together compose a prayer for the new officers. (An easy approach is for one leader to help the children compose the prayer while the other writes the prayer down.) Pray the prayer together and promise the children that you will deliver it to the officers—then *do* it! (Your minister may be willing to take it to their first meeting.)

Closing

Sing "Take My Life and Let It Be Consecrated," using the song chart already made. Then conclude with a prayer about dedicating our feet and hands and mouths to doing God's work at church and at home.

Session 34: Worshiping God with Music

Worship Focus: We worship God with music because we often sense God's presence when we sing and hear music. Musicians often create beautiful songs as gifts of love to God.

There is something about music that makes us more aware of God's presence and helps us express ourselves more fully to God. A popular poster for a choir room is one that says, "When we sing, we pray twice." Often we turn to a familiar hymn that says more in its combination of words and music than we can articulate on our own. Music also calls to mind entire experiences. When we hear "Silent Night," we can be flooded by the meaning of the entire Christmas story and a lifetime of Christmas celebrations.

Musicians also use music as a way of giving God gifts of praise and thanksgiving. Some of the greatest church music was written specifically as a gift to God. Choirs generally see their work as a way of giving God a gift of praise.

We all grow in the way we incorporate music in our worship by adding and evaluating new experiences with music. Today we offer the children a series of experiences with music, in which they will be exposed to its emotional power, and we will introduce them to people who can share their love of worshiping with music.

Getting Ready

This session is unlike the others in this book. It offers no planned progression of worship activities. Instead it offers a series of activities with music. Your task is to select the ones that fit your church's use of music and your musical resources.

To create your session plan, follow these simple steps.

1. Read through all of the activities and determine who in your congregation could provide the needed leadership. Flag the activities that you *could* do.

2. From the flagged activities, select several that offer a variety of actions and exposure to a variety

of musical worship experiences. Arrange them in a logical order and check the estimated time allowed for each activity to be sure you have planned enough but not too much.

3. Contact the needed leaders asking for their help. If you need to borrow choir members, solicit the support of the choir director.

Possible Worship Activities with Music

Psalm 150 with rhythm instruments (five minutes). Read Psalm 150 from a simple version, such as *The Good News Bible.* Point out that people have used many different instruments to praise God. Distribute the rhythm instruments. Then prepare to praise God with the following version of the psalm. Repeat the psalm several times, swapping instruments each time.

Praise God at church! *(all say "Praise God!" and play instruments)*
Praise God in heaven! *(repeat above)*
Praise God for the mighty things he has done!

(Stop here the first time through the reading to ask, "What mighty things has God done?" Help the children identify such mighty deeds as God's creation of everything in the world, including ourselves, caring for us, sending Jesus, and so on. All say "Praise God!" and play instruments.)

Praise God with . . . *(name and play an instrument and say "Praise God!" Continue until all instruments have been named).*
Praise the Lord all living things! *(voices only, "Praise God!")*
Praise the Lord! *(voices and instruments)*
Praise the Lord! *(repeat)*

(The last time you go through the psalm, repeat the last phrase several times, getting quieter until you are whispering your praises. Then whisper instructions to put instruments back in the box.)

Sing favorite worship songs (five to ten minutes). Spend some time singing songs you have enjoyed together this year. Let the children suggest some of the songs. If at all possible, arrange for an instrumentalist to accompany you as you sing. This addition will give the music new power for the children.

March to the hymn "God of Our Fathers, Whose Almighty Hand" with trumpet or drum accompaniment (ten minutes). This stirring hymn focuses on the power and majesty of God. Especially for children, such power is often felt forcefully in marches worthy of a king. The words of the hymn say less to kindergarten children than do the feelings of the music. So simply introduce it as a hymn about God's greatness and power. Present one verse of the music by: (1) playing a tape of your choir singing it, accompanied by the organ; (2) inviting a pianist and drummer to play the hymn together; or (3) inviting a trumpeter to play it alone or with accompaniment.

After playing the first verse, teach the children to clap the fanfare at the beginning of each verse. Then have them stand up and march in a circle as the music is played. The march begins with the leader lining out and the children repeating the first two verses of Psalm 150. At the beginning of each verse, stop the march for everyone to clap the fanfare with the drummer. (A pause in the piano accompaniment will help the children recognize this point.)

Dance to a hymn of joy (five minutes). Select a joyful hymn, such as "Joyful, Joyful We Adore Thee" or "All Things Bright and Beautiful." Play the songs on the piano or another instrument. Read one of the verses to the children and briefly explain what we are happy about when we sing the song. Then give each child a pastel colored crêpe paper streamer about 24″ long to wave as they dance to the music. Dance with them, enjoying the happiness of the song.

Go to the sanctuary to hear special music sung by the choir (ten minutes). If your choir will be providing music that is especially interesting to the children, plan to visit the sanctuary to hear it. Sit outside a door that can be opened at the appropriate time and then closed when the choir concludes its anthem.

Meet a storytelling, guitar playing David (ten minutes). Invite a man who plays guitar, costumed as David, to visit your group to tell about David's music using the story below. The guitar playing is limited to strumming a few chords before each line of a psalm.

When "David" arrives, introduce him to the group, then let him tell his story something like what follows.

I have seven older brothers, and you know what that means. I get to do what none of the others wants to do. For me, that means that I get to spend lots of time watching our sheep. Most of the time it's kind of boring. I just sit and watch the sheep eat grass. But I also watch the flowers grow and bloom. And I have seen birds build their nests, lay their eggs, and feed their babies. Seeing those things makes me think of God, so I make up poems for God, like this one.

(Play the chords then say the words dramatically.)
(strum a chord) O Lord, our Lord, your greatness is seen in all the world!
(strum softly) Your praise reaches up to the heavens!
(strum softly) It is sung by children and babies.
(strum a second chord) When I look at the sky, which you made,
(strum it again) and the moon and stars which you set in their places—
(strum a third chord) Who are we that you think of us—
(strum it again) just people that you care for us?
(strum a fourth chord) Yet you have made us inferior only to yourself
(strum it again) and crowned us with honor and glory.
(strum it again) You placed us in charge of everything you have made,
(strum first chord) O Lord, our Lord, your greatness is seen in all the world!

But watching sheep is not always quiet like this. I have to protect the sheep from bears and wolves. I once killed a lion by myself. That was scary. When I am scared, I pray.

(strum fast) When I am afraid, O Lord Almighty,
(strum one chord) I put my trust in you.
(strum again) I trust in God and am not afraid.

Invite the children to sing these lines with you. Conclude by telling the children that music makes us feel close to God.

Invite a soloist to sing for you (ten minutes). Ask someone to visit your group and to sing a lively worship song and one quieter, more reflective worship song. If possible, both songs should be ones that are sung frequently in your congregation. When you invite your guest, state the focus of this session and ask him or her to share with the children his or her love of music in the way the songs are sung and to tell briefly how he or she worships God with each of the songs sung. Urge the guest to select short songs or plan to sing only one or two verses of a longer song. If the soloist chooses a song your children know, plan for them to join in singing it a second time. If the soloist selects a song with a short singable chorus, ask the soloist to teach it to the children so that they can sing along on the chorus while the soloist sings verses.

The point is to expose the children to a person who uses music especially well in worship. So choose your guest carefully.

Finger-paint to taped hymns (ten minutes). Find a record of hymns or ask the choir to tape several hymns for your group. Look for a variety of hymns—happy hymns of praise, reflective hymns related to Jesus' death and resurrection, marching hymns of dedication, and so forth.

Send the children to the work tables in aprons. Once everyone is placed, turn on the music for the children to listen to as they paint.

Session 35: Special Jobs in Worship

Worship Focus: When we worship together in the sanctuary, there are special jobs that different people do to help us worship.

As they worship with the congregation, children see the worship leaders in action. Today we will take time to learn about those leaders, the particular tasks they do, and the special robes they may wear. There are two reasons for doing this: (1) to help the children understand what they are experiencing in worship and (2) to introduce them to the possibility that they might one day want to be one of the leaders.

Warning: Watch out for stereotypes and biases. Unless your church expressly forbids it, encourage both boys and girls to try on all of the robes. Present *all* kinds of leadership as being equally important. Emphasize that the people who assume leadership and the worshipers in the pews are equally important to God.

Time	Worship Activity	Materials/Resources
5 min.	1. Conversation about who children saw in worship	
5 min.	2. Minister(s) identify task and try on robes	picture(s) of minister(s) robe and stole full length mirror
5 min.	3. Music leaders and choir identify tasks and try on robes	pictures of music leaders choir robe
5 min.	4. Ushers interviewed to identify tasks and special badges	picture of ushers badges (if used)
10 min.	5. Make puppets and worship robes	pre-cut puppet forms heads from catalogs crayons or pens glue straws or pencils or craft sticks and tape
15 min.	6. Using puppets, stage a worship service	order of worship posters prepared puppet robes (offering plate and change)

Getting Ready

1. Decide which of your worship leaders to feature in this session. If possible, arrange for one of them to visit with your group and talk about his or her job in the church. If possible, ask a minister to leave

worship wearing a robe to visit with the children and to explain what his or her job in worship is and to let them try on the robes being worn that day. If a minister is not available, an usher can usually visit briefly.

2. Get pictures of your congregation's worship leaders in the appropriate robes and borrow robes for the children to try on. (If your minister has only one robe and will be wearing it, check with the music folks. An old black choir robe could be an acceptable substitute.)

3. Copy enough puppet forms from the pattern section of this book so that each child can choose either the male or the female one. From catalogs and magazines, cut out a variety of people's heads for the children to glue to the blank head space on their puppet forms. Prepare the puppets' robes using the directions on the pattern page. Get out the glue and crayons or marking pens for completing the puppet bodies. Use masking tape to mount the bodies on pencils, straws, or craft sticks.

4. Get out your order of worship posters to use in the puppet worship service.

Getting Started

As you walk back to the room or as soon as you arrive and get settled, ask the children who they saw in worship today. Hear their descriptions of various leaders and worshipers who were in the sanctuary. Be sure to show interest in those who are not "leaders" but were noticed by the children as you direct them to think about the special tasks of the leaders.

The Minister(s)

Show the children the photograph(s) of your minister(s) in worship robes. Ask the children to identify the photograph(s); help them with names if necessary. Then ask whether anyone knows something about a person in any of the photographs. Combine this information with yours to talk about who is in the minister's family, what the minister likes to do, and anything else that identifies the minister as an individual person. Then ask what that person did in worship this morning. After the children identify what they saw the minister do, you will have to add other things a minister does in worship that the children have not seen, or did not see this morning. Repeat the process for each of the ministers if there were more than one in today's worship.

Finally ask what the minister wore. Show the robe and explain its use in your church.

In most Protestant traditions, ministers wear simple black robes so that worshipers are not distracted by looking at their clothing. The simple robe says, "This person is not important. What the person *says* is important." Many ministers also wear a stole, or broad ribbon, around their necks. The stole is a reminder of the yoke of Christ. Kindergarten children need only hear that the stole reminds the ministers that they are doing God's work, not their own. The color of the stole generally follows the liturgical colors.

As you explain the meaning of the robes, use one child as a model. For best results, stand your model on a chair or a stool. Having a full length mirror handy also adds to the experience. Several children may want to try on the robes and stole. Remember that as the children try on the robes they are seeing themselves in that role. Such experiences are important. But, you will have to judge how long you can do it and maintain the children's interest for the other worship leaders.

If older children serve as acolytes in your congregation, you may want to describe their leadership and try on their robes at this point.

Music Leaders and Choir

Repeat the above process for the music leaders of the congregation. In most churches you will want to talk about the organist and the choir members.

Choir robes serve the same function as the minister's robes. They aim our attention to what the organist is playing and the choir is singing rather than at what they are wearing.

The Ushers and Others

Repeat the process for these leaders, too. If possible, invite one of them to visit your group to tell what these leaders do to help us worship together. Help the children to try on the boutonnieres, badges, and whatever else these persons wear to identify themselves to worshipers or to visitors.

Making Worship Puppets

Show the children a puppet form and a completed puppet in "street clothes." Explain how you glued on the face and colored in the clothes. Give each child a puppet form and send the children to work tables that have been supplied with a small pile of "heads" and crayons or marking pens with which to color the clothes.

As the children finish, they join a leader on the rug. The leader tapes the puppet to a pencil or a straw or a craft stick. Also have on hand the prepared robes for the puppets to try on. Encourage the children to take turns trying different robes on their puppets and playing out the role a little with one another.

Worship with Puppet Leaders

When all of the children have arrived on the rug, explain to the group that they are going to have a worship service. They will take part with their puppets acting the parts of different leaders. Decide who will take each role. (Remember you can have several ministers with each leading one part of the service.) Be sure to stress the value of those who are acting as the worshipers.

Set up chairs or sit on the floor in the configuration of your sanctuary. Send all of the worshipers to the back to be led to their places by the ushers. Then let the worship leaders take their places in the way they do in your congregation. Go through your order of worship, following your order of worship posters and with lots of stage managing. For instance, you may say, "It is time for the call to worship. Reverend Susie, please stand up and call us to worship by saying 'Come, let us worship God.' "

The order of worship is as follows.

1. Call to worship: "Come, let us worship God."
2. Song: choose a favorite song for the worshipers to sing.
3. Minister leads the worshipers in praying the Lord's Prayer together.
4. Choir sings a song all the children know.
5. Minister "reads" to the congregation the two great commandments, "Love the Lord your God . . . " and "Love your neighbor as you love yourself" (Matt. 22:37, 39) by repeating them after an adult.
6. Adult asks the minister to possibly say something to the worshipers about those two rules.
7. If you wish, ushers collect the offering and the worshipers sing the doxology. If you do this, have an offering plate and some change for each worshiper.
8. All sing one last song.

Session 36: Praising God with Psalms

Worship Focus: We can use the prayers in the book of Psalms in the Bible to worship God.

The psalms are physically at the center of our Bible and at the center of our worship. We use verses of the psalms throughout our worship because in them we find beautiful expressions of all the movements of worship. When Christians are asked to cite passages of scripture that have been meaningful in their lives, most often they point to a psalm.

The aim of this session is to give the children a chance to worship God. The psalms are simply the form we will use to enable that worship. Our only teaching aim is to point out the book of Psalms in the Bible and to let the children hear the word *psalm* several times so that it will begin to be familiar to them.

Time	Worship Activity	Materials/Resources
5 min.	1. Conversation about Bibles and looking at Psalms	collection of Bibles
5 min.	2. Praise God with musical instruments (Ps. 150)	rhythm instruments
5 min.	3. Being Forgiven (Ps. 103)	
20 min.	4. Illustrating Psalm 104	chart paper tempera paints brushes
5 min.	5. Story about psalm for help and praying for help	
5 min.	6. Closing: Praise God for psalms	

Getting Ready

1. Obtain several Bibles to show the children as they gather. Be sure that an open Bible is in your worship center.
2. Get out the rhythm instruments.
3. Decide how your group will create its creation mural. Then mix the tempera paints (don't forget the squirt of detergent), get out the brushes, and be sure you have the paint aprons and clean-up supplies handy. Decide where you will mount your mural and have the necessary tape or tacks.

Getting Started

After the children have settled their belongings, gather on the rug with your collection of Bibles on the floor. Explain where the Bibles have come from. Note who they belong to, when the person got the Bible, where it is kept, and how it is used. Listen to the children's accounts of the Bibles at their homes.

Open one of the Bibles to the book of Psalms. Pronounce the word *psalm* and help the children to pronounce it, taking care to feel the "l" with their tongues as they say it. Point out the difference in the sounds of the words *songs* and *psalms*. Then explain that the book of Psalms is a collection of prayers that we can use in worshiping God. Explain that today we are going to use several of them as we worship God together.

Praise God with Musical Instruments (Psalm 150)

Follow the directions on pages 142-43 in session 34 for praising God using rhythm instruments and Psalm 150.

Being Forgiven (Psalm 103)

Once the instruments have been put aside, say to the children something like the following.

> It makes me feel good to praise God. God *is* very great and good. And God made me. Most of the time that makes me feel good, but sometimes. . . .
> I look at these hands *(look at your hands),* and I remember that they have hit when they could have helped and grabbed when they could have shared. I am sorry, God.

I look at these feet *(look at feet)*, and I know that they have kicked when they could have been still, and they have stamped to demand their own way when they could have run to help. I am sorry, God.

I think about this mouth *(touch your lips)*, and I know that I do not always say, "Praise God!" Sometimes I say mean, unkind words to friends. I am sorry, God.

(pause) When I think about these things, I am glad that there is a promise in the psalm book in the Bible. I am thankful that God has promised . . . *(go into the "As High as the Sky" promise of forgiveness, which is Psalm 103:11-12; see page 202).*

If you present this in a mood of prayer, the children will join you in looking at and thinking about their hands and feet and mouths. They will also say and do the motions to the promise of forgiveness.

Illustrating Psalm 104

Psalm 104 is a psalm to praise God for the world God created and sustains. Read the excerpts below, urging the children to listen for things God created that they would like to paint onto a mural.

> Praise the Lord, my soul!
>   O Lord, my God, how
>   great you are! . . .
> You have set the earth firmly on
>   its foundations,
>   and it will never be moved.
> You placed the ocean over it like
>   a robe. . . .
> You make springs flow in the
>   valleys,
>   and rivers run between the
>   hills.
> They provide water for the wild
>   animals;
>   there the wild donkeys quench
>   their thirst.
> In the trees near by
>   the birds make their nests and
>   sing.
> From the sky you send rain on
>   the hills,
>   and the earth is filled with your
>   blessings.
> You make grass grow for the
>   cattle,
>   and plants for [us] to use,
> so that [we] can grow [our] crops. . . .
> The wild goats live in the high
>   mountains,
>   and the rock badgers hide in
>   the cliffs.
> You created the moon to mark
>   the months;
>   and the sun knows the time to set.
> You made the night, and in the
>   darkness
>   all the wild animals come out.
> The young lions roar while they
>   hunt,
>   looking for the food that God
>   provides.
> When the sun rises, they go back
>   and lie down in their dens.

Then people go out to do their
    work,
  and keep working until
    evening.
Lord, you have made so many
    things!
  How wisely you made them all!

(Psalm 104:1-24 GNB)

Proceed to paint the mural in the way outlined below that suits your situation and children best.

Option One. Lay a long, wide strip of chart paper on the floor. The children will gather around it to paint things God created. Do not worry about things being upside down and sideways. Just enjoy the great variety of God's creation.

Option Two. Paint on a narrow strip (approximately 12″ wide) of shelf paper. Turn the strips into a frame for a window in your room or in a hallway near your room.

When the mural is complete, gather around it. Create your own psalm to praise God by asking each child in turn to point to what he or she painted and say, "Thank you, God, for. . . . ." If you have framed a window with your mural, one of the adult leaders follows the last child who speaks to describe what God made that can be seen outside the window.

Continue the time of praise by singing a few favorite songs. End with "Kum Ba Yah" with the motions (page 205).

Praying for Help

Open a Bible on your lap. Note that just as the song "Kum Ba Yah" asks God to stay close to us and to help us, the book of Psalms includes many prayers that ask for God's help. Briefly cite the following examples.

When David was captured and thrown into prison, he prayed, "When I am afraid, O Lord Almighty, I put my trust in you" (Ps. 56:3 GNB) and asked God to protect him from his enemies.

David did get out of prison, but he still had to hide from people who wanted to kill him. He got tired of running and hiding and trying to figure out what to do next. Once he prayed, "I call to the Lord for help. . . . I tell him all my troubles. When I am ready to give up, [God] knows what I should do" (Ps. 142:1-3*a* GNB).

When another person was worried about what to do, that person prayed, "Teach me, Lord, what you want me to do, and I will obey you" (Psalm 86:11).

I think someone who had said mean words to friends and had been unkind, but wanted to do better, added the prayer, "Lord, place a guard at my mouth. . . . Keep me from wanting to do wrong" (Ps. 141:3-4 GNB).

I'll bet one psalm writer was still in bed to pray, "Fill us each morning with your constant love, so that we may sing and be glad all our life" (Ps. 90:14 GNB).

Invite the children to join you in composing a psalm prayer to ask God for help you need. Start it with "Fill us each morning with your love, that we may sing and be glad all our lives" or a similar request in your own words. Then use the questions below to help the children create prayer requests.

* What are some new things we have to do that are a little scary?
* What do you worry about?
* What do you need to learn to do?
* Who do you know needs help from us or from God?

The easiest way to compose this prayer is for one adult to lead the discussion and the other to act as secretary. When your prayer is complete, invite the children to pray it with you by repeating each line after you say it.

Closing

Close with the following "thank you" litany and any songs time allows. Each line of the litany begins with an increasing number of hand claps. When not clapping, the children hold their hands up, palms forward. If you use your hands dramatically like you are using cymbals, the children will follow your lead.

> *(clap once)* God, you are the greatest and the best!
> *(clap twice)* Thank you, God, for loving us.
> *(clap three times)* Thank you, God, for being close to us when
> *(clap four times)* we know your power in the strong, beautiful world you made;
> *(clap five times)* when we feel your forgiveness when we have done wrong; and
> *(clap six times)* when we need your help.
> *(clap lots of times)* Thank you for the psalms that help us worship you.
> *(clap lots of times)* Thank you for music we can sing for you.
> *(clap once)* But most of all, God, thank you for loving us.
> *(drop your hands into your lap to indicate the end)*

Session 37: God Is with Us Always (Benediction)

Worship Focus: God is with us always. Like a good shepherd taking care of sheep, God takes care of us.

One of the chief fears of childhood is the fear of being lost or abandoned. As adults, we know that we are never totally free from that fear.

One of the promises of the Bible is that God is with us and will take care of us. We are never totally alone. Today we will explore and celebrate this truth using several biblical stories, and we will highlight the weekly repetition of that promise in the benediction of our worship in the sanctuary. The focus is not on teaching facts but on providing an opportunity for the children to express and to strengthen their trust in God's loving, guiding presence.

Time	Worship Activity	Materials/Resources
5 min.	1. Call the role and talk about being lost	
10 min.	2. Good Shepherd stories: Calling the sheep into the fold by name The lost sheep is found	sheep, shepherd, and sheepfold figures Bible
5 min.	3. "The Lost Sheep" game	"sheep"
15 min.	4. Hearing and illustrating Psalm 139:1-12	paper and selected drawing medium
10 min.	5. The Benediction: Great Commission story Visit to sanctuary	

Getting Ready

1. Find or make figures of the Good Shepherd, several sheep, and a sheepfold. Check old nativity sets for the shepherd and the sheep. If you cannot find freestanding figures, cut some from old curriculum

pictures or from Christmas cards. A spring-clip clothespin or a lump of clay makes a fine stand. The sheepfold can be a small box with a gate cut on one side, through which the shepherd and sheep can enter and leave. A long piece of poster board or cardboard can also be folded to shape a pen with a side entry.

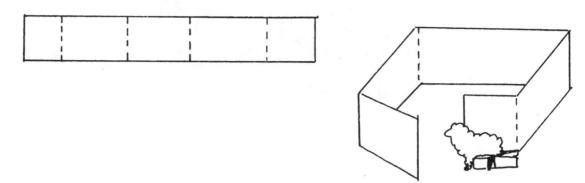

2. For "The Lost Sheep" game, any object the size of a chalkboard eraser can be a "sheep," but a stuffed toy sheep or a sheep puppet will be more attractive and interesting.

3. Gather supplies for the children to use in drawing pictures that illustrate places where God is with us. As a last resort, use crayons and drawing paper, but consider using colored chalk, tempera paints and brushes, or marking pens. Have handy a marking pen with which to write the children's captions on their pictures and tape or tacks for mounting the pictures in the display area.

4. Plan the group's visit to the sanctuary to witness the benediction.

5. Be sure that you know how your congregation uses the benediction. Usually the minister concludes worship by sending the congregation out to be God's people in the world and reminding them as they go that God will be with them. Some ministers use the same benediction each week. If yours does, be sure you know that benediction and its meaning. In some congregations, the choir sings the benediction. If yours does, be sure you know what they sing and why. Your pastor might want to invite the children to the front just before the benediction to speak to them and the congregation about the meaning of the benediction.

Getting Started

As the children leave the sanctuary, gather them by calling each one by name. Ask, "Is ——— here?" about some of them and respond positively when each one is accounted for. Ask about children who are not with you and wonder where they are. As you get ready to go to your room, note to the whole group that it is good to be together and that you miss each one of them when they are not there.

Once in your room, set aside belongings, then gather on the rug for conversation about being lost. Hear stories about being lost and talk about how it feels to be lost. Listen for or add stories of your own that describe (1) finding yourself away from the people with whom you went to the store or park or the like; (2) getting lost going somewhere you thought you could find, like the bath house at a campground; and (3) going where you are not supposed to go by accident or on purpose.

Conclude the conversation by affirming the children's fears about being lost. Being lost *is* frightening. Then tell them that it is impossible to get lost from God. God is with us always and will always love and take care of us. Sing "Jesus Loves Me" and other songs the children know about God's love.

The Good Shepherd

Show the children the shepherd, sheep, and sheepfold figures. Briefly explain the use of the sheepfold as a safe place for the sheep to sleep at night. Then tell the following story.

Jesus said "I am like a good Shepherd." He told lots of stories about the good shepherd.

He said that when the shepherd comes to the door of the sheepfold *(set up the sheepfold)*, the shepherd calls each one of the sheep by name, and they follow the shepherd out of the sheepfold. *(Call several sheep, using the children's names, and ask the children to move the sheep out of the sheepfold.)* At night, the shepherd brings the sheep back to the fold. Again the shepherd calls each one by name, and the sheep go in.

(Repeat the name-calling as the sheep are moved into the sheepfold. Repeat this part of the story several times to give several children a chance to move the figures and to help the children grasp the events of the story. Then proceed to another "Good Shepherd" story.)

Jesus told another story about the good shepherd who had one hundred sheep. One evening as he brought them into the fold, he counted each one and called it by name. One was missing. There were only ninety-nine sheep. The good shepherd knew which one was missing. So he went back to the fields, and he looked and looked until he found that one lost sheep. When he found it, the good shepherd was so happy that he gave the sheep a ride back to the sheepfold on his shoulders.

"The Lost Sheep" Game

Play a version of "Hide and Seek" using a chalkboard eraser "sheep." The children close their eyes while an adult hides the sheep in the playing area. At the word *go,* players look for the lost sheep. When it is found, the leader says, "Bring the lost sheep home" to call everyone back to the starting point. Repeat this as many times as you like. On a pretty day, play outside, with clearly defined boundaries.

Exploring Psalm 139:1-12

Open your Bible to Psalm 139 and introduce it as a prayer written by a person who knew that God was always very close. Read from the *Good News Bible* or this paraphrase.

> Lord, you know me better than anyone else does.
> You watch me when I am working and playing and resting.
> You know everything I do.
> Even before I speak, you know what I will say.
> You are all around me on every side.
> You protect me with your power.
> You know me better than I can understand.
>
> There is no place I can go and be away from you.
> If I go to heaven, you are there.
> If I go to faraway mountains, you will be there to
>   lead me.
> If I go into dark forests or dry, treeless deserts,
>   you will protect me.
> If I hide deep in the darkness of a cave,
>   you will see me even in the dark.
> Yes, wherever I go, you will be close beside me to
>   guide me and help me.

Point out that you think the psalm writer was trying to think of places where we might forget that God is with us. The writer thought of dark jungles or deep caves. Ask the children to name some places where they think we might forget that God is with us always. If they need suggestions, mention some places close to home, such as in a swimming pool or on the playground. Once the children have thought of several ideas, send them to tables to make drawings of these places for a display wall that will be your own "God Is with Us Always " psalm. Talk informally with them about God's presence in the situations they are drawing. As they finish, one adult writes on each drawing a phrase dictated by the artist to say how that artist knows that God is with him or her in the situation drawn. The other leader helps those finishing up at the tables.

Once all the pictures are on display, gather around them as a group. Turn them into a litany psalm by looking at one picture at a time. An adult leader reads the caption for each one, to which the group responds, "God is with us always."

The Benediction

Explain to the children that we remind ourselves that God is with us always each Sunday at the end of the worship time. Describe your congregation's practice concerning benediction.

Visit the sanctuary for the benediction. Sit outside a door from which the children can see the minister. While one adult keeps up with what is going on in the sanctuary, the other opens a Bible to Matthew 28 and tells the story of the Great Commission, emphasizing that Jesus gave his friends some jobs to do. He sent them to places all over the world, and he promised them that wherever they went, he would be there with them. Open the door just in time to see the minister pronounce the benediction.

After the benediction, return to your room. In a circle, remind the children that God is with them always everywhere they go. Then help them get ready to go home.

Session 38: Talking to God About Our Church

Worship Focus: We think with God about our church. We thank God for the church. We pray for our church.

This is not a lesson about the nature and function of the church. It is an opportunity for the children to talk to God about the church as they experience it. It is a chance for praise and thanksgiving, celebrating the variety of things we do together as a church. It is also a chance to pray for the church, to ask God to be with us and to take care of us and to help us take care of others. It may even be a time of confession. The activities are designed to help the children express their feelings and ideas about the church. Your challenge is to listen to what they say and to help them share it with God.

Time	Worship Activity	Materials/Resources
8 min.	1. Call to worship and conversation about what the children do at church	call to worship poster photos of church activities
15 min.	2. Create a mural about your church	mural paper selected media aprons, if needed
10 min.	3. Finger play, song, and dance about the church	recording of "Blest Be the Tie That Binds"
12 min.	4. Worship service about church Call to worship Song Prayer Song/dance	order of worship posters finished mural dance music

Getting Ready

1. If your church has them, gather photographs of church activities.
2. Get out or make "Order of Worship" posters.

Also make a "Call to Worship" poster to use today. On a piece of stiff paper or poster board, glue a picture of your church's building (from the bulletin or newsletter cover) and draw a smiling face. This will recall the verse, "I was glad when they said to me, 'Let us go to the house of the Lord' " (Ps. 122:1 RSV).

3. Plan how you will provide music for the "Blest Be the Tie That Binds" circle dance. One of the leaders can play the music on a piano or other instrument. Or you can make a recording of a musician (maybe the choir director) playing the music through four times. Be sure to have a tape player on hand if you need one.

4. Gather supplies for making a mural. You will need one long strip of chart paper and crayons, marking pens, and either paint and brushes or colored chalk.

Getting Started

Set personal belongings aside and gather on the rug. Show the children the "Call to Worship" poster and read Psalm 122:1 from the Bible in your worship center. Then ask the children what they do when they come to the house of the Lord. Share stories of the church activities in which the children participate. Show pictures of several church events that are important to the children, but that they might not remember without prompting. Or ask questions such as, "Who went on the church retreat?" or "What did we do at church during Christmas?" to stimulate thinking.

Create a Church Mural

Place your "Call to Worship" poster in the middle of a strip of mural paper on a table or on the floor. Invite the children to think of one thing they do at church to paint or draw on the mural. Hear ideas about what each child is going to paint. Try to have a variety of activities represented. Then sit around the paper and go to work. If you are going to paint, remember to use the aprons. Continue individual conversations about what the children do at church. Talk about what they enjoy, what they feel, and what they wish.

Singing About the Church

As the children finish their work on the mural, gather them on the rug to do the "Here Is the Church" finger play below, sing a song, and learn a song and dance about the church.

Here is the church, *(interlock fingers to form building)*
Here is the steeple, *(form steeple with index fingers)*
Open the doors, *(open thumbs)*
See all the people. *(open hands to reveal finger "people")*
Here is the church *(interlock hands with fingers on the outside)*
Here is the steeple *(form steeple with index fingers)*
Open the doors *(open thumbs)*
Where are the people? *(open hands to reveal "empty church")*
You can have a church *(interlock hands with fingers on the inside)*
Without any steeple,
But you can't have a church *(shake head "no")*
Without any people. *(open hands to reveal finger "people")*

Sing "We Are the Church" with the motions (see page 204).

Introduce the hymn "Blest Be the Tie That Binds," which celebrates the love we share in church. Kindergarten children can worship with this hymn not through the words, which are beyond their understanding, but by dancing it as a circle dance. So play the music through once. Sing the first verse, emphasizing the words *blest, hearts,* and *Christian love.* Tell them that it is a happy song to thank God for all the love that is part of our church.

Stand in a circle and hold hands. Teach the following motions. (I am using the words of the song to show you where the motions fit. There is no connection between the words of each phrase and the motion with it. You may dance to the music without the words. The dance as a whole celebrates the love that connects us.)

Blest be the tie that binds
(holding hands, form one big circle with joined hands raised over your heads)
Our hearts in Christian love;
(continue holding hands, but lower them)
The fellowship of kindred minds
(all side-step lightly to the left)
Is like to that above.
(side-step lightly back to the right)

Play the hymn several times, repeating the motions. Adults may want to sing the first verse over and over with the music. Or you may choose to let the music and motions speak for themselves.

A Worship Service About Our Church

Gather on the rug. If possible, put the mural on the floor in the center of the circle or on a nearby wall. Invite the children to plan a time of worshiping together about your church.

Place the "Order of Worship" posters in order against a wall or on the chalk tray of the chalkboard. Put the "Call to Worship" poster in first place. Repeat the verse once more as practice. Put a song poster up next and select a song about the church (maybe "We Are the Church"). Put the praying hands third, saying that praying for the church is important and that you have a plan for your prayer. Put a second song poster up last. Plan to sing and dance "Blest Be the Tie That Binds."

When everything is ready, give the children a moment of silence, then point to the "Call to Worship" poster. Say the verse together and sing the selected song.

Tell the children that you will use your mural to pray. The first way you will pray is to take turns pointing out what the children drew and their telling about it. After each person has spoken, the whole group will say, "Thank you, God, for our church!" Then one of the leaders begins a prayer something like that below.

God, we do thank you for our church and all the love we share. But we have to tell you that we do not always do what we should. Sometimes even at church we say mean words to one another. We are selfish. (*Add some statements about the kinds of things that go wrong at some of the events the children have drawn on the mural. For instance, "We argue over our games at parties."*)

We are sorry. Help us to do better. (*Ask the children to look at the mural and suggest some things we need to ask God's help. After each suggestion, the group says, "Please, help us, God."*) Thank you, God, for your promise that you will love us and be with always. Amen.

Close by dancing "Blest Be the Tie That Binds."

Session 39: Let's Plan a Worship Service

Worship Focus: We can plan a worship service for God together.

This is not one session but a process with which you can create an unlimited number of sessions. The basic format is that you and your children plan and carry out a short worship service built around the theme of a selected biblical text. In the process, the children will learn that worship services do not just happen. People plan them and prepare them as gifts to God. They will also see themselves as people who can create prayers and choose songs for a group to use. This is their first step in learning to pray publicly and to take responsibility not only for their own worship but also for that of the group.

Time	Worship Activity	Materials/Resources
5 min.	1. Conversation about the last week and introduction of the project	
?? min.	2. Plan scripture presentation	open Bible poster
?? min.	3. Select songs to sing	2 song poster
?? min.	4. Prepare the prayer	prayer poster
?? min.	5. Plan the offering	offering basket dedication posters
5 min.	6. Preparing the room and setting up order cards	
10 min.	7. Worship together	

Getting Ready

1. Begin your preparations for this session by reading the entire session plan. Then, using the ideas in the "Plan the Scripture Presentation" section, select the Bible story that you will use as your text for the day. Put the message of the text into one sentence your particular children can understand. Decide which method you will use to present the text to your children.

Once you know how your text will be presented, work through the various sections to plan for prayers, songs, and an offering or dedication. Some of the suggestions offered for each one will take very little time with the children. Others will take considerable time. So plan to use one or two of the more time-consuming activities and one or two of the short activities for the session. Estimate the time for each activity and for the whole session.

Possibility to consider: By the end of the year, the children will be able to use what they have practiced and created during the session for a short worship service at the end of the session. However, at the beginning of the year you might want to worship with each item as you create it or practice it instead of waiting until the end of the session. For them the whole session interweaves preparations and worship.

2. Once you complete your plan, gather materials for the various activities. If you have not already made them for another session, make the parts of worship posters.

Getting Started

As the children gather on the rug, talk about what they have done during the last week as a way of learning what is uppermost in their thoughts today.

If the children have spent time in the sanctuary, ask them what they did there. Help them to identify ways they worshiped by singing, listening, and praying. Then tell them the story about how your worship services are planned. If the children have not been in the sanctuary, move directly to your story. You will have to "write" the story so that it fits your congregation. Some steps to mention include the following.

* a minister or committee picks the scripture passage
* someone picks the songs to sing
* the musicians and choir members practice the music
* someone (minister or liturgist) plans the prayers
* a secretary (or someone else) prepares the bulletin
* someone cleans the building

After describing the way congregational worship is planned in your church, invite the children to plan a worship service together.

Plan the Scripture Presentation Together

The heart of a worship service is the selected Bible text. Its message affects the choice of songs we sing and the prayers we pray. Select one of the stories below or another of your choosing as the heart of today's worship with the children. Plan how you will present it with the children.

Some possible biblical texts:

1. Noah (Gen. 6:5–9:19)—God cares for people and animals.
2. Abraham and Sarah move (Gen. 12:1-7)—God is with people as they move to a new place.
3. David takes care of Mephibosheth (II Sam. 9)—We can take care of each other.
4. Jesus blesses the children (Mark 10:13-16)—Jesus loves and cares about children.
5. Jesus befriends Zacchaeus (Luke 19:1-10)—Jesus befriends lonely people.

Some ways of presenting the texts:

1. Read directly from a simple translation of the Bible or read the story from a Bible storybook. (For the story of Noah, try *Noah's Ark* by Peter Spier, which is all pictures. The children will have to tell you the story.)
2. Tell the story in your own words, emphasizing the feelings of the people involved. As you speak, show those feelings with your face and body. Invite the children to show the feelings with theirs, also. Divide the children into groups with each group pantomiming the feelings of one character or group in the story.

3. Make puppets using any of the patterns at the back of this book. Draw biblical clothing onto the body patterns or select different kinds of socks to represent different characters in the story; for example, Abraham could be a man's business sock, while Sarah is a lacy girl's sock. Pull the sock over your hand and lower arm. React with exaggerated motions to the feelings and actions of the story. For example, make Abraham and Sarah wrinkle up with worry about packing and leaving. Show them trudging along wearily. Detailed faces are not necessary to express these feelings.

4. If your church has a filmstrip or video of your chosen story that is appropriate for your children, show it.

Depending on what presentation method you have chosen, you may at this point simply read or tell the story to the children. You may have to practice it several times as preparation for presenting it in your worship service. If you plan to show a video or filmstrip of the story during the worship service, try reading or telling it at the beginning of the session so that the children are introduced to the theme early and meet the story in two media during the session.

Put the open Bible poster for proclamation in place leaning against the display wall or chalk tray.

Select Songs to Sing

Present the two song posters and ask the children to select two songs to sing in your worship. The children may simply select favorite songs, or they may want to sing songs that are connected to the story for the day. If you know such a song that is worshipful, teach it to the group now to sing during the worship service. Place the song posters in the proper sequence along the display area.

Prepare the Prayer

Prepare a prayer time by using one of the following methods.

1. Talk about what you want to say to God today. Identify several topics based on your earlier conversation and the children's suggestions. Identify possible prayers of praise, thanksgiving, confession, and petition. As the group talks, one leader makes notes to use in voicing a prayer on behalf of the group.

2. To create a litany prayer, ask the children to complete some of the following phrases or others of your design: "God, today we thank you for. . . . " "God, you are so great! You. . . . " "God, we need your help in our families. Help us. . . . " "God, we need your help at school. Help us. . . . "

Again one adult leads discussion while the other takes notes about these prayer phrases. At the appropriate time during the worship service, the adult reads aloud each of the children's prayers with the children responding, "Lord, hear our prayer."

3. The children draw a prayer picture for God. At the prayer time, each child in turn shows his or her picture and briefly says the prayer behind it.

4. Pray the Lord's Prayer.

Place the prayer poster at the appropriate place in the order of worship sequence.

Preparing a Dedication Time

Choose one of the following to do.

1. Give each child a coin to put in an offering basket as it is passed. Be ready to tell the children about one way the church uses money that is related to the theme of worship; for example, for Abraham and Sarah, show a picture of refugees and tell about the church's helping people who have to move from their homes. Say a prayer of dedication that mentions that use of money. Collect the offering, pray, and sing following whatever pattern your congregation uses on Sunday mornings.

2. Do a service project as your dedication. (1) Make an audio or videotape of your group singing to send to a shut-in member of your congregation (especially good with the David story). (2) Plant flowering plants to give with a card of appreciation to members of the church staff. (3) Plant bedding

plants around the church as a way to keep the earth beautiful if you are working with the Noah theme. (4) Paint a mural of the Bible story for the day. Mount it just outside the nursery door as a gift to the nursery children and their parents.

Keep the finished product near your worship center so that you can refer to it at the dedication time in your service. An adult needs to offer a prayer of dedication to offer this gift to God and to God's people.

Prepare the Room for Worship

As you finish your preparations, take time to put your worship area in order. This can be a matter of simply straightening the worship center and checking the order of worship posters, or you can divide into work teams to dust the room, arrange chairs in rows like pews, gather flowers or natural items for the nature center, and so on.

Worship Together

Follow your planned order of worship. Point to the "Order of Worship" posters as you go to remind the children of what is next.

Session 40: Praise God of the Seasons: Fall

Session 41: Praise God of the Seasons: Spring

Worship Focus: We praise God, who created the world with its changing seasons.

The changing seasons often alert us most pointedly to God's plans for the natural order. Because children are fascinated by these changes, we can use them to lead the children to praise the God behind the changes. This session is really two sessions. It can and should be done once in the fall and once in the spring or early summer with emphasis on the characteristics of that season. You can follow the same basic session outline, but select the most appropriate activity from the nature walk activity list. Repeating the other activities in the session will only reinforce learning, understanding, and enjoyment.

Again, remember that all your talk about and enjoyment of changes in nature should point to God who created it all. This is an opportunity to praise God!

Time	Worship Activity	Materials/Resources
5 min.	1. Conversation about this season	one seasonal nature item
20 min.	2. Praising the Creator: "I Sing the Almighty Power of God" Doxology "God Made the World" story picture litany Line out Psalm 8	props and recording for "I Sing the Almighty Power of God" Doxology Song Book pictures for litany
30 min.	3. Nature walk and selected follow-up	check directions
5 min.	4. Closing singing	props for "I Sing . . ."

Getting Ready

1. To learn and enjoy "I Sing the Almighty Power of God," you will need two resources. First, make a tape recording of yourself or another person or a group (maybe the choir) singing the first verse of the hymn. Be sure that the words are understandable. Second, make props for the children to use as they sing. Mount on stiff poster boards a picture of some mountains, an ocean picture, and a picture of clouds. Cut from stiff poster board a bright yellow sun, a white sliver of a moon, and some stars (cookie cutters make good outlines) to mount on a dark colored piece of poster board. As they sing, the children will raise each prop as it is mentioned.

2. For the picture litany, collect fifteen to twenty nature pictures that reflect the current season. Choose pictures that focus on one or two central plants, animals, or rocks rather than on sweeping landscapes. The children will identify specific things they see in each picture as part of a praise litany. Use big magazine pictures or projected slides.

3. Practice lining out Psalm 8 aloud using the directions. Read and sing with dramatic flair. If you relax and enjoy the praise poem, the children will enter into it with you. Remember, you are not performing for the children but leading them in worshiping God.

4. The "Nature Walk" section offers a variety of activities to use as a follow-up to the actual walk. Select one for this session and prepare accordingly.

Getting Started

As the children arrive, one leader greets them and helps them find safe places for their belongings. The other leader gathers the children on the rug to talk about whatever is going on in the natural world. Display one sign of the season (colored leaf in the fall, budding branch in the spring) to start the children's thoughts about what they have seen. Talk about what you see and do during this season that you cannot do during other seasons.

Praise the Creator with Songs

When most of the children have arrived, sing some familiar praise songs related to God in nature. Use your picture song books to sing the doxology and "For the Beauty of the Earth." When you sing the doxology, take time to think of the "blessings that flow" in this particular season.

Listen to your recording of "I Sing the Almighty Power of God" and encourage the children to listen for words they know. Use the words they hear to introduce the hymn as a song to praise God for some of the wonderful things in the natural world. Hand out your poster board props and instruct the children to raise their props when they hear that word. Help them by handing out the props in the order they appear in the song and by pointing to each one at the proper time. To give everyone a turn and to build familiarity with the song, repeat the process several times, giving different children the props. The first few times, keep the props in order, then mix them up. Sing along with the recording.

Praise the Creator with a Story

Read this story about God, the Creator.

God Made Our World
(Genesis 1 and Ecclesiastes 3:11a)

It is hard for us to imagine that once there was no world at all. We wonder about that long, long ago time when there was no earth, no sun, and no water and when there were none of the things we see in our world today.

But always there was God. "In the beginning God created the heavens and the earth." God made the water, the land, and the sky. God made day and night. God created fish, birds, and animals. God made plants and all growing things. "And God saw everything that he had made, and behold, it was very good." Then God created people who were able to think, to work, and to worship.

People have always wondered at the richness and the beauty of God's world. We wonder, too.

We wonder at the beauty God has made in things that are very great. God made the high mountains and the great oceans. God made the sun, the moon, and the stars.

We wonder at the beauty God has made in little things. We see brightly colored butterflies and hummingbirds. We may see small blue-speckled eggs in a little nest. We may see a green and gold June bug, a fuzzy, striped caterpillar, or a shiny, orange beetle.

We wonder at the special kinds of beauty God planned for different seasons of the year. In winter, when the snow makes a soft, white covering on the ground and icicles sparkle in the sunlight, we say, "God has made everything beautiful in its time."

When spring brings new green leaves and the first yellow jonquils, we think again, "God has made everything beautiful in its time."

In summer we enjoy the long, warm days of playtime outdoors. We see the beauty of flowers, orchards, and gardens. We watch the summer rain and are glad that "God has made everything beautiful in its time."

When autumn leaves turn red and gold, ripe fruit and harvest fields remind us of God's love and care, and we give thanks that "God has made everything beautiful in its time."

We are thankful, too, that God created us and gave us minds so that we can think about God and love and praise God for all this goodness.

Praise the Creator with a Picture Litany

Present your selected nature pictures or slides to the children one at a time. Either let the children call out what they see or go around the circle asking each child in turn to identify what is in one picture. The group response to each picture is "Praise God for _____!" This can be a rather spirited noisy litany with high participation. That's fine! Praise is not always quiet and refined.

Praise the Creator with Psalm 8

Line out Psalm 8 as below.

O Lord, *our* Lord,
Your greatness is seen in all the world!
Your praise reaches up into the heavens!
(loudly) Praise the Lord!
It is sung by children and babies.
(whisper) Praise the Lord.
You are safe and secure from all your enemies,
You stop anyone who opposes you.
When I look at the sky *(sweep your arm over head)*
  which *you* have made,
at the moon and the stars which you set in their places *(form big moon around your head with arms and sprinkle stars with your fingers),*
what are we that you think about us? *(hands on hips, head tilted to side with questioning look)*
Just people that you care about us? *(hands turned up with questioning look on face)*
Yet, you have made us inferior only to yourself. *(fold hands in lap)*
You have crowned us with honor and glory. *(make a crown on your head with your hands)*
You have put us in charge of everything you have made. *(point to yourself and to one another)*
You have placed us over all creation—*(spread arms out to side to include the whole world)*
sheep, *(ba-a-a)*
and cattle, *(moo)*

and the wild animals, too, *(make antlers with fingers)*
the birds *(flap your arms like a bird)*
and fish and the creatures of the sea. *(swim with your arms)*
O Lord, *our* Lord,
Your greatness is seen in all the earth! *(arms up over head in victory salute)*

Nature Walk

Go outside together to look at what is going on in God's world. Before leaving, be sure the children understand your purpose and do not expect to play. On your trip, gather what you need for one of the following activities.

1. Create a worship center that features natural items of the season. Cover your worship center with fabric or spread the fabric on the floor. Open a Bible to Psalm 8. Add a hymnbook. Then go out to look for signs of God's work in the world to add (nuts and colored leaves in fall; buds and green leaves in spring; and who knows what else any time of year). When you return to the room, each child will add his or her contribution, explaining how God is working in it.

2. The children gather natural items to bring back to the room and glue onto individual Styrofoam meat trays for a seasonal collage. If you have enough adult help, have each child dictate a one-line prayer for an adult to write on paper that the child then glues onto the tray with the nature items.

3. During spring, search for items that show that things change. For example, get a bud and a flower or an acorn and an oak twig. Take time to identify where each item came from and what it will become. To get started, you may want to show the children some paired pictures of baby and adult animals and seeds and flowers. As you talk, remember to speak of God's plan for growth.

4. During the summer or fall, focus on leaves. On your walk gather leaves that have prominent veins. When you get back to your room, make chalk rubbings of them. (Lay a piece of typing paper over the leaf and rub all over the leaf with the side of colored chalk. The outline of the leaf and its vein system will stand out.) After finishing the rubbings, talk about God's plan for the veins to carry food to and from the leaves. Compare the veins in the leaves to the blood veins in our wrists, which carry nourishment to our fingers.

Closing

Today's closing will grow out of the nature walk activities you selected. If you did activity one or three, your discussion may lead into a prayer of praise, and you may sing praise songs, including "I Sing the Almighty Power of God." If you did activity two or four, gather with your completed projects for a prayer and some singing. If the children dictated some of their prayers onto their trays, read each child's prayer. The children respond to each prayer, "Praise God's wonderful plan!"

Session 42: And God Created Animals

Worship Focus: We will praise God, who created the animals, and we will think about our responsibility for the animals.

Children's fascination for animals can be the entry point to celebrating the fact that God created the animals and that God put us in charge of the animals. We praise God for the beauty and good we see in the created order, and we think seriously about our role in it. We will end the session with dedication to promises about acting responsibly toward the animals we encounter. In so doing, we offer the children a chance to worship God by thinking about their own world and we begin building values that will make the children good stewards of God's creation now and throughout their lives.

Time	Worship Activity	Materials/Resources
8 min.	1. Conversation about pictures of animals children have brought from home	
7 min.	2. "And God Created . . ." story and prayer	Bible from worship table
15 min.	3. Making scrappy animals	background sheets pre-cut "paper" shapes glue
5 min.	4. Singing game about animals	animal cards
10 min.	5. "God Created People" Discussion Promise making Singing	

Getting Ready

1. Contact the children in advance to invite them to bring a picture of their pets or of some animal they saw in a zoo or on a vacation. Explain to the parents that the children will be thinking about their responsibility for animals as they worship this Sunday.

Because some children will arrive without a picture, collect several interesting animal pictures. The children can choose one of them to use as "their picture."

2. Put your imagination to work to gather a supply of different kinds of paper that the children can use to create pictures of animals. For background sheets on which to construct the animals, provide brown construction paper or grassy wall paper samples or sheets of sandpaper. For animal shapes, provide construction paper or textured wall paper samples (slick and shiny or flocked and furry) or solid colored gift wraps. For whiskers and tails, use yarn or string or wire.

Cut your animal papers into appropriately sized circles (big for heads, small for eyes), rectangles (some for bodies, others for legs), ovals (bodies), triangles (manes, ears), and other shapes. Divide your collection between the work tables and put them in shallow boxes. Be sure you have ample glue. Make one sample animal to show the children.

3. To make the card deck for the song-game, gather index cards or cut stiff paper into approximately 4″ × 6″ cards. For each child, glue a picture of one easily recognizable animal on a card. If your group is large, you will need several cards for some animals.

Getting Started

As the children arrive, help them set aside their belongings, except the animal pictures they have brought. Gather on the rug and give the children turns to tell briefly about the animals in their pictures. Offer the children who came without a picture a chance to tell about a picture they have selected from your pile of animal pictures. As the children talk, point out in a mood of happy wonder all the differences in the animals.

As the children tell about their animals, ask them to put their pictures on the worship table. Be sure that the children's names are on the back of the pictures.

During this conversation, the other leader needs to listen carefully and take notes about the names of pets and the children's interest in animals. After the following story, this leader will lead a prayer of thanksgiving, mentioning the children's pets by name and noting other of the children's interests and concerns about animals.

Hearing the Creation Story

Open the Bible in the worship center to Genesis 1 to tell the story of creation with the focus on the animals.

And God Created . . .

The very first story in the Bible is the story of the beginning of the world. The story begins with God.

God made the world and everything in it. The first thing God did was to separate the day from the night. And God was pleased with both day and night. That was the first day.

On the second day, God made the sky, and God said of the sky, "That is good."

On the third day, God separated the land from the water. God made the water into oceans and lakes and rivers and streams. God shaped the land into mountains and valleys and hills and plains. God was pleased, but did not stop there. God covered the earth with grass and flowers and bushes and trees. There were even plants to grow under the water in the oceans and streams. And God said, "That is good."

On the fourth day, God worked more on day and night. For the day, God created the bright sun to rise in the morning and set in the evening. For the night, God created the glowing moon and millions of twinkling stars. And God said, "That is good."

When the sun rose over the mountains and oceans on the fifth day, God's world was beautiful, but it was quiet. So God said, "Let the water be filled with many kinds of living beings, and let the air be filled with birds." God created great sea monsters, all kinds of fish, and all the birds. God blessed them all, saying, "That is good."

When the sun rose over the earth on the sixth day, the birds were singing in the trees and the fish were jumping in the rivers. Then God made the animals that live on the land. God made big animals, like elephants and buffalo and cows and horses. And God made tiny animals, like ants and beetles and mice. God made wild animals———like lions and tigers———and God made tame animals———like dogs and cats and goats. When God looked at all the animals, God said, "That is good."

(pause) I agree with God. The day and night; the land and water; the sun, moon, and stars; and most especially the animals *are good.* God did a great job of creating animals. *(Then voice a simple prayer of thanksgiving in which the children's pets are mentioned by name and other animal concerns noted.)*

Making Scrappy Animals

Show the children an animal you made from scraps. Then send them to tables to make their own. As they work, talk about the characteristics of each animal. Pepper your conversation with phrases like "I like the way God made the———able to———" or "I wonder why God made the———that way?" When they are finished, have the children leave the animals on the tables to dry. Be sure each child's name is written on or near his or her animal. As the workers finish, one leader gathers them on the rug to begin the singing game. The other leader helps the others finish their work and join the game on the rug.

Animal Song and Game

Teach the children the song below by singing to the tune of "Old MacDonald Had a Farm" a verse about one animal.

> God, our Father, made the earth,
> A-la-le-lu-ia!
> And for the earth God made the _____(name an animal),
> A-la-le-lu-ia!
> With a _____ (sound animal makes) here,
> And a _____ (sound animal makes) there,
> Here a _____ (repeat),
> There a _____ (repeat),
> Everywhere a _____ (repeat sound twice).
> God, our Father, made the _____ (name the animal),
> A-la-le-lu-ia!

After shuffling your deck of animal picture cards, deal one to each child. Then begin singing the song as a group. When you get to "And for the earth God made the . . . " point to a child. The child shows his or her card to the group and calls out the name of the animal. Sing the rest of the song together, making the appropriate animal sounds.

"God Created People": Story, Discussion, Promises

As the game winds down, ask the following questions as the entry into the rest of the creation story. After each question, the children will answer "God did," creating an informal litany.

1. On the very first day of the world, who made the day and the night?
2. On the second day, who made the wide blue sky?
3. And who, on the third day, separated the water and the land to make oceans and mountains and lakes and valleys?
4. And on that same day, who covered the mountains and plains with grass and flowers and trees, and who planted seaweed in the ocean?
5. Then who created the sun to shine all day and the moon to glow and the stars to shine all night?
6. Then who created the fish in the sea and the birds in the air and all the animals that walk around on the land?

After asking all the questions, say:

> You are right, but God was not through yet. God looked at everything in the world and said, "That is good." But then God said, "Now I am going to make *people*. People will be like animals, but different. They will be like me. So God made people. God made men and women. Then God told them, "I am putting you in charge of the fish and the birds and the animals. I have planned for food for all the animals and for you, but you are in charge." Then God looked at the whole world. God looked carefully at each thing, and God was pleased. God said, "That is good."

Pause and then ask the children, "What did God say about people and the animals?" To help them explore the meaning of their answers, ask such questions as:

* How are you in charge of _____? *(name some of their pets)*
* If I find a bird's nest or a baby animal outside, how am I in charge of it?
* Did God mean for us to be in charge of the animals by pulling the legs off beetles for fun or by picking the cat up by its tail just to see what it will do?

As the discussion proceeds, change the focus to creating some promises that we can make to God about how we will treat and take care of the animals. As the group shapes the promises, one leader should write them down. When the promises are complete, you are ready for a time of dedication.

Ask the children to stand up straight and tall. State each promise individually and ask the children if they are willing to make that promise to God. If they are, they reply, "I promise." After the children have made the promises, one leader offers a prayer to praise God for the animals and to ask for God's help in taking care of them.

Close by singing for the children the chorus to the hymn "All Things Bright and Beautiful." If they know it, they may sing it with you. Then sing other praise songs. If you have time, play again the song-game "God Created People!"

Be sure the children take home the pictures they brought as well as the scrappy animals they made.

Session 43: Praise God Who Made You!

Worship Focus: We praise God, who created each one of us wonderfully!

God made each of us with a unique set of talents and characteristics that are part of a good plan. Today we celebrate both those plans as we see them in each of the children and in God, who created the plans. It is a time to focus on what is unique about each child in your group. More important, it is a time to call them to praise God, who is behind the persons they are. Lace your conversation with statements like, "I'm glad God gave you such pretty red hair" and "I wonder what plan God has for someone who runs as fast as you do, Tony?"

Time	Worship Activity	Materials/Resources
5 min.	1. Mirror conversation	mirror big pieces of chart paper
20 min.	2. Make life-sized self-portraits	crayons
5 min.	3. "And God Created" story	Bible
5 min.	4. Sing: "He's Got the Whole World in His Hands" Doxology	Doxology Song book (?)
2 min.	5. Line out Psalm 100	Bible
3 min.	6. Confession and Pardon	
5 min.	7. "Follow the Praise Leader"	
10 min.	8. God Made Us Able to Help	supplies for selected project
5 min.	9. Story of Jeremiah Prayer Praise songs	Bible

Getting Ready

1. Prepare to tell the children about themselves as being God's incredible creations. Point to their physical characteristics with pleasure. Focus on some gifts or special interests as part of the special way God made each child.

2. For each child, cut a piece of chart paper large enough for the child to lie on while you draw an outline of him or her with a dark crayon. Also gather baskets of crayons for the children to use in coloring their faces, hair, and clothes. You may want to use large crayons on their sides to fill in spaces for clothes. Have masking tape handy to mount the portraits on the wall for the remainder of this session and to hold the paper in a roll to take home at the end of the session.

3. Choose one of the activities described below and gather the necessary supplies.

Getting Started

As the children arrive, one leader helps them put their belongings in a safe place before sending them to join the other leader, who has a mirror, on the rug. Give each child a chance to look in the mirror and talk about what each sees. Discuss all their differences in hair, eyes, smiles, and the like.

Making Life-sized Self-portraits

When all have arrived, give the children strips of chart paper larger than themselves. The children lie on the floor on their paper while the adults draw around them on the paper. The children then color in their faces and hair and clothes. (You may need extra space for this.) As the children finish, mount their masterpieces on the wall around the room. As the children finish their work, one leader gathers them on the rug to sing favorite songs until the other children finish their work.

"And God Created . . .": A Story

When all have gathered on the rug, open a Bible on your lap and tell the children that the Bible begins with this story about God and the world.

Read Genesis 1:1–2:4, using *The Good News Bible*. Each time you come to the statement "And God was pleased with what he saw," replace it with "And God said, 'That's good!' " The first time you come to it, ask the children to say it the way they think God said it. Practice it a few times. The next time the statement comes up, simply say, "And God said. . . ." Look at the children and pause for them to say together, "That's good!"

When you come to the end of Genesis 2:4, continue with, "But God did not stop there. One day God said, 'I'm thinking of a little girl with soft black hair and big brown almond-shaped eyes that shine when she sings. So I think I'll make her voice as pretty as her eyes.' So God created Lu Ling and said. . . . " Go around the circle and describe each child, concluding each description with, "So God created *(child's name)* and said. . . . " Let all the children add, "That's good." If there is a visitor or new child, say something about the child's appearance, then add, "And God wrapped up some surprises in _____ for us to learn about as we get to know him." Conclude with, "That's good." If you have a large number of children, keep your descriptions to one brief sentence, but do not omit anyone.

Sing for the God Who Made Us

After stating that this makes you want to praise God, invite the children to sing some familiar praise songs. Try "He's Got the Whole World in His Hands," with verses about all the different kinds of people God holds. If you have not used your Doxology Song Book in a while, this would be a good day to bring it out.

Psalm 100

As a response to the good feelings of the creation story and your singing, line out Psalm 100 together. Read the short phrases in verses one and two with expansive joy for the children to repeat. Present the phrases in verse three more quietly and thoughtfully. Return to the mood of joy for verses four and five. Then repeat the phrases in verse three and add an "Amen." Ask the children what it means to say, "God made us. We belong to God. We are God's people. We are God's flock." This discussion sets the stage for confession.

Confession

Say something like the following.

> *God* made each of us with a special plan. *God* made us different and wonderful. *God* thinks we are a special creation. We know that, but sometimes we forget. We forget who we are.
> We say "I can't."
> We feel dumb and stupid.
> We compare ourselves to others, saying: "I'll never be able to sing like she does"; "I'll never be able to run as fast as my brother"; "My hair won't curl like hers does"; "I'll never be able to read as well as they do." *(use statements you've heard from your children)*
> God, help us remember that:
> *(clap once)* You made us!
> *(clap twice)* You made each one of us wonderfully different!
> *(clap more)* You made each one of us with a special plan.
> *(clap more)* When you made us, you said, "That's good."
> *(clap more)* You love us. Amen. *(more clapping)*

The children may join you in clapping as you progress.

Follow the Praise Leader

The children are probably ready to move around, so play "Follow the Praise Leader." Tell them to say and do what the leader (an adult) does. Begin with, "Praise God for bodies that stand tall," and stand up. Continue with, "Praise God for feet that hop . . . children who skip . . . arms with strong muscles . . . " and so on. Move around the room and even down a hall and back, if that is possible. End the game with the children standing where they need to be to begin your "Helpers' Project" or back on the rug for the closing.

God Made Us Able to Help Other People

If you have time, end "Follow the Leader" with "Thank God for people who can . . . " *(do whatever they need to do for the project)*. Then introduce and do one of the following. (1) Empty garbage cans in all church school classrooms. (2) Plant flowers around the church (have the soil prepared for the children to plant bedding plants using tablespoons as trowels). (3) Sing a song over the telephone to a shut-in church member (Show the children the person's picture as they get ready to make this call.)

Closing

When the project is complete, gather on the rug. Introduce the children to Jeremiah by showing them the book in the Bible that bears his name. Tell the story from Jeremiah 1:1-9 in your own words. (The word *spokesman* might be easier to understand than *prophet*.)

Ask when it was that God said he began to know and care about Jeremiah. Point out to the children that before each of them was born God knew and loved them, too. Go around the circle and say to each one something like, "Before you were born, God knew all about you and loved you." Then close with a short prayer to praise God for making all the children just the way they are and to thank God for love that started before we were born and never stops. If you have time, sing a praise song.

Session 44: God, You Gave Us Hands

Worship Focus: God gave us hands with which to work and play and take care of others.

Kindergarten children are interested in learning new things to do with their hands. In this session, they will have a chance to celebrate and enjoy their hands, to confess and be forgiven for the wrong ways they have used their hands, and to dedicate their hands to a project in which they serve others.

Time	Worship Activity	Materials/Resources
??	1. Children in the sanctuary	
5 min.	2. "Follow the Leader" game on the way from the sanctuary; talk about hands	
5 min.	3. Singing and clapping praise	worship center Bible
15 min.	4. Making things with our hands: torn paper art clay modeling tower building	construction paper glue clay building blocks
2 min.	5. Confession and forgiveness with hands	
3 min.	6. Story: "Jesus' Hands"	
10 min.	7. Serving with our hands	supplies for selected project
5 min.	8. Closing	

Getting Ready

1. Gather materials for the three "Using Our Hands" activities.
2. Select one of the service projects described or one of your own. Gather the needed supplies.

Getting Started

As you walk from the sanctuary to your room, play "Follow the Leader," using different hand activities, such as holding a finger to your lips to indicate silence as the group tiptoes away from the sanctuary, stretching to touch something up high with your hands, opening and closing a door, turning a handle on a drinking fountain, and clapping your hands as you walk. Once you get to your room, gather the children on the rug. Point out that you are glad everyone has hands and name some of the things you did with your hands.

Praising God with Our Hands and Mouths

Open the Bible to Psalm 47. Read the first line, then leave the Bible open in your lap as you sing "Clap Your Hands, All You People" to the tune of "She'll Be Coming Around the Mountain" (see session 45). Make up other verses about snapping your fingers, slapping your knees, and other hand motions.

Sing the doxology, making a praise flower as you sing. To make the flower, everyone sits in a circle with hands held high and the palm of each hand touching the palm of a neighbor's hand. Each time you sing the word *praise,* clap hands with both neighbors. From the top, this looks like a flower.

Sing other favorite praise songs, including "He's Got the Whole World in His Hands."

To create a praise litany, have the children slap their legs once, clap their hands once, and snap their fingers once, in this order. Then add the words below. Once the children get the hang of it, invite them to offer the praise prayers while the whole group claps the pattern.

> Praise *(slap)* God *(clap)* for *(snap)*
> The bright morning sun *(hands up and out)*.
> Praise *(slap)* God *(clap)* for *(snap)*
> The friends we know at church *(hands up and out)*.
> Praise *(slap)* God *(clap)* for *(snap)*
> Hands for work and play *(hands up and out)*.

Using Our Hands to Make Things

Invite the children to try one or more of the hand activities you have prepared.

1. Make torn paper designs. Each child selects one piece of construction paper as a background for a picture made by gluing scraps of construction paper onto the background. They cannot use scissors, but must use their hands to tear the scraps into the shapes they want. Some children will make animals or people. Others will prefer free-form designs with a variety of colors and shapes.

2. Make something out of clay. Each child works with a lump of modeling clay. A finished product is not the goal here. Instead, the children are free to enjoy making and remaking a variety of objects.

3. Make towers with wooden blocks. Work as a group to build taller and taller towers. Record the height of each tower on a piece of paper mounted on the wall or a table leg. As you work, talk about how you use your hands in building towers.

Clap your hands several times in rapid succession to get the children's attention when you want them to finish their work and come to the rug.

Confessing and Forgiven Hands

As the children gather on the rug, talk about what they did with their hands and what they like about each project. Then begin the slap, clap, snap sequence again without words. Do it several times to focus the children's attention on you and on the activity that is about to start. Then after a snap, turn your hands palms up. Look at your hands and then at the children. Do the following confession.

> God gave us hands, wonderful hands that can do many things! But we decide how to use them. And sometimes we do not use them in wonderful ways. When that happens, we need to say, "I'm sorry." Let's tell God. I'll tell God with my mouth. You use your hands.
>
> Let's pray. *(fold hands in prayer)*
> God, you gave each one of us hands to use *(turn palms up for your own inspection)*. And we thank you. But

we also have to tell you that we have used our hands to grab *(grab with your hands)* and say, "That's mine!" We have even grabbed what is not ours and said, "I want it!" *(grab again)*

We have pushed people away with our hands, saying, "Go away! I don't like you" *(push hands in front with palms out)*. We have even hit others when we were angry *(mime hitting)*. And we have hidden our hands when there was work to do *(hide hands behind your backs)*.

Forgive us, God *(lay hands in lap, palms up)*. We are sorry. Amen.

(pause)

When we say we are sorry, God promises to forgive. God says, "That's okay. I have work for you to do. I need people to share *(turn palms out and up in offering)*. I need people to make friends *(shake hands with neighbors)*. And I need people who are ready to join hands and work together" *(hold hands with neighbors)*.

In response, sing the doxology.

A Story: "Jesus' Hands"

Point out that just like you and me, Jesus had two hands to use each day.

Jesus' Hands

When Jesus woke up in the morning, he stretched his arms *(stretch your arms above your head)* and his hands *(flex your hands)*. He got out of bed and went outside to pray. His hands lay quietly in his lap *(lay your hands in your lap)* while he talked with God. Then he got busy.

Everywhere Jesus went he made friends. When he saw someone who looked sad and lonely, he would say, "I want to be your friend" *(reach out to shake hands with one of the children)*.

When two friends were fighting, Jesus would put his hands on their shoulders and say, *(put your arms around the children on either side of you)* "Let's work this out. God wants us to love one another."

When people came to listen to Jesus, he would teach them about God. One day he said, "Think *(point to your head)* about the birds *(make the same hand fly like a bird)*. They are so tiny, and there are many of them, *(cup your hand as if holding a bird)* but God cares about each one of them. I tell you that God loves the birds, but God loves each of you *(point to the children)* even more."

When sick people came to Jesus, he would touch them with his hands *(reach out to feel the forehead of a child near you)*, and they would get better *(hug the child)*.

By the end of the day, Jesus was tired, and his hands were tired. He lay his hands quietly in his lap *(do the same with yours)* and talked with God about what had happened that day. And then he went to bed.

If you have already learned the Lord's Prayer, fold your hands and pray it together.

Serving Others with Your Hands

Suggest that just as Jesus used his hands to help others, so also we can use ours to help others. Give directions for one of the service projects described below.

1. If it is winter, spread crunchy peanut butter on pine cones. Roll the cones in birdseed to make bird feeders.

2. If your church has a mailing (maybe the newsletter) that needs to go out, ask the children to help by putting the folded letters into envelopes and sealing the envelopes or by putting stamps on the envelopes or postcards. If the mailbox is nearby, mail the letters together. Be sure the children know why the letters are being sent.

Closing

Gather back on the rug and repeat the slap, clap, snap pattern a few times. Then begin saying one-line prayers again. Pray about things you have done with your hands during this session, saying,

171

"Praise God for . . . " "Thank you, God, for . . . " and so on. Allow the children to add their prayers. Then move into the following benediction.

God *(slap)* be *(clap)* with us *(snap)* all week long *(hands up)*.
God *(slap)* be *(clap)* with us *(snap)*. Keep us safe and strong *(hands up)*.
God *(slap)* be *(clap)* with us *(snap)*. Help us love and care *(present hands as if offering to help)*.
God *(slap)* be *(clap)* with us *(snap)* and with people everywhere *(open your hands and arms as if to include the whole world)*.

If you have a few extra minutes, sing "He's Got the Whole World in His Hands" and other praise songs.

Session 45: Take My Life and Let It Be Consecrated

Worship Focus: We can use our bodies and lives to praise God and to do God's work.

Obviously *consecrated* is not part of the kindergartner's vocabulary. Adults' familiarity with the word often depends on the part of the Christian family with which one worships. *Consecrated* means "set aside for holy (or God's) use." Kindergartners can begin to think about setting aside or using their bodies to praise God and to do God's work. We will explore that concept today. But we will introduce the big word *consecration* simply to enjoy such a big word and to begin experiencing this and other big words that are used in worship as being interesting and friendly, rather than strangely incomprehensible, words.

Time	Worship Activity	Materials/Resources
5 min.	1. Consecrated Treasure Hunt	letter cards
15 min.	2. Sing and make puppet heads	"Take My Life . . ." picture book puppet bodies paper bits glue and toothpicks
5 min.	3. Confession about using our hands and make hands of the puppet	puppet hands
15 min.	4. Story: "Andrew's Feet" Make feet and assemble puppets	puppet feet, shorts, shoes, and shirt brads crayons
5 min.	5. Sing with the puppets	

Getting Ready

1. Cut three sheets of colored construction paper into fourths to make cards. On each card, write one letter of the word *consecrated*. In a lower corner of the card, number the letters to show the order in which they appear in the word. Write another letter on the extra card to show the children what they are looking for as they start on their hunt. Scatter the cards in sight but in a variety of places along your group's path from the sanctuary to your room. Be sure to scatter them late enough so that no

well-meaning church member will pick them up to clean up the hall.

2. Copy one puppet pattern sheet for each child. Cut out the major body pieces from this copy. Cut the clothing pieces out of different colored paper. Sort the pieces so that you have all the hands, shirts, and the like together.

Tape the tabs on each arm into a loop, through which the children will slip their thumbs or fingers. The loops will be flattened while the children create the puppet, but they will be easy to open up when the puppets are ready to use.

Cut scraps of construction paper into tiny bits with which the children can make eyes, mouths, and hair for the puppet faces. Pour white glue into shallow dishes and find toothpicks for the children to use to drip glue onto their puppets. Supply two brads to fasten the feet to each puppet.

Getting Started

Just outside the sanctuary doors, gather your group and explain that on the way to your room everyone is to look for cards that have letters on them. They will be scattered high and low. Show them the extra card so that they know what they are looking for. Then walk to your room. Be sure each of the letters is found.

Once in the room, settle belongings and gather the children on the rug. Point out the little numbers on the cards. Then call out the numbers for the finders to put the cards in the proper order on the floor or on the chalkboard chalk tray. When all the letters are in place, challenge the children to sound out the word. Give lots of help and have fun with it. Say the whole word, inviting the children to say it. Enjoy its length and sound. Point out that in worship we use lots of big words and that this is one of them. Define *consecrated* as "set aside to be used by God."

Consecrating Our Voices to Praise God

Invite the children to consecrate their voices to sing several praise songs to God. Then try singing Psalm 47 to the tune of "She'll Be Coming Around the Mountain."*

(chorus)
Clap your hands, all ye people. Clap your hands.
Clap your hands, all ye people. Clap your hands.
Clap your hands, all ye people.
Clap your hands, all ye people.
Clap your hands, all ye people. Clap your hands.
Verses:
1. Sing a mighty song of joy—Allelu!
2. Stomp your helping feet. Stomp your feet.
3. Shake friendly hands, all ye people. Let's shake hands.

———————
*Chorus and first verse by Pat McGeachy III. Used by permission.

Also relearn the third verse of "Take My Life and Let It Be Consecrated" using the picture song book you made in session 9. Talk about ways we use our mouths to sing praise songs for God and to say loving things to other people.

Give each child a puppet body form. At the work tables, the children will glue little bits of paper in place to make faces and hair for their puppets. It will be easier for the children to put the glue on the puppet than on the tiny pieces of paper.

As they finish their puppet heads, instruct the children to leave them on the tables to dry. Fast artists may want to color their puppets' shirts.

Consecrated Hands: Confession and Puppet Hands

Gather again on the rug. While the children gather compare hands and talk about what we do with our hands. Include such things as how we use our hands when we eat, when we play on the playground, and when we help out at home. Then invite the children to talk to God with you about their hands.

> Thank you, God, for hands; *(hold hands up)*
> Hands we can use to wave
>   "hello" to new friends; *(wave)*
> Hands we can use to pet a soft furry puppy or kitten. *(mime petting an animal)*
> Hands that we can hold with
>   a good friend *(hold a neighbor's hand)*
>   and swing as we walk together. *(both swing hands)*
> Hands we can use to help
>   set the table, *(mime setting a table)*
>   hold the baby, *(mime rocking a baby in your arms)*
>   or hug people we love. *(hug self)*
>
> But, God, we also
>   use our hands to hit when
>   we are angry. *(slapping motion)*
> We reach out with our hands
>   to grab what is not ours. *(grab)*
> We use our hands to cover our
>   ears when we do not want to hear
>   what other people want and need. *(cover ears)*
> Sometimes we hide our hands when
>   someone needs our help. *(hide hands behind your back)*
> We are sorry. *(lay hands palms up in your lap)*
>   *(pause)*
> God knows when we are sorry.
> God loves us anyway.
> God says we can wash our hands *(mime washing hands)*
> And try again to
>   be a good friend. *(shake hands with neighbors)*

Sing a praise song to thank God. Then give the children pre-cut hands to glue onto their puppets.

Consecrated Feet: Story and Puppet Feet

Sing the verse about mouths and hands and feet in "Take My Life and Let It Be Consecrated" using your song book.

Tell the story "Andrew's Feet" to show how feet can be consecrated to God's work.

Andrew's Feet

When Andrew first woke up, his feet were snuggled way down in the covers. They felt soft and warm. When he wiggled his toes, it felt like the covers were trying to hug him tight. But his feet did not stay there long.

He smelled pancakes and bacon. So his feet jumped out of bed onto the cool, smooth floor. They ran down the hall and stretched up on tippy toes to give Mother a big good morning hug. Then they climbed up in his chair. Andrew wrapped his feet around the chair in his own special way. But they did not stay there long—only long enough for Andrew to gobble down three pancakes and two pieces of bacon.

He ran out into the backyard. The cool dew on the grass made his feet jump and his toes curl. He high-stepped out to the swing and pumped until he was swinging high into the air. He reached up with his feet as high as they would go. It felt like he could almost touch God with his toes. So he whispered, "Good morning, God" on the way up, and he could almost feel God touch his toes and whisper, "Good morning, Andrew," as he swooshed back to earth. It felt good, but his feet did not stay there long.

"Andrew, come put on your shoes so we can go to the store. I need a helper to carry the sack." So Andrew ran inside and found his blue shoes under his bed, and even tied the laces all by himself. Hop, hop, hop, he went down the sidewalk, jumping the cracks. There were two big bags to carry home. Step, step, step, Andrew walked, being careful not to drop the bag he was carrying.

"I don't know what I would do without your strong feet to help me," said Mother as they climbed the stairs at home.

After lunch, Andrew sat in Daddy's big chair. Mother asked Andrew to hold baby Chris for a while. So Andrew curled his feet around Chris to make a little hole for Chris to lie in. It felt good and strong to hold Chris like that with his feet. Andrew liked it, and so did Chris. And they stayed there, but not too long. There were many things to do and places to go all day long.

Finally, Andrew wiggled his feet in the bathtub. He washed between each one of his toes. He kicked his bubble bath into piles of bubbles. Then he rinsed off and dried with a big red towel.

His feet walked slowly down the hall and crawled into bed. "My feet are tired," Andrew told Daddy. "They played outside, helped carry groceries home, and took care of Chris."

"I guess they are tired," Daddy replied. "But I think they are also happy. They have helped and loved and enjoyed. That is all happy work for feet."

(look up from your story and pause) And you know what I think? I think Andrew had happy, consecrated feet.

To make feet for the puppets, give each child two foot patterns. Show the children how to match the holes in the shorts to those on the legs. Then let them select colors of "shorts" to glue to the tops of the legs and the style of shoe to glue to the feet. The children may want to color the shoes and add patterns to the shorts before gluing them in place.

To assemble the puppets, give each child two brads. Show the group how to use them to attach the legs to the body.

Again, let the puppets dry for a few minutes while you clean up and, if you have time, play a game the children like.

Closing

Show the children how to hold the puppets by slipping their thumbs through one arm loop and their little fingers through the other one. Let the children experiment with manipulating their puppets. Then sing several verses of "Clap Your Hands, All Ye People" and verses two and three of "Take My Life and Let It Be Consecrated."

Session 46: Thank You, God, for Families

Worship Focus: We talk to God about our families.

The lives of most kindergarten children center on their families. In today's session, the children are presented an opportunity to celebrate the good things about their families, admit their wrongs against members of their families, and make a gift to take to their families.

Underlying these activities is the belief that God planned for us to live in families and that God cares about what happens in our families. We can share with God the joys and sorrows of family life. Be careful to affirm all sorts of family groupings and remember that not all families live under one roof.

Time	Worship Activity	Materials/Resources
5 min.	1. Sing praise songs	
10 min.	2. Draw pictures of your families	large drawing paper crayons or marking pens
5 min.	3. A praise litany celebrating our families	
2 min.	4. Confession and forgiveness for families	
3 min.	5. "A Family That Loved Each Other"	worship center Bible
15 min.	6. Making a gift for members of our families	cookies plates and wrap to cover them icing
5 min.	7. Closing	

Getting Ready

1. Gather large sheets of drawing paper and crayons for the family portraits.
2. Buy or make plain sugar cookies 2″ to 3″ in diameter with an even surface. (You will need one for each member of each child's family.) Choose one of the two methods of decoration described and prepare accordingly.

Getting Started

As you walk to your room from the sanctuary, talk with the children informally about members of their families. Once belongings are set aside and the group has gathered on the rug, sing several favorite praise songs together.

Drawing Our Families

Ask the children to tell how many people there are in their families. Go around the circle so that each child may answer. Note the variety of answers. Then invite the children to draw a picture of their family. As they work, talk individually with the children about members of their families.

When all have finished, gather on the rug. Create an informal praise litany by asking each child to introduce his or her family using the picture of it. After each description, the group replies, "Thank you, God, for ———'s family." In smaller groups, the children's descriptions can include somewhat detailed comments. In larger groups, limit descriptions to naming family members and pointing to them. The challenge is to give each child enough time to reflect on his or her family without losing the interest of the whole group.

Confession and Forgiveness for Families

Point out that despite all the good things about our families, we each do and say things in our families for which we need to say, "I'm sorry." Ask each child to think about the following wrong things that we all tend to do in our families. Raise the following list of family sins thoughtfully and sadly to set the tone for confession.

Raise your hand if you ever fight with a brother or sister.
Raise your hand if you ever get so angry that you hit another person in your family.
Raise your hand if you sometimes call a brother or sister a mean name.
Raise your hand if you sometimes talk back when your mother or dad asks you to do something.
Raise your hand if you have pouted when you had to do something other people in your family wanted you to do, but you did not want to do it.
(fold your hands in your lap in prayer) God, we love the people in our families, but we do not always treat them right. We are sorry about the mean, fighting things we do. Help us to be kinder. Help us to remember not to hit and kick when we get angry. Help us to love each person in our family. Amen.
When we tell God that we are sorry, what does God promise? *(Briefly hear the children's responses, then continue.)* God says, "That's all right. I forgive you, and I will be with you to help you. You *can* remember not to hit. I will help you. You *can* stop before you say mean names. I will help you. You *can* do happily what other people want you to do, even if you do not really want to do it. I will help you. You can even keep from fighting with your brothers and sisters. It is hard, but I will help you with that, too.
Remember that I am always with you, and I love you very much."

Sing one favorite praise song to thank God for understanding and for helping.

Hear a Story About a Family

Open your Bible to the book of Ruth to introduce this story about a family that loved and took care of each other.

A Family That Loved Each Other

Young Ruth and old Naomi were a family. Once Naomi's husband and Ruth's husband had been part of their family, but both husbands were dead. So now Ruth and Naomi were the whole family. They loved each other very much. Because they were very poor, they never had enough money or food.
When they moved to Bethlehem, Ruth said, "I will go out to the fields. Maybe a kind farmer will let me gather grain so that we can make bread for dinner." A kind farmer named Boaz did let her pick up the leftover grain in his field. Ruth worked hard all day. She wanted to have enough for a good dinner for Naomi.
Boaz watched Ruth. It made him happy to see her working so hard to take care of Old Naomi. He could see that she loved Naomi very much. At the end of the day, he gave Ruth an extra sack of grain to take home.
Naomi was surprised and happy when Ruth came home with so much grain. While Ruth rested, Naomi made a big loaf of bread. She knew that Ruth was hungry and wanted her to have a good supper. They ate the bread while it was still warm and enjoyed every bite.
While they ate, Naomi smiled. "I think Boaz likes you. I think our family is going to grow."
Naomi kept smiling as she washed Ruth's best dress and found a beautiful necklace for her to wear to a party. She brushed Ruth's hair until it shone and braided it with a beautiful ribbon. She wanted Ruth to be pretty and to enjoy the party. She also hoped that Boaz would want to marry her.
And he did. When Ruth and Boaz got married, Naomi and Ruth moved into Boaz's big house. They became a family together. Later Ruth and Boaz had a son named Obed. Together they were all a happy family. Boaz worked in the fields to grow their food. Ruth cooked the food from the fields for them to eat. And Naomi helped Ruth take care of Obed. They worked and played and were happy together.

Ask the children to tell you what Ruth did to take care of Naomi, what Naomi did to take care of Ruth, and what each of them do to love and take care of the people in their families.

Making a Gift for Our Families

Invite the children to ice one cookie for each member of their families, including themselves. As one leader gives each child the appropriate number of cookies, the other helps the children start to work. Place the cookies flat on a stiff paper plate. The children can use the plates as work space and trays for the trip home. Some children may need two plates to accommodate larger numbers of cookies or to package cookies for families living in two different places. (Consider having the children wear painting aprons.) Choose one of the following decorating methods: (1) Spread icing (provide several colors in shallow plastic bowls) with plastic knives, then decorate the iced cookies with pieces of cherries or nuts or small candies. (2) Use tubes of icing or gel to decorate the cookies.

In each case, encourage the children to prepare a special cookie for each member of their families. Use foil or plastic wrap to cover the plates for the trip home.

Closing

After the children have finished and washed their hands, one leader gathers them on the rug to sing. When the whole group has gathered, offer a prayer to thank God for families and to ask God to be with them in their families. Then go around the circle and charge each child to love his or her family this week. Say such things as "Karen, take care of your family"; "Derrick, be kind to your brothers and sister this week"; and "Alice, give your grandmother lots of hugs this week." End by saying to all of them, "Remember, God loves you and your families. God is with you every day in your families. Amen."

Session 47: Thank You, God, for Friends

Worship Focus: We thank God for friends and try to be loving friends.

Warm, loving friends are one of the most treasured blessings of life. In worship today, we will thank God for our friends and think about being a loving friend. We will explore Paul's teachings about love in I Corinthians 13 as they apply to being a loving friend. We will paint rocks to give to our friends as love offerings.

Time	Worship Activity	Materials/Resources
5 min.	1. Sharing grapes and singing	small bowl of seedless grapes
10 min.	2. Drawing a friend	drawing paper crayons tape or tacks for mounting pictures
3 min.	3. Prayer for our friends	
7 min.	4. Prayer using I Corinthians 13:4-6	Bible
15-20 min.	5. Making a gift for a friend	two rocks per child foil or plastic work pads tempera paints brushes clean-up supplies
5 min.	6. Closing: "Hurray for God!" litany	

Getting Ready

1. Prepare seedless grapes to share with the children.

2. On the work tables, gather drawing paper and crayons for the children to make drawings of their friends. Have on hand tape or tacks to mount the drawings on a display wall during the session.

3. Gather two fist-sized rocks (with smooth edges if possible) for each child in the group. Prepare small containers of tempera paints in several different colors. Cut pieces of plastic or foil for the children to work on and to lay the rocks on to dry. Gather medium brushes, paint aprons, and clean-up supplies.

Getting Started

As they arrive, help the children to set aside their belongings, then gather on the rug. Set a bowl of seedless grapes in your lap and say how much you enjoy them. Ask the children whether they like grapes. Then point out that you could eat the grapes all by yourself, or you could share them. Decide to share them and offer each child one or two. End with "For the Beauty of the Earth," using your song book. After singing the first verse, point out how much more we enjoy the beauties of the earth and sky when we share them with friends.

Drawing Our Friends

Help the children to name some of their friends. Remember that family members, people of all ages, and other children at school or church or in the neighborhood can all be friends. Once everyone has named one or more friends, invite them to go to the tables to draw a picture of one of their friends. Some of the artists may want to add pictures of what they like to do with that friend. As they draw, talk informally with the children about their friends.

"Thank God for Friends" Prayer

When most of the artists have completed their work, gather them and their drawings on the rug. Give the children a chance to show their pictures and tell about their friends. While each one talks, mount the drawings on a wall or door for all to see (they will take their pictures home at the end of worship today). Conclude each child's description by saying or praying together, "Thank you, God, for friends" or "Thank you, God, for _____(child's name) and _____ (friend's name).

Prayer Using I Corinthians 13:4-6

When all of the children are with the group, open the Bible from your worship center. Read from it the following description of a loving friend, based on I Corinthians 13:4-6.

A Loving Friend

> A loving friend is patient.
> A loving friend is kind.
> A loving friend is not jealous of what others have.
> A loving friend is not selfish and grouchy.
> A loving friend thinks about what others want as well as about what "I want."
> A loving friend tells happy stories about friends and forgets the unhappy ones.
> A loving friend never stops being a friend.

Based on the children's accounts of their friends, go through the reading a second time and use what the children have said to illustrate each sentence. Also use examples you have observed as the group works and worships together. (Be brief!) Then present the truth that as much as we want to be loving friends, we do not always succeed. Say or pray thoughtfully,

God, we want to be patient, but sometimes we say "It is *my* turn *now!*"
We want to be kind, but sometimes we hit or kick before we think about it.
We do not mean to be jealous, but sometimes our friends get such wonderful toys and wear such pretty clothes.
We do not want to be selfish and grouchy, but we say, "It is mine!"; "You can't play with it!"; and "I don't want to."
We do try to think about what others want, and to tell only happy stories about our friends, and to be always a loving friend, but sometimes we just forget.
For all the times we are not loving friends, we are sorry, God.

Sing "Forgive Me, God, for the Things I Do" as a prayer. As an assurance of pardon, go through the sequence below. If the second adult leader joins in on the refrain, the children will also start saying it.

Leader: Even when we are not patient,

Children: God loves us.

Leader: When we are not kind,

Children: God loves us.

Leader: When we are jealous,

Children: God loves us.

Leader: Even when we are selfish and grouchy and never think about anyone but ourselves,

Children: God loves us.

Leader: God loves us and forgives us and is always our friend.

Children: God loves us.

Making a Gift for Our Friends

Give the directions for painting one rock to keep and one rock to give to a friend. Some children may want to paint the rock to look like an animal or a person. Others will prefer to do free-form designs. After they have put on their painting aprons, have the children go to the tables to work. (Placing two rocks at each place in advance avoids the scramble for rocks.)

Closing

As the children finish painting and cleaning up, one leader gathers them on the rug to sing songs about love and friends; also enjoy some favorites as time allows. Conclude by singing the first verse of "For the Beauty of the Earth" again.

On the spot, create an exuberant litany in which one leader says "Praise God for _____" (name one of the following: grapes, friends, the beauties of the earth, and anything you have enjoyed together this morning). The other leader and the children will reply loudly, "Hurray for God!" Repeat until you run out of things to mention. The last line is "Hurray for God!" spoken by the first leader. The second leader, with the children, then repeats it. Repeat the phrase several times, getting quieter each time. End with "Amen."

Session 48: God Understands Our Angry Feelings

Worship Focus: Because we can share all our feelings with God, we can share our angry feelings with God. God understands angry feelings.

Today we are going to deal with anger as a very real response to situations that seem unfair or that hurt. A child's outrage at getting the smaller cookie feels much the same as an adult's outrage at economic injustice. Both are anger. Though our anger is aroused by different things, each of us experiences anger.

We often give children the idea that anger is bad when it is neither good nor bad. What we really want to communicate is that some ways of expressing anger are good and others are bad. We need to give children permission to feel angry and let them know that God can accept their anger. Therefore, today's session focuses not on how we act out our anger, but on the fact that we can always share our anger with God. When anger can be shared with God, it can be directed by God to healthy expression.

Time	*Worship Activity*	*Materials/Resources*
5 min.	1. Identifying our feelings with pictures and a song	feeling faces pictures
15 min.	2. Finger-painting feelings	finger paint paper, finger paint, aprons clean-up supplies
5 min.	3. Songs and a prayer about God's love and our feelings	
5 min.	4. Exploring our anger: "How do you feel when . . ." angry motions	angry music
10 min.	5. "Angry Jonah" story and "If You're Angry" song	rhythm instruments
5 min.	6. Closing: list what makes us angry litany singing	

Getting Ready

1. From newspapers, magazines, and old curriculum cut out pictures of people expressing a variety of feelings. Use pictures of children if possible, but include a few pictures of adults to point out that people of all ages have feelings. Find pictures representing both happy and sad feelings.

2. Get out your rhythm instruments. If you wish to use it, find a tape or record of angry sounding music to play while the children move.

3. For finger-painting, gather the paint, the slick finger paint paper, the children's painting aprons, and the needed cleaning supplies.

Getting Started

As one leader helps the children set aside their belongings, the other gathers the children on the rug to look at pictures of people expressing feelings. Ask the children which picture they feel more like at the moment. Let the children explain why they feel the way they do today. Accept all answers without judgment.

Sing several homegrown verses of the old song "If You're Happy and You Know It" (see page 183) in a particular feeling, picking up on both the happy and the unhappy feelings most children identified with in the pictures.

Finger-Painting Feelings

Give the children directions for finger-painting and have them put on their paint aprons. Give them some time to enjoy and experiment with the paints. Then encourage the children to paint their feelings. Move among the children and ask such things as "How does *sad* feel?" or "Show me *joyful*." Some children will paint their way through a variety of feelings, while others will spend more time on the one feeling that most interests them at the moment. Ask the children to finish by painting *anger*. Then have them leave their paintings to dry so that they can clean up and gather on the rug.

God Loves Us No Matter What We Are Feeling

While one leader oversees the cleanup, the other gathers the children on the rug to talk about how it felt to paint those feelings. After hearing the children's comments about the feelings they painted, point out that God loves us no matter what we are feeling. Sing some songs about God's love ("Jesus Loves Me," "Jesus Loves the Little Children," and "He's Got the Whole World in His Hands").

Follow the songs with a brief teacher-led prayer to thank God for being near us no matter what we are feeling.

Exploring Anger

Ask the group (or ask individual children) to show you how they would feel in the following situations.

1. Your class is going to the zoo. Your two best friends get to ride together. The teacher says that you have to go in another car.
2. Your mother insists that you turn off the TV in the middle of your favorite show to eat dinner.
3. You want to play "Chutes and Ladders," but everyone else wants to play "Old Maid" so you have to play "Old Maid."
4. You wanted to wear your green sweater. It is dirty, so you have to wear the old yellow one.
5. Your big brother just kicked you out of the tree house. He says you are too little to play with his friends.
6. Add any others that are appropriate for your group.

Talk about how anger feels in your eyes, mouth, hands, and so on. Have everyone stand up in a circle. As you describe ways we show our anger with our bodies, act them out and invite the children to follow your lead.

Angry feet stomp. *(stomp around in a circle)*
Angry fists pound. *(keep stomping and pound with fists)*
Angry mouths frown. *(do other motions and frown)*
Angry heads shake. *(do other motions and shake head)*

(If you want to get further into displaying angry feelings, play "angry" music while the children continue the motions for a minute or two. When you stop the music, freeze in place. Pause, then begin the following prayer.)

God, anger feels tight and tense and stiff. Thank you for loving us even when we are angry. When we are angry, help us loosen our heads *(slowly roll your head)*. Help us to relax our hands *(shake out your fists and wiggle your fingers)*. Help us to quiet our stomping feet *(sit on the floor and stretch your legs out in front of you and bounce them lightly)*, so that we can find a way to smile again *(turn a frown into a smile)*. Amen.

The children may naturally follow you into this prayer. If they do not, call on some by name to do the actions with you.

God Loves Angry Jonah and Us

After the prayer, remind the children that as bad as anger feels, we know that God is with us when we are angry, and God understands how we feel. To illustrate this point, tell the following version of the story of Jonah.

Angry Jonah

The Bible tells stories about happy people and sad people and frightened people and excited people. The Bible even tells stories about angry people. Of all the people in the Bible, the angriest was probably Jonah.

Oh, Jonah was angry! He was so angry that his head hurt, and his fingernails were digging into the palms of his hands. Jonah was angry at the people of Nineveh. And Jonah was angry at God. Jonah was angry because God sent him to tell the people in Nineveh that God loved them. Jonah said that he would tell anyone in the whole world that God loved them—but not the lousy, no good people in Nineveh.

At first, Jonah tried to talk God out of the whole idea. God listened, but he still sent Jonah to Nineveh. Then Jonah tried to run away. But God found him and sent him back to Nineveh. Finally, Jonah went and did what God asked. He told the people of Nineveh that God loved them. And they believed him! Those lousy people of Nineveh began loving one another and living by God's rules. Now you would think that would make Jonah happy, but it did not. It only made him angrier.

Jonah walked out of the town and sat down on a high hill. "I told you it was a dumb idea to come to Nineveh," Jonah whined to God.

You would think God would be disgusted with Jonah by this time. But God kept on loving him. God listened to him and talked to him. God said again and again, "I love you, Jonah, and I love the people of Nineveh."

We don't know whether Jonah ever stopped being angry at the people of Nineveh or at God. What we do know is that God kept loving Jonah and listening to him and talking to him.

If God kept loving Jonah after he argued and ran away and pouted and fussed, we know that God can keep loving us—even when we are angry.

Rephrase the song "If You're Happy and You Know It" to sing about anger. Accompany yourselves with rhythm instruments, playing them with great anger at the appropriate places. This time sing:

If you're angry and you know it, tell it to God.
(everyone makes angry music with rhythm instruments)
(Repeat line one)
If you're angry and you know it,
God, who made you, wants to share it.
If you're angry and you know it,
Tell it to God.
(lay your hands quietly in your lap in prayer)

Closing

As a group, make a litany by listing what makes you angry. An adult leader reads the list one item at a time. After each item, the group responds, "We can tell God. God understands." Close by singing "If You're Angry and You Know It" with the lyrics above. First sing about anger, then sing about other feelings, including both happy and unhappy feelings. Be sure to end with a happy one.

Session 49: God's World of Happy Differences

Worship Focus: Let's celebrate and enjoy all the differences God planned into the world. God made us all different, but God made us all members of one family.

The world is full of differences. People look different, wear different clothes, eat different foods, speak different languages, and govern their lives differently. As transportation and communication improve, we all become much more aware of these differences.

If God's love is to include the entire world, it is essential that all of us learn to appreciate rather than to fear our differences. That is not a simple task. At this point in global history, the brightest people in all cultures are struggling with how to respect one another's differences and maintain our own heritages. There are few easy, obvious answers.

All of that is beyond the children's understanding for now. But they can begin to know and experience as nonthreatening people who are different and they can celebrate the worldwide family of God, which includes a variety of people. That is the focus of today's worship.

Time	Worship Activity	Materials/Resources
	1. Children in the sanctuary	
10 min.	2. "Differences" activities	paper strips and pens for recording bathroom scale fruit tray pictures of children
5 min.	3. Singing about our differences and God's love	
5 min.	4. Confession and forgiveness about our fear of differences	magic slate
10 min.	5. Discussion about another culture	
10 min.	6. Weaving project	prepared bases and strips stapler and staples
5 min.	7. Closing	small ball of yarn recorded hymn and recorder

Getting Ready

1. The heart of this session is a visit by a person who has lived or traveled in another country or culture. The purpose of the visit is to introduce the children to some people who are very different from themselves in the ways they look, dress, eat, and live, but who are part of God's family and, therefore, potential friends. Explain this purpose clearly to your guest when you call. Encourage your guest to bring or wear native clothes, a sample of a native food that your children might like, and other objects that would help the children to imagine this different way of living.

2. Decide how many of the "differences" activities to do and gather the necessary supplies. Gather

pictures of attractive children from a variety of racial and cultural backgrounds from *National Geographic* magazines, travel magazines, or any other source.

3. For the weaving project, copy one of the bases from the Craft Patterns section for each child. Cut along the parallel lines. From a variety of colors of construction paper, cut strips ½" wide and 12" long. Weave one strip through several slits and staple it at the end to give each child a start. Each leader will need a stapler and staples to secure the end of the children's work when they have woven all the strips.

4. Find the magic slate and stylus you bought for one of the confession sessions at the beginning of the year.

5. If you have not already made a recording of "Blest Be the Tie That Binds," record or recruit a good pianist to record the music of the hymn several times without interruption. Save the recording.

Getting Started

On your way from the sanctuary to your room, make several stops to compare differences among the children, using some or all of the following activities.

1. On a strip of paper mounted on a door, mark how high each person can jump. Compare the marks as differences without paying undue attention to who can jump higher.

2. Weigh each of the children on a bathroom scale. Note their weights on a wall chart and comment on all the different weights for children who are almost the same age.

3. Identify all the different eye colors among the children.

4. Offer each of the children a choice of one piece of fruit from a plate of bite-sized fruit pieces. Comment on all the different choices as the children eat.

5. Back in your room, show the children a collection of pictures of children of different races and cultures and ask the children to identify the differences among the children. Enjoy both.

Sing Praises for God-created Differences

Sing "He's Got the Whole World in His Hands" making up new verses about differences in people. For example, sing:

He's got the people with black or white skin in his hands.
He's got the people with yellow skin in his hands.
He's got the people with red or brown skin in his hands.
He's got the whole world in his hands.

Have the group invent other verses about eye color or other differences the children have identified. Then sing "Jesus Loves the Little Children," "Praise Him, All Ye Little Children," and other praise songs.

Confession and Forgiveness

Point out that as much as we enjoy all of the differences in people, we sometimes use those differences in hurtful instead of loving ways. When we do, we need to say, "I'm sorry." Draw figures on the magic slate as you offer the following prayer.

(fold hands in lap, holding slate) God, you made us each different. Most of the time we enjoy those differences, but not always. Sometimes we say, "His eyes are not like mine. I don't like him! *(Draw angry looking eyes on the slate.)* Or we say, "Her hair curls funny. I don't like her!" *(Add frazzled hair to figure.)*

Sometimes we meet someone who has different clothes, and we say, "I don't want to play with that weird looking person!" *(Draw a shirt with one long sleeve and one short sleeve and a slanted hem.)*

When we eat at a friend's house and are offered strange food, we say, "I won't eat that. It's different."

"We are sorry, God. Help us to be kind and good to all people and to enjoy our differences. *(Sing "Forgive Me, God, for Things I Do.")*

When we say, "I'm sorry," God promises to say, "That is all right." God promises to erase the wrong *(erase *the slate)* so that we can start over again. We can say a happy hello to *(draw happy looking eyes)*. We can learn about new hair *(draw curly hair with a ribbon in it)*. We can play with people who wear different clothes *(redraw the odd shirt)*. And we can try out some new foods. We may even like some of them! *(draw a big smile on the face)*.

In response sing "Jesus Loves the Little Children."

Learning About Some People Who Are Different

Introduce your guest, who will talk briefly about the people of his or her native culture or a country that the guest has toured. Encourage the children to ask questions. Keep attention focused on the people of the country the guest talks about and the ways they are different from your children. Also keep the tone of the discussion positive so that the people described sound like interesting folks who would be fun to have as friends.

Weaving Project

Show the children how to weave a strip of paper under and over the base paper. This will be a challenging project. Do not insist on uniform weaving; a child may choose to skip some slots or change direction. If they are pleased with the effect, share their pleasure.

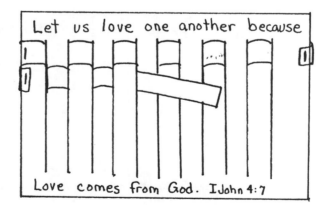

Closing

Review some of the differences you have explored today. Then point out that in spite of all those differences, we can all be friends because God is our Father. Sing through or play on your tape recorder one verse of "Blest Be the Tie That Binds." Pass the end of a long piece of yarn to the child on one side of you. Ask that child to pass the end to the next child but to keep holding on to the yarn and let it slide through his or her fingers. Continue the process until the end of the yarn has gone all the way around the circle and back to you with all of the children holding on to it. As you tie the end to the other end of the yarn in your lap, explain that the yarn is like the tie in the song. The song says that God's love ties us all together just like we are held together by the yarn. Stand up and keep holding on to the yarn. Dance to the hymn following the directions on page 155.

After dancing through several verses, sit down and lay the yarn ring on the floor in front of you. If your children know the Lord's Prayer, point out that the Lord's Prayer belongs to all of God's family. It does not say "*My* Father, who art in heaven." It says, "*Our* Father, who art in heaven." Invite the children to pray it together, remembering that lots of other people who look and eat and dress differently than we do pray this same prayer.

Close by charging each child with a specific charge related to valuing differences in people—for example, say, "Sara, love all people this week"; "Sam, smile at all kinds of eyes this week." Conclude by saying, "And remember, God loves each one of us with all our differences, and God takes care of us always."

Session 50: God, I'm Going Back to School

Worship Focus: God will be with us as we go back to school.

Going back to school is an intense time for children. There is the prospect of starting new classes, meeting new friends, and having new things to do. As they get ready to go back to school, most children will get at least one or two pieces of new clothing and some school supplies. The new things add to the excitement.

With the anticipation there is usually some concern about the unknown or what was unpleasant last year. This session is an opportunity to raise both the anticipation and the fears to God in worship. In doing so, we remind the children that God is interested in whatever interests or concerns them. We also remind them that God will be with them at school.

Time	*Worship Activity*	*Materials/Resources*
8 min.	1. Conversation about getting ready for school Praise litany	
7 min.	2. Singing praise songs	
5 min.	3. "Getting Ready" story Create petition prayer	
20 min.	4. Make "God Is with Me" reminder	wooden disks sandpaper thick paint, sponges prepared stencils paint aprons clean-up supplies
5 min.	5. Closing story and benediction	sample disk

Getting Ready

Making the "God Is with Me" reminder requires one disk of wood approximately 2" in diameter and ¼" thick for each child. Such disks may be cut from dowels using an electrical saw. If a member of your congregation works with wood, enlist that person's help to cut the wooden disks and with the project on Sunday, or you may get them from a lumberyard or hardware store.

In addition to the disks, you will need a piece of sandpaper for each child, pre-cut stencils from the patterns at the back of the book, shallow dishes of thick tempera paint, and pieces of sponge with which to dab the paint onto stencil covered disks.

Set up one or two stencil tables with an adult at each table. Prepare one stencil for every three children. Tape the stencils to the table on one side to form a hinge. Position each disk under the stencil, then secure the stencil with tape on the side opposite the hinge. After the disk has been painted, lift one piece of tape, remove that disk, position the next one, and tape the stencil in place again. If the stencil sheets are just a little larger than the disks, they keep the disk from sliding.

Have paint aprons handy. Enlist some extra hands for this project.

Getting Started

As you walk to your room, talk about the coming school year. Once you have set aside your belongings and have gathered on the rug, continue the conversation. Find out which school each child will attend. Talk about preparations for school by asking for a show of hands to such questions as: "Who has bought something new to wear to school?"; "Who has bought pencils?" (and other kinds of school supplies); "How will you get to school—on a bus, in a car, walk?

Use what the children have said to produce a "thank you" litany that reflects their excitement. The adult leader makes statements to which the children and the other leader respond, "Thank you, God, for a new year at school." Use the following suggestions as a starter: (1) Thank God for the summer, noting some of the things you know your children have done and enjoyed. (2) Tell God that the children will be going to school. Name the schools and the children who will attend each one. (3) Tell God about the excitement of getting new clothes, and thank God for all the colors and textures of different kinds of clothing. (4) Tell God about the school supplies the children are buying, and thank God for new things to learn. Focus your statements on praise and thanksgiving.

Singing Praises

Keeping alive the mood of the praise litany, sing the doxology and note that one of the "blessings" that flow to us is the blessing of going back to school. Then sing several favorite praise songs, such as "Praise Ye the Lord, Alleluia!"

"Getting Ready": A Story and a Prayer

Tell the following story. If you have a boy hand puppet, let the puppet be Ricky and tell the story.

Getting Ready

Tomorrow will be the first day of school. My name is Ricky. I am going to be in the first grade. And I can hardly wait. Kim and Kerry, my big sisters, are excited, too.

This morning, Mother and I went to my school to register and to meet my teacher, Ms. Chunn. We had to stand in a long line. Mother filled out forms. Then we went to my room. It is a big room with a tank of fish in the corner. I saw my name on my desk.

When we got home for lunch, a box from Uncle Earl was in the mail. He sent Kim, Kerry, and me each a book bag to use at school. Mine is green.

After lunch, we all went to the store to buy new shoes and sweaters and paper and pencils.

We had hamburgers for dinner. When we finished, Dad brought out the Bible. "Tonight," he said, "is a good night to think about Moses." He told us how God asked Moses to do something very exciting and very hard. God wanted Moses to lead his people away from a mean king in Egypt. Moses was excited because he knew the people needed to get away from the king. But he was a little frightened, too. It was going to be hard work, and he was going to have to do new things. He told God about his fears. God promised Moses that he would never be alone. God was going to be with him always. God promised to help him know what to say when he met the wicked king. God even sent Aaron along to be Moses' friend and helper.

Dad said we were starting something new just like Moses was. Dad said that he knew we were all excited about our new clothes and our book bags from Uncle Earl and our new classes. But he also knew that school was going to be hard work and that we were going to need God's help just like Moses did. So the whole family made a "back to school prayer" together. Kerry prayed that the work in fifth grade would not be too hard. Kim asked God to help her find friends in her new class and to help her be a good friend to everyone. And I prayed that Ms. Chunn would be a good teacher and that school would be fun. Dad thanked God for being with each one of us always wherever we are, and he asked God to help us have a good year at school and a good year in our family.

Create your own "back to school" prayer together by thinking of what is needed for a good school year. Work with the children to shape their concerns into prayer requests. While one leader works with the children, the other writes down the prayers created. When the prayer is complete, bow your heads and allow a moment of silence for the children to get ready. One adult leader then prays the prayers aloud on behalf of the group. Close by praying the Lord's Prayer together.

Make a "God Is with Me" Reminder

To make a reminder that can be carried to school in a pocket, give each child a wooden disk and a piece of sandpaper to sand the edges.

The next stop is the stencil table, where the children will place their disks under the prepared stencil and paint in the stencil with a small piece of sponge dipped in thick tempera paint. To avoid smears, have an adult handy to remove the stencil. Set each disk aside to dry on a paper towel with the child's name on it.

One adult needs to be ready to gather the children as they finish. Sing or play a quiet game on the rug while the others complete their work.

Closing

Show the children a completed "God Is with Me" reminder disk, then use it to tell this story.

God Is with Latoya at School

Latoya bounced out of bed. Her school clothes were waiting for her on the chair. She got dressed. The last thing she did was pick up her reminder. It was smooth between her fingers (rub your disk between your fingers and slide it into a pocket or hide it in your lap). She put it in her pocket and prayed, "God be with me at school today."

Larry walked with her to school. He had promised to help her find her room. There were lots of people! When Larry stopped to talk to his fifth grade friends, she lost him. She looked up the hall (shade your eyes and look one way) and down the hall (look the other way), but she could not see Larry. Trying to feel brave, Latoya put her hand in her pocket. There was the disk. As her fingers closed over it, she remembered that God is with her. That did make her feel safer and braver. Suddenly, she heard Larry calling her name.

They finally found her room. Latoya's teacher had a big friendly smile and showed Latoya a desk with her name on it. No more sitting at tables this year—she had a desk of her own! (Pantomime sitting up straight at a desk and running your hands across its top) "Thank you, God, for a desk with my name on it."

All morning she got new things to put into her desk. There were two big pencils, a book about a turtle, and a picture that she drew. At lunch, Latoya was hungry. As she sat down to eat, she remembered to say, "Thank you, God, for food to eat, and thank you for being with me at school" (fold hands in your lap as you pray).

After lunch, she got a book with lots of numbers in it. Everyone was counting things (look concerned and count on your fingers). And everyone could count faster and higher than she could. Numbers were hard. "God, help me with numbers," she prayed, and she tried again.

That night when she got ready for bed, her "God Is with Me" reminder fell out of her pocket. Latoya picked it up and rubbed the smooth side on her face (pick up your disk and rub it on your cheek). "Thank you, God, for being with me at school today. Be with me every day." And then she went to bed.

Point out that just as God was with Latoya, God will be with the children as they go to school. Urge them to carry their reminders in their pockets or put them in their desks at school to help them remember.

For the benediction, all stand in a circle. Ask the children to do what you do and repeat what you say.

(raise arms over heads) God, be with us.
Keep us growing stronger this year.
(place hands on head) God, be with us.
Help us learn new things.
(hold hands with neighbor) God, be with us.
Help us find new friends and be good friends.
(fold hands) God, be with us.
And bring us back together next week. Amen.

Session 51: Celebrating God's Power on Halloween

Worship Focus: No person, no thing, and no force anywhere is as powerful as God.

The celebration of Halloween, or All Hallow's Eve, began in the Middle Ages, when people were keenly aware of the vastness of the universe and their vulnerability in it. At that time people generally believed that demons and all sorts of spirits roamed the world interfering in personal affairs. On Halloween, people confronted these evil powers by gathering at night to light huge bonfires to scare off the demons and thus prepare for All Saint's Day, which followed. On All Saint's Day, they celebrated the good powers that were at work in the world.

For children today, Halloween is a time to dress up in costumes and enjoy parties or trick-or-treating. At some point between the ages of five and seven, the focus shifts to dealing with frightening powers. Especially among the boys, super hero and monster costumes become the favorites. Haunted houses become a frightening delight, and horror stories are popular. Just like their medieval counterparts, the children try to conquer fear by taming it.

In this worship service, the children are invited to think about powers. We will begin by identifying and celebrating the children's own powers. Then we will let them name some of the real and imaginary powers in their world. This is an opportunity to compare God's loving power to the powers that confront the children in cartoon stories ("Masters of the Universe" or whatever is currently popular), the ghosts and spirits in "haunted" houses, and the "monsters" in their bedroom closets at night. Sorting out which powers are real and which are imaginary is difficult at this age. What is important is for the children to know that God is stronger than any power, real or imagined. Comparing the good or evil qualities of the various powers is also beyond the mental abilities of kindergarten children. For now, they simply need to know that God is the most powerful of all.

Time	Worship Activity	Materials/Resources
7 min.	1. Conversation about children's powers	3 weights to lift
3 min.	2. Praise and confession about our powers	
15 min.	3. Power building centers	materials for selected centers
5 min.	4. Singing about God's power	
20 min.	5. Making masks	prepared grocery bag mask forms construction paper glue or paste crayons
10 min.	6. Closing: Nothing separates us from God's love	Bible

Getting Ready

1. Find several items the children can lift—one very light, one heavy but liftable, and one that no child will be able to lift.

2. Set up several power-building centers. (1) *Tower Power*. On the wall beside a pile of blocks, mount a strip of paper on which the children can mark the height of the towers they build as they work together to build the tallest towers. (2) *Bobbing Power*. Tie one end of a length of thread snugly around a slice of apple. Tie the other end to a yardstick or tack it onto the top of a doorway so that the apple slice is at a child's mouth level. The children's challenge is to eat the apple slice on the thread while holding their hands behind their backs. Plan for several children to try eating an apple slice at the same time. (3) *Music Power*. Invite a musician to teach the children a short, VERY simple tune on an instrument. (4) *Puzzle Power*. Bring "new" puzzles from home or make puzzles by gluing magazine pictures onto cardboard, then cut them into pieces following the shapes in the pictures. (5) Offer any challenging but attainable activity for which you have the materials and leadership. You will need one activity for every five children. Each center will require one youth or adult leader. It would be wise for at least one of the regular leaders to oversee the activity of the whole room.

3. Gather enough plain brown grocery sacks to make a mask for each child. Before class cut two eye holes in each bag in the appropriate places and, if your bags need it, shoulder spaces at the sides.

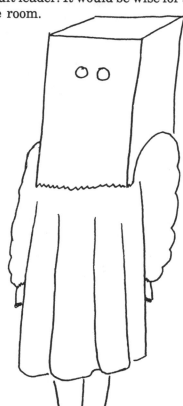

To turn the bags into masks, the children will need construction paper scraps that can be torn and glue sticks or paste with which to mount the paper scraps on the bag masks. Some children will want to use crayons as well.

On small cards, print, "I know that nothing in the world is powerful enough to stop God from loving and taking care of us" (see Romans 8:38*a*). Staple a card to the lower edge of each child's mask to give parents an idea about why their children made monster masks as part of a worship time.

Getting Started

As one leader meets the children and sets aside their belongings, the other leader gathers the children on the rug for conversation and experiments about their powers. Begin with experiments about physical powers. (Be careful not to let this become a competition.) Take turns trying to lift your light and heavy objects. Next try jumping to touch a high object (the object may be a leader's hand held at different levels). Turn attention to mental powers by asking simple questions that the children can answer—the days of the week, facts about today's weather, and what is going on during this season. Introduce the power to make people happy and help the children to tell you about some of the ways they can make people happy. Throughout the above conversation, comment about how powerful the children are.

Praise and Confession About Our Powers

Invite the children to join you in praising God for these powers by repeating your motions and words.

(all stand up tall)
Thank you, God, for bodies that are strong. *(flex arm)*
Thank you for bodies that are growing so that we can reach higher, *(stand tall and reach up on toes)*
and run faster. *(run in place)*
Thank you for fingers *(hold up hands, wiggling fingers)*
that can hold crayons and pencils and paintbrushes *(mime drawing)*
and can learn to tie shoelaces. *(mime tying laces)*
Thank you for a mind *(point to head)*
that can learn about your world. *(sweep arms)*
(sit down with hands in lap)
You made us so powerful, God.
But we do not always use our powers.
Sometimes we say, "I can't do that," *(turn palms up and out in resignation)*
When what we really mean is "I don't want to do that." *(fold hands across chest)*
Sometimes we are afraid *(worried look on face)*
to try something new.
Sometimes we will not even try to learn how to do something new. *(fold arms across chest and shake head "no")*
And sometimes when we could help, *(hands palms out to help)*
We do not. *(hide hands behind back)*
We are sorry, God. *(fold hands in your lap)*
Help us to use all of our powers.
Help us to be powerful people who love others.
Amen.
(pause before continuing)
When we say we are sorry,
God promises to forgive us.
God promises to say, "That's all right."
God helps us to be stronger, *(flex arm)*
and grow taller, *(sit up very tall)*
and learn powerful new things, *(point to head)*
and make other people even happier. *(smile broadly and shake hands with neighbor)*

Working in Power-building Centers

Explain that one way we grow more powerful is by using our powers. Then invite the children to try out some of the power builders around the room. If you have guests, introduce them and what they will be doing.

At the appropriate time, warn the children and the leaders that in two minutes the group will gather again on the rug. This allows time to finish working and to put equipment aside.

Singing About God's Power

As the children gather on the rug, talk briefly with them about which tasks were easier or harder and which they enjoyed trying to do most. Then turn their attention from their powers to God's powers. Sing songs that describe God's power, including the doxology and "He's Got the Whole World in His Hands." Point out God's powers as you sing.

Making Masks

Ask the children to tell who is the strongest, most powerful in the whole world. Listen to their answers and be ready to explore all possibilities with them. The final answer is, of course, God. But unless that is the immediate and unquestioned response from the children, take time to compare God's power to those of cartoon super heroes, people the children have personally met, and any other person or thing mentioned.

Since it is Halloween, invite the children to make paper bag masks of powerful things or people. These can be specific things or people they know, or they can be invented monsters and powerful creatures. Using a child as a model, show the children how the prepared mask forms fit. Invite them to tear construction paper into ears, hair, mouths, teeth, fangs, helmets, and the like to glue onto their bags to make powerful masks.

As the first children finish their masks, one leader gathers with them on the rug. Have them set their masks on the floor in front of them while you play a quiet game, such as "Simon Says," together until the others finish and join you.

Closing: God Is More Powerful!

Ask the children one at a time to put on their masks and briefly tell or show the group who you are.

When everyone has had a turn, open the Bible from your worship center to Romans 8. "Read" the following version of Romans 8:38*a*: "I know that nothing in the world is powerful enough to stop God from loving and taking care of us." Explain that all the creatures they have talked about and created have special powers, but none of them is as powerful as God. Create an informal litany prayer about this by inviting the children to say something that one "hero" or monster can do. As a group, respond to each one by saying, "God, you are stronger!" Close with:

> God, you *are* stronger. It is good to know that nothing and no person in the world is strong enough to keep you from loving us and taking care of us. Thank you for keeping us safe. In Jesus' name, amen.

Sing songs about God's power, beginning with "Jesus Loves Me" and a comment about how wonderful it is that the most powerful One in the world loves each one of us.

Session 52: You Are Growing Up
(Last Sunday of the Year)

Worship Focus: Let's celebrate our growth. We are old enough to be in worship every Sunday for the whole service!

This final session of the year is a time to celebrate what has been done and learned during the past year and to anticipate the children's move into the sanctuary as full-time participants in the congregation's worship.

This session also provides some practical preparation for the move into the sanctuary. For one thing, the children need to know before they arrive at church next Sunday that they will spend all of the worship hour in the sanctuary. That change will be presented as an exciting milestone. The children will also put together a kit of items that will help them participate in worship during the coming weeks. The session also includes a letter to parents to prepare them for this new stage in their children's worship lives.

Time	Worship Activity	Materials/Resources
3 min.	1. Look at pictures from early in the year to discuss growth	photos from year name necklaces
5 min.	2. Sing songs you have learned this year	big song books
4 min.	3. Creating a psalm about growing	
3 min.	4. Confessing prayer	
5 min.	5. "Children Grow As Worshipers": story	
20 min.	6. Making a worship tool kit	prepared envelope bookmark forms pre-cut yarn tiny pictures and/or stickers offering envelopes
5 min.	7. Closing	

Getting Ready

1. Dig out all of the photographs you have made of the children during the year. Look especially for ones from early in the year that will show how the children have grown or changed.

2. Gather all of the big song books and charts that you have made during the year.

3. Prepare a sturdy envelope for each child to use as a worship kit. For simplicity, choose a sandwich-sized ziplock bag, or ask someone to design a print on the front of a 6″ × 8″ manila envelope.

4. From colored poster board, cut bookmarks 1½″ × 6″. If you plan for the children to add yarn ties, punch a hole in the center of one end with a hole punch. Add the number of Bible readings in your worship to the number of hymns and multiply by the number of children to find out how many bookmarks to make.

For the Bible bookmarks, gather stickers or familiar Bible characters or small pictures of Bible stories cut from old Sunday school books, glue or paste, and gold yarn (metallic is especially great) cut into 4″ lengths for tassels.

For the hymn bookmarks, gather stickers or small pictures of singers or musical figures (your choir director might be a good source for these), glue or paste, and a second color of yarn cut into 4″ lengths.

5. If your church provides the children with offering envelopes for their worship offering, get a set for each of the children.

6. Most important of all, prepare a letter to mail to parents. Use the one at the end of this session as a starter. You will have to tailor it to fit your situation. The goals of the letter are to tell parents that their children will be with them for the entire worship service starting on a specific date and to give them some ideas of how to help their children enter into worship.

194

Enlist the help of the church secretary or a parent to copy and mail this. Check the mailing list carefully to be sure that parents of all the children get a letter.

Getting Started

As you walk to your room, start conversations about what the children have been doing during the week. Hear stories about school and family. Listen to hear what is on their minds today. Once you have gotten your belongings settled and gathered on the rug, show the children pictures you took of them at the beginning of the year. Note all the ways they have grown or changed (haircuts, glasses, and so on). If you have the name necklaces you used in the fall, get them out. Talk about how well you know one another now after needing name necklaces to remember names last fall.

Singing Our Songs

Bring out all of your song books. Sing through all of the songs you learned this year. Include some of the Christmas and Easter songs and group favorites. Compliment the children on how well they sing and how well they know these important worship songs.

Creating a Psalm About Growing

The poets who wrote the psalms in the Old Testament did not rhyme sounds in each line. They rhymed ideas. Rhyme ideas to create a psalm with the children. Give them a general line and help them to state similar lines. For example, you say, "God, we are growing!" The children add such lines as, "We are taller now than we were last year"; "We need new shoes and clothes!"; and "We can run faster and jump higher."

Use the following lines (or similar ones) to create a psalm about growth. Have one adult leader write it down as the other works with the children to create it.

> God, we are growing in so many ways!
> God, we know new songs to sing for you!
> God, we are learning about your church!

When it is complete, line your psalm out, concluding, "Thank you, God, for growing. Alleluia! Amen."

Confessing

As you finish the psalm, go straight into the following prayer of confession and indicate to the children that they are to do what you do.

> It feels great to grow, God (*sit up very straight*). It is good to be able to reach high things (*stretch arms over your head*). It makes us feel strong (*flex muscles*) and happy (*smile*).
> But we do not always use our strong bodies well, God. Sometimes we use them (*flex muscles again and look threatening*) to make others do what we want them to do (*pause and look sad*). Sometimes we stretch out (*stretch arms out*) to take things that are not ours (*pause sadly again*).
> We do not feel so big then, God (*turn palms up in gesture of resignation*). We feel small (*hunch down*) and mean (*frown sadly*).
> We are sorry, God (*fold hands in your lap*). Amen.

Sing "Forgive Me, God, for Things I Do." Conclude by saying the words and doing the motions to the "As High as the Sky" promise of forgiveness (page 202).

Children Grow in Our Church Story

To describe the way most children in your congregation grow as worshipers, select the appropriate paragraphs below and edit as needed.

When a baby is born in our church, there is a rose up front on the very next Sunday. We all ask God to keep the baby safe and strong. The baby is one of God's people, but the baby does not know it.

When a baby is still very tiny, some parents bring the baby to church to be baptized. We put water on the baby's head and ask God to help the baby to grow up strong and kind and good. We promise to teach the baby about God and about Jesus. The baby just watches or cries or laughs. The baby is one of God's people, but does not know anything about what is happening.

Soon the parents bring the baby to the nursery. *(Name the nursery workers if they are known by name to your children)* ———— love them and play with them and take care of them. Even in the nursery, the baby is one of God's people.

When the baby gets older, it is time for Sunday school. In the two-year-old class and the three-year-old class and the four-year-old class, the children learn about God and Jesus. Every once in a while they visit the big church just to see what it looks like, but they do not go during worship. They are part of God's people, but they are too young to be in worship.

Now, when the children get to be five years old, they know a lot. They are almost ready to go to worship in the sanctuary. They come to _____ *(fill in the name of your group)* to learn about what we do in worship and to worship God. They learn songs, and they pray prayers. They go to parts of the worship service. They are not quite old enough to stay for the whole time, but they are still part of God's people.

Finally the day comes when they are old enough. They are ready to worship with God's people. Next Sunday, you will be old enough. You will begin going to worship every Sunday. You will pray the Lord's Prayer and sing the doxology and put money in the offering plate and listen to the Bible. You will be one of God's people who can sing and pray with the whole church. You are not a baby who does not know what to do.

Talk briefly about what will happen when they go to church with their families next week.

Making a Worship Tool Kit

To help the children participate in the full worship service, make a small kit of worship tools that they can carry to worship for a while. Give each child a prepared envelope or ziplock bag. Then add the tools and explain the use of each one before making it.

Tool one. Show the children a Bible like the ones they will find in the pews in the sanctuary. Point out that the Bible is read every Sunday in worship. Tell how many lessons your congregation generally reads. Give each child that number of bookmark forms.

The children then select several pre-cut pictures or stickers of familiar Bible stories to glue on their bookmarks. Warn them to keep the holes at the bottom of the bookmarks open. When the pictures are in place, give each child 4″ of yarn to tie through each hole. Put the finished bookmarks in the envelopes.

Gather the fast workers on the rug to try out the bookmarks. Let the children point to one of several marks you have placed to mark familiar stories in the worship center Bible. Open the Bible to the selected mark and read the verses. Let the children enjoy their recognition of the stories or verses.

Tool two. When all have finished their Bible bookmarks, show the children a hymnbook. Point out the way the songs in it are numbered. Using a bulletin, find the number of the hymn that was sung while the children were in worship today. Let children select one sticker to decorate each of the hymn bookmarks. If you have time, give each child yarn of another color to tie through the holes in these bookmarks. Provide as many bookmarks as the number of hymns generally sung. Add these bookmarks to each kit.

Tool three. If your congregation uses envelopes for offerings, provide a box of envelopes for each child. Talk about their use and store them in the kit.

Tool four. If your congregation uses prayer request cards, show one to the children and explain its use. Suggest that the children draw their prayer requests on the cards.

Tool five. Show them today's bulletin. Talk about how it is used. Assure the children that their parents are getting a letter that will tell them how to help the children use this tool kit.

Closing

Sing one or two of your favorite songs. Stand in a circle. One leader says a brief prayer to thank God for friends who can worship God together.

One teacher should be near the door to be sure that all parents have received the letter and to remind them that this is the last week of kindergarten worship for their children. Have extra letters on hand for those who have been missed.

(put this letter on your church's stationery)

Dear ___ :

After a year of learning about worship, attending parts of the worship service, and worshiping with other children, it is time for your child to become a full-time participant in congregational worship. (Date) will be the last Sunday of (name of your group) for this group. On (date) they will be welcomed in the sanctuary. (Describe any public recognition to be given the children.)

As your child joins you full time, there are a few simple things you can do to help him or her participate more fully.

(1) Sit where your child can see.

(2) The children have learned the Lord's Prayer and the doxology. Help your child to recognize them and join in praying and singing them in the sanctuary.

(3) Your child will make (or has made) a kit of bookmarks to use in worship. Before worship begins, help your child to find and to mark the Bible readings and hymns for the day. The hymns are easier for the children to find because they can be located by their numbers. Until your child reads well, you will have to help more with the Bible bookmarks. Turn the bookmarks sideways and use them during the scripture readings and hymns to follow the reading and singing. Even before they can read every word, children get a feeling of participation by following along.

(4) Be sure your child has money to add to the offering plate as it is passed. (If your congregation has envelopes for the children to use, explain the plan.)

(5) The sermon will be the last part of the service your child fully appreciates. Help your child to learn to listen is to give them pencil, paper, and a task to do while listening. Suggest that your child draw something based on a hymn you sang, the scripture reading, or something else that has happened during worship. Discuss the work on the way home.

We are glad your child has been part of (name of your group) this year and hope that it will prove to be a beneficial first step toward worshiping with God's people.

Sincerely,

AN AFTERWORD

The last session was a celebration for you as well as for the children. I hope you caught at least a hint of what the children have gained from your work and love. As you think back over the year, evaluate:

* songs and prayers the children learned;
* the movements of worship they explored;
* patterns in your congregation's worship that they will recognize as they worship in the sanctuary; and
* worship experiences that you shared.

Each part of the experience is valuable. I hope that the experience has been a rich one for you and for your children.

Finally, I urge you to keep in touch with these children. You are all part of God's family. You belong to one another. So speak to them in the sanctuary and when you see them around church. Watch their continued growth as worshipers as they sing in choirs, become acolytes, share in the sacraments, and are confirmed into membership. Continue to love and pray for them and to enjoy their love.

WORSHIP RESOURCES

The songs and prayers on the following pages are used and are not readily available in hymnbooks and in children's church music books.

READINGS AND PRAYERS

Practice reading this aloud with great drama. Shout when it says shout. When it talks about being too excited to sit still, wriggle and put some excitement into your voice. Add whatever vocal inflections and motions are appropriate to create the feeling of praise.

*What Is Praise Like?**

Praise is being so excited about something that you can't sit still or keep quiet!
It is shouting, "Hip, hip hooray!"
It is saying softly, "That makes me feel good."
It is taking off your shoes, feeling sand and mud,
   water and moss on your toes and feet.
It is running in quick circles like a foal, or sniffing
   every smell in the air like a hound.

Praise is being with lots of other people who want to do and say the same thing!
It is singing together, "For he's a jolly good fellow."
It is crowding up to the curbing to see the parade.
It is waving flags and flying balloons.
It is hearing the organ get louder and louder,
   and feeling a tingling in your ribs.
It is everyone shouting after a home run hit in the
   ball game.

Praise is being all by yourself and knowing wonderful things.
It is feeling cooling raindrops on a hot, hot day.
It is feeling warm and safe in bed.
It is making up your own song to sing and dancing your
   very own dance.
It is walking along a fence or wall and not falling off.

Praise is feeling very good about yourself, and believing that God feels good about you, too.
It is saying, "Give us this day our daily bread,"
   knowing there will be bread to eat, and saying,
   "Thank you, God!"
It is hearing someone say, "I don't like what you did,
   but I still love you," and saying "Thank you, God!"
It is going to church and knowing, "This is the day the

---

* From *All Our Days Laugh and Praise* by Morris D. Pike, copyright 1974 by Friendship Press, New York. Used by permission.

Lord has made," and rejoicing and feeling glad.
It is saying, "Let me tell you . . . " and having someone
    really listen. Then you can say, "That's good!
Thank you!"

Praise is the glad, happy feeling that comes from knowing and believing God feels good about all these things!

AS HIGH AS THE SKY

(A Promise of God's Forgiveness)

As the heaven is high above the earth,
  (stretch arms high over head pointing to sky)
so great is God's mercy!
  (turn palms upward as if releasing something that will float up and away)
As far as the east,
  (point one direction)
is from the west,
  (point the other direction)
so far has God removed our transgressions from us!
  (turn palms out as if pushing back a wall on each side)

A PSALM OF THANKSGIVING*

LEADER:

1. O give thanks unto the Lord, for God is good.

2. O give thanks unto the God of gods.

3. O give thanks unto the Lord of lords.

4. To our God who does great things.

5. To our God who made the heavens.

6. To our God who made the earth and seas.

7. To our God who feeds every living thing.

8. O give thanks unto the God of heaven.

CHILDREN'S RESPONSE:

For God's love will last for - e - ver!

* By Lynette Johnson. Used by permission.

FORGIVE ME, GOD, FOR THINGS I DO

ST. FLAVIAN

JOHN DAY'S *PSALTER*

1. For-give me, God, for things I do That are not kind and good,
2. When some-one is un-kind to me Then help me, God, to see

For-give me, God, and help me try To do the things I should.
How I can keep on lov-ing him · As you keep lov-ing me.

Stanza 1, Elizabeth McE. Shields
Stanza 2, Beverly Schultz Mullins

LORD'S PRAYER

West Indies

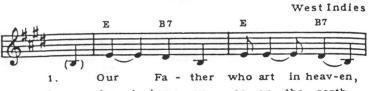

1. Our Fa-ther who art in heav-en,
2. As in heav-en, so on the earth;
3. And for-give us Fa-ther all our debts;
4. And lead us not in-to temp-ta - tion;
5. For Thine is the King-dom, pow-er and glo-ry;
6. A - men, a-men, it shall be so;

Hal - low - ed be Thy name;

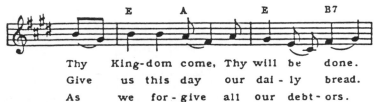

Thy King-dom come, Thy will be done.
Give us this day our dai-ly bread.
As we for-give all our debt-ors.
But de-li-ver us from all e-vil.
For - ev-er and for-ev-er and ev-er.
A - men, a-men it shall be so.

Hal - low - ed be Thy name.

KUM BA YAH

African (Angola)

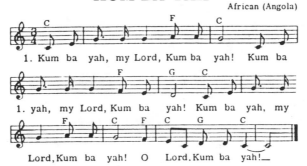

1. Kum ba yah, my Lord, Kum ba yah! Kum ba
1. yah, my Lord, Kum ba yah! Kum ba yah, my
Lord, Kum ba yah! O Lord, Kum ba yah!

2. Someone's crying, Lord...
3. Someone's singing, Lord...
4. Someone's praying, Lord...

CHORUS	MOTIONS
Kum Ba Yah	*Rotate hands around each other On Yah turn both hands out, plams up in acceptance*
My	*With first finger point up*
Lord	*Draw one hand diagonally across your body from a shoulder to opposite hip*
(Repeat three times)	
O	*form "O" with first finger and thumb of one hand*
Lord	*Same as above*

VERSES

1. Someone's crying . . .	*Trace tears on face with fingers*
2. Someone's praying . . .	*Fold hands in prayer*
3. Someone's laughing . . .	*Throw hands out to the side, palms out, and smile*

WE ARE THE CHURCH

RICHARD AVERY
DONALD MARSH

Dedicated to Ethel Davis

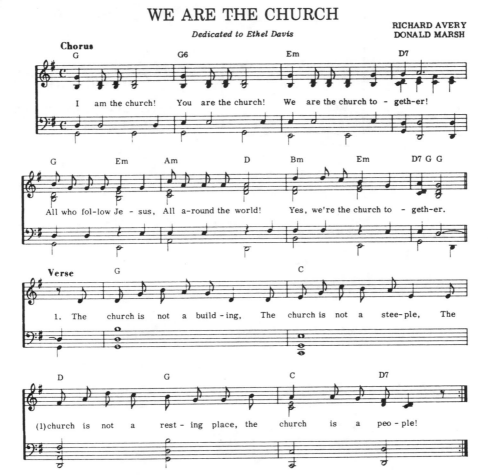

Chorus

I am the church! You are the church! We are the church to - geth-er!

All who fol-low Je - sus, All a-round the world! Yes, we're the church to - geth-er.

Verse

1. The church is not a build-ing, The church is not a stee-ple, The

(1)church is not a rest-ing place, the church is a peo-ple!

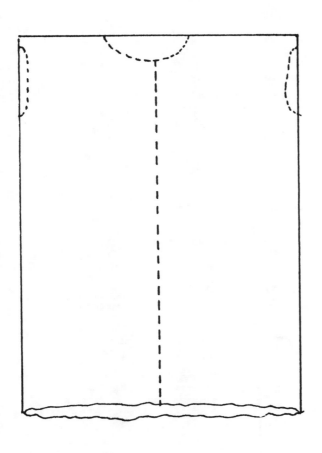

Plastic Bag Painting Aprons

1. Cut a shallow neck hole in the sealed bottom of a large kitchen garbage bag.

2. Cut shallow long holes in the sides of the bag at the neck hole end.

3. Cut a slit in one side from the neck hole to the end of the bag.

These aprons are worn with the slit down the children's back. You can tape them closed with masking tape.

The aprons can be dried off with a paper towel after small spills or discarded after major spills.

GOD

cut heavy circles of
separate piece to
mount on top of
petals or rays piece

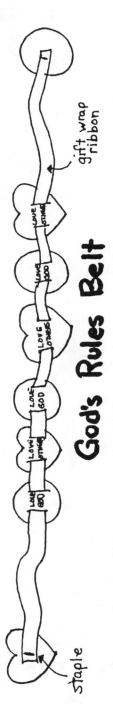

God's Rules Belt

1. Copy this page on stiff colored paper for each child.
2. Cut out circles and hearts. (Try cutting circles with pinking shears.)
3. Cut 2 slashes in each figure as shown.

gift wrap ribbon

staple

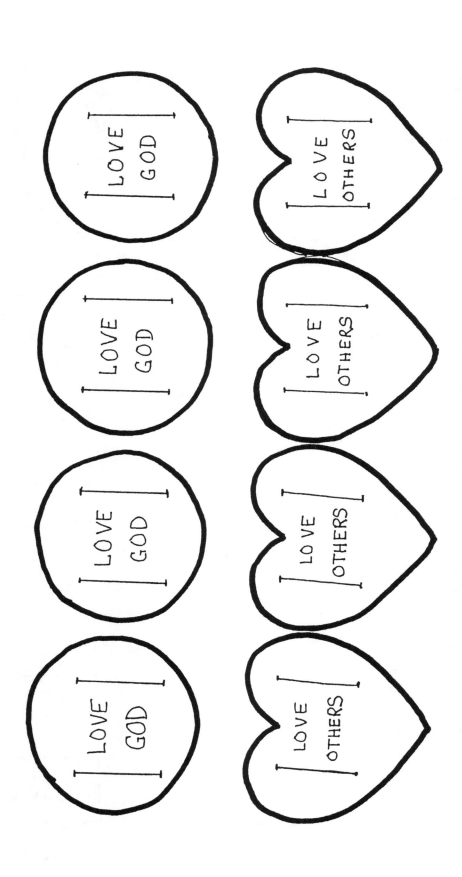

[LOVE GOD]

[LOVE GOD]

[LOVE GOD]

[LOVE GOD]

[LOVE OTHERS]

[LOVE OTHERS]

[LOVE OTHERS]

[LOVE OTHERS]

To prepare finger puppets

1. copy this page onto stiff beige paper
2. cut along heavy lines (curved fingernail scissors are great for cutting the finger holes)

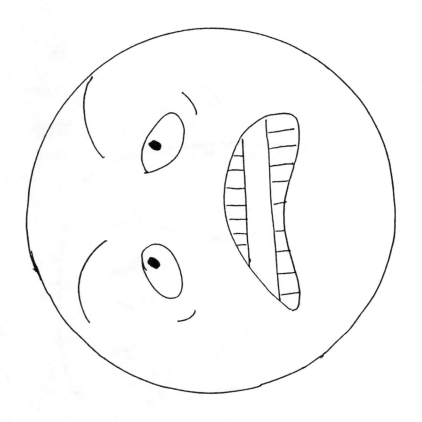

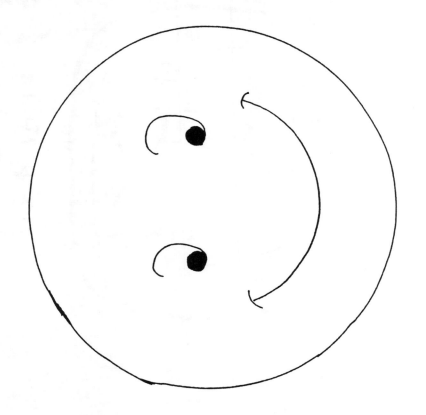

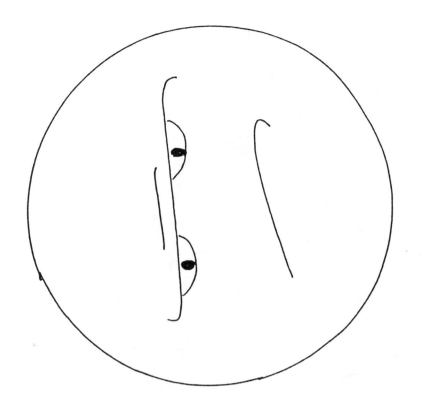

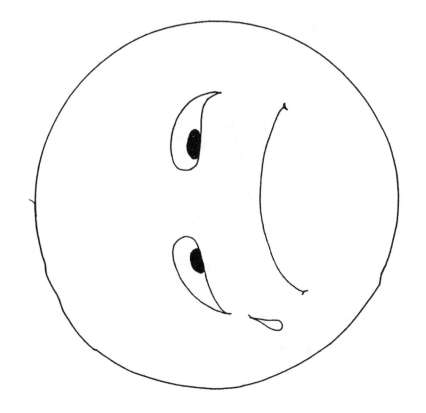

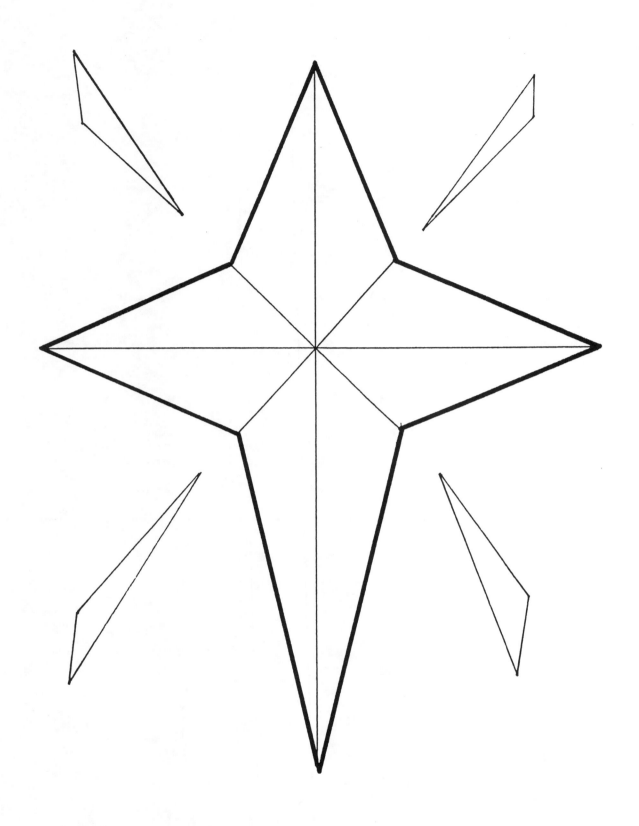

Epiphany Star

Easter Flowers

1. Copy this page of patterns onto stiff paper.
2. Use circles to cut flower centers from gold construction paper.
3. Cut petal patterns into colored tissue paper petals.

(I gave you several patterns so you can enlist helpers!)

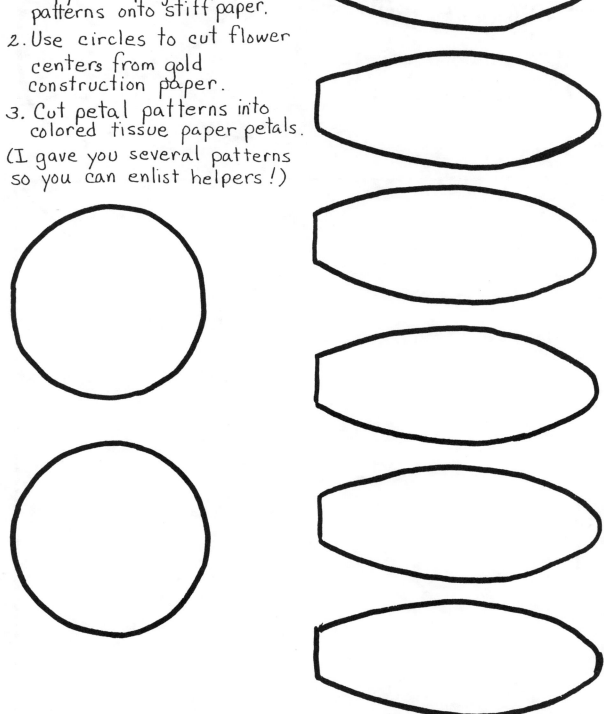

Pentecost
Flame Patterns
and
Pinwheel Forms

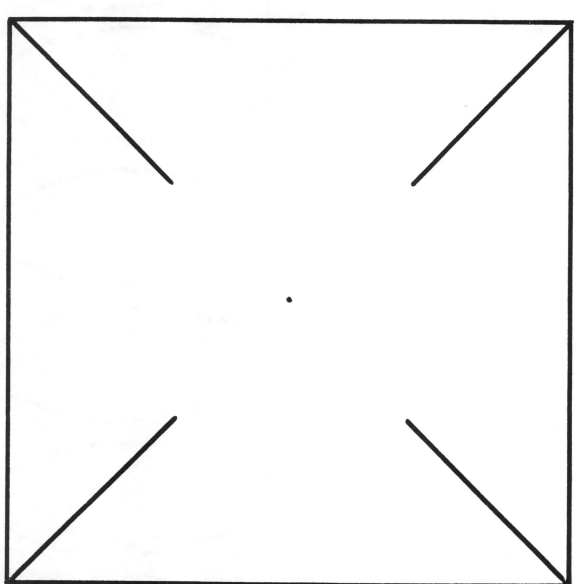

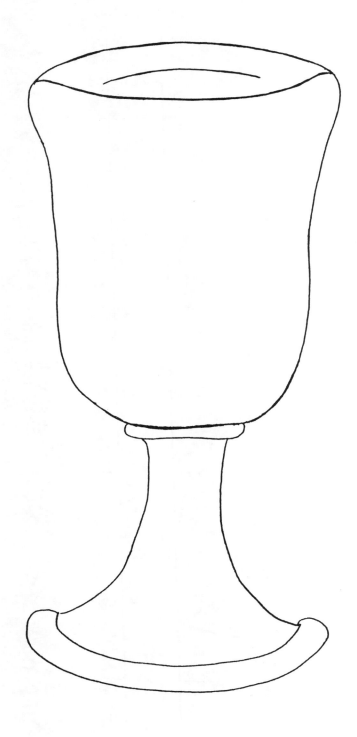

Consecrated
Puppet

↪ cut from construction paper
• make **O**'s with a hole punch

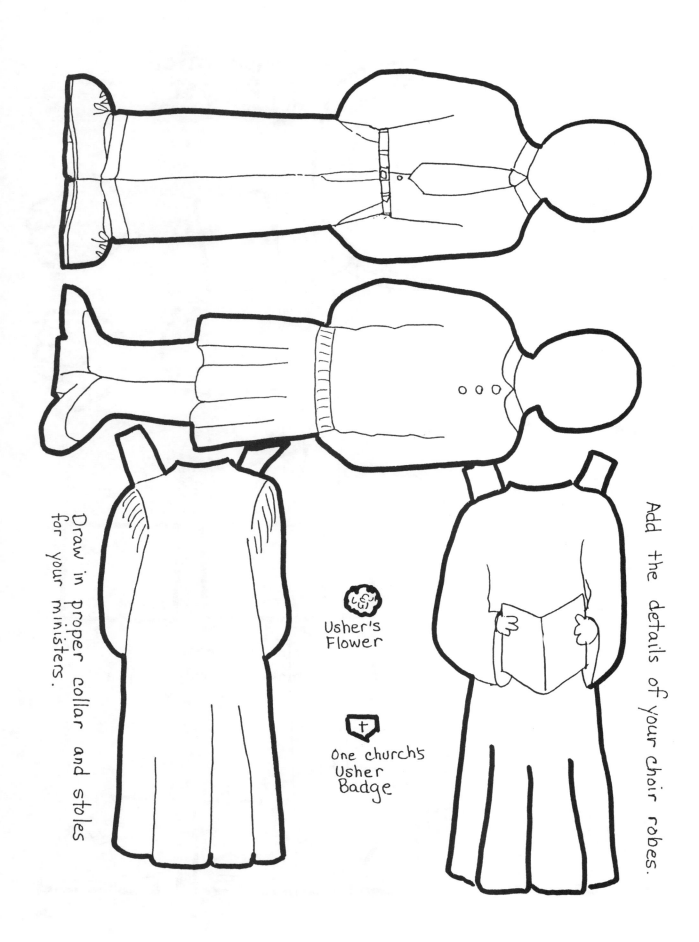

Draw in proper collar and stoles for your ministers.

Usher's Flower

One church's Usher Badge

Add the details of your choir robes.

ORDER OF WORSHIP POSTER
Directions

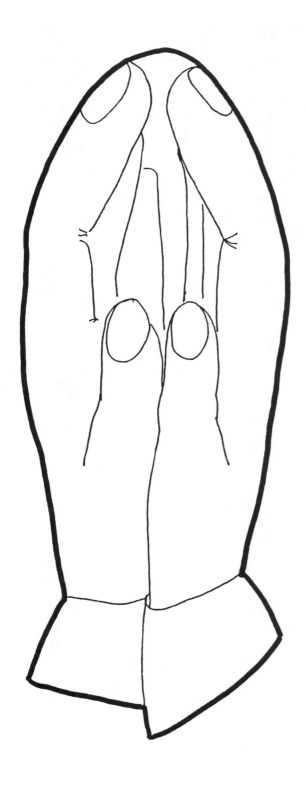

1. Find five posterboards approximately 9" x 12" in attractive pastel color(s).

2. To make 2 song posters cut out 2 pictures of people singing. (Old teaching pictures are a good source.) Mount each picture on one of the posters.

3. To make the prayer poster, copy the praying hands pattern onto stiff tan paper. Cut the hands out and mount them on a poster.

4. To make the proclamation poster, copy the open Bible on stiff white paper. Color the cover and the book mark. Cut the figure out and mount it on a poster.

5. To make the dedication poster, cut the plate pattern from heavy paper. Cut coins and bills from appropriate colors. Mount the coins and bills on the plate. Mount the plate on the poster.

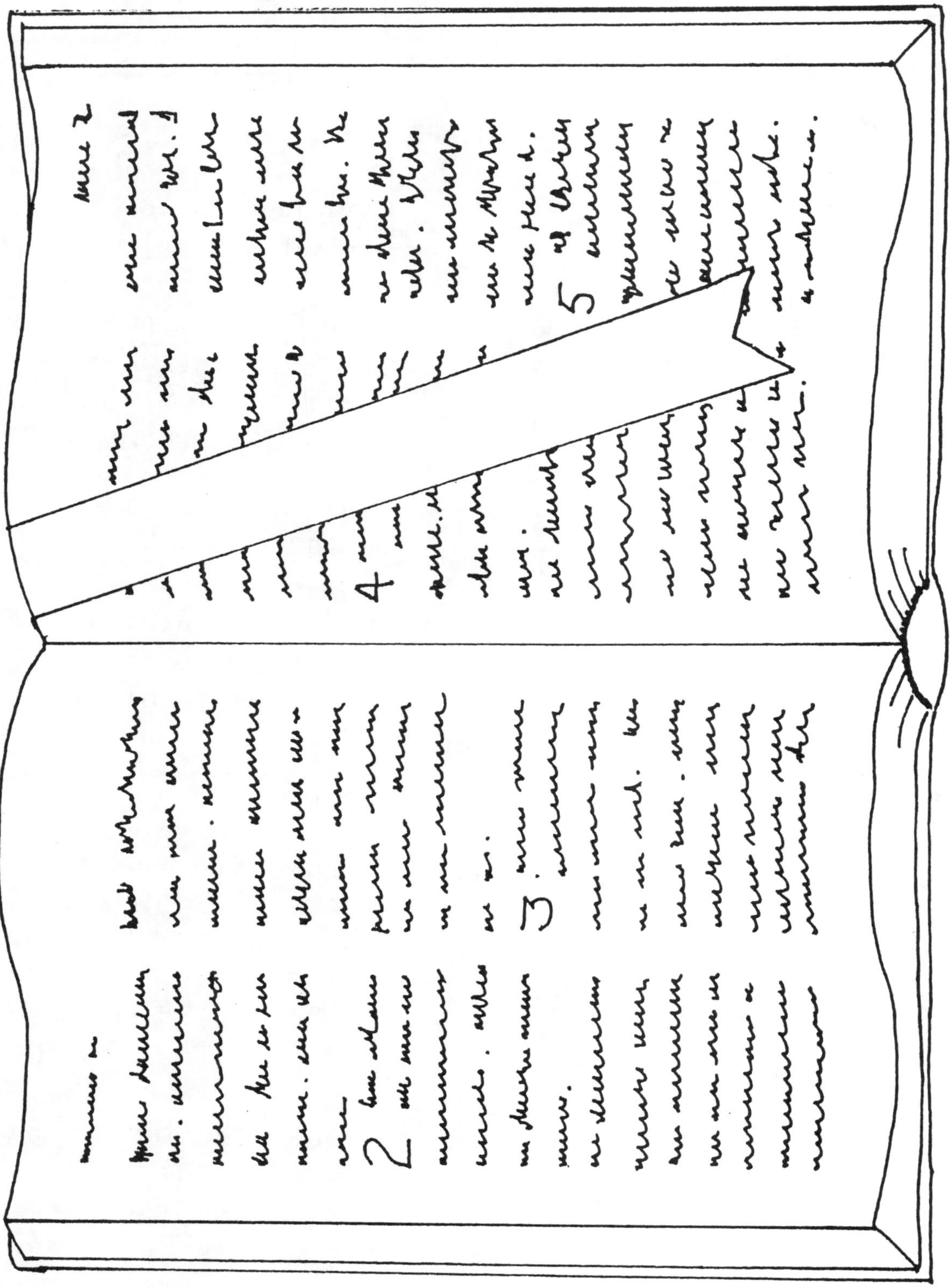

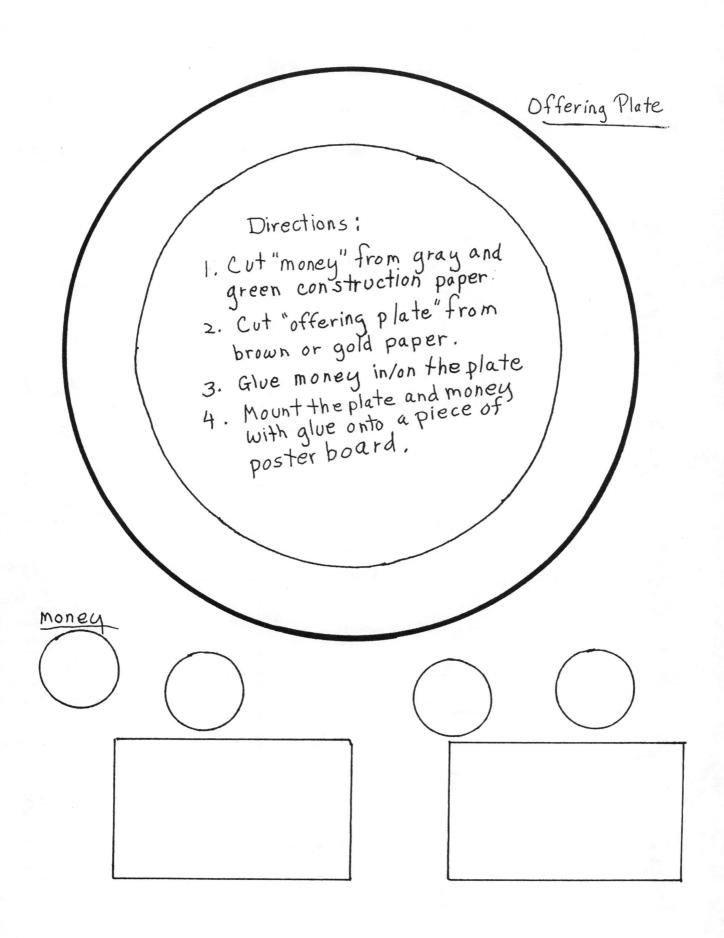

Offering Plate

Directions:

1. Cut "money" from gray and green construction paper.
2. Cut "offering plate" from brown or gold paper.
3. Glue money in/on the plate
4. Mount the plate and money with glue onto a piece of poster board.

money

Let us love one another because

_____

_____

_____

_____

_____

_____

_____

Love comes from God. (I John 4:7)